K £1·

MORAL THEO
Dead Ends and Wa

Liberation and Theology Series

Titles in the series
(latter volumes in preparation)

Introducing Liberation Theology
by Leonardo Boff and Clodovis Boff (Vol. 1)

Trinity and Society by Leonardo Boff (Vol. 2)

Ethics and Community by Enrique Dussel (Vol. 3)

The Holy Spirit and Liberation by José Comblin (Vol. 4)

The Memory of the Christian People
by Eduardo Hoornaert (Vol. 5)

The Bible, the Church and the Poor
by Jorge Pixley and Clodovis Boff (Vol. 6)

Mary, Mother of God, Mother of the Poor
by Ivone Gebara and Maria Clara Bingemer (Vol. 7)

Being Human: A Christian Anthropology
by José Comblin (Vol. 8)

Moral Theology: Dead Ends and Ways Forward
by Antônio Moser and Bernardino Leers (Vol. 9)

Creation and History by Pedro Trigo (Vol. 10)

The God of Christians by Ronaldo Muñoz (Vol. 11)

. . . "this is going to be a series which both illuminates Latin American realities and provokes thought about the relevance to the rest of the world of a theology which springs very powerfully out of these realities - out of the people's suffering and out of a still vibrant faith." —David L. Edwards, *The Church Times*

Antônio Moser
Bernardino Leers

MORAL THEOLOGY

Dead Ends and Ways Forward

Translated from the Portuguese by
Paul Burns

BURNS & OATES

First published in this translation in Great Britain in 1990
by Burns & Oates Ltd, Wellwood, North Farm Rd,
Tunbridge Wells, Kent TN2 3DR
and in the United States of America
by Orbis Books, Maryknoll, New York 10545

Published originally in Brazil under the title
Teologia moral: Impasses e alternativas
by Editora Vozes Ltda, Petrópolis, R.J.

ISBN 0 86012 171 2

Typeset by Selectmove Ltd, London
Printed in Great Britain by BPCC Wheatons Ltd, Exeter

Liberation and Theology Series

In the years since its emergence in Latin America, liberation theology has challenged the church to a renewal of faith lived in solidarity with the poor and oppressed. The effects of this theology have spread throughout the world, inspiring in many Christians a deeper life of faith and commitment, but for others arousing fears and concerns.

Its proponents have insisted that liberation theology is not a sub-topic of theology but really a new way of doing theology. The Liberation and Theology Series is an effort to test that claim by addressing the full spectrum of Christian faith from the perspective of the poor.

Thus, volumes in the Series are devoted to such topics as God, Christ, the Church, Revelation, Mary, the Sacraments, and so forth. But the Series will also explore topics seldom addressed by traditional theology, though vital to Christian life – aspects of politics, culture, the role of women, the status of ethnic minorities. All these are examined in the light of faith lived in a context of oppression and liberation.

The work of over a hundred theologians, pastoral agents, and social scientists from Latin America, and supported by some one hundred and forty bishops, the Liberation and Theology Series is the most ambitious and creative theological project in the history of the Americas.

Addressed to the universal church, these volumes will be essential reading for all those interested in the challenge of faith in the modern world. They will be especially welcomed by all who are committed to the cause of the poor, by those engaged in the struggle for a new society, by all those seeking to establish a more solid link between faith and politics, prayer and action.

"This is a most enterprising series which should enable those of us who live in the West to listen to what the liberation theologians themselves have to say. It may well open the eyes of Western Christians to the need for liberation in the First World as well." – *The Expository Times*

Contents

Foreword

by Rt Rev. Valfredo Tepe

Bishop of Ilheus and Member of the Congregation for the Doctrine of the Faith

Both authors of this book are well known in Brazil as distinguished teachers and authors of respected works in the field of moral theology. I regard this, their latest work, as both courageous and balanced.

Courageous because, starting from the sure church patrimony of revealed truths, from tradition and the magisterium, they face up to the new challenges and problems raised by historical change. The task of theologians is not just to teach established doctrine, but also to work out currently valid responses to challenging new situations.

Vatican II took the risk of inserting the church into the modern world with its giddying historical changes, and invited theologians "to seek continually for more suitable ways of communicating doctrine" (GS 62c). In the development of moral theology, it asked for a more biblical and christocentric approach, and said that it should show "the nobility of the Christian vocation of the faithful and their obligation to bring forth fruit in charity for the light of the world" (OT 16d). The Medellín and Puebla conferences, spelling out the option for the poor, set the contextual guidelines for moral theology in Latin America, setting it to study the specific questions arising from the clamour of the oppressed masses and to place itself at their side, reflecting from their point of view. A theology responsive to the historical development and social context of

Latin America is, in the words of the Vatican's "instruction" on liberation theology, "not merely opportune, but useful and necessary." It was brave of the authors to apply this to the field of moral theology, in which liberation theology has so far had little to say. Their book is timely and fills a gap; if "praxis" is such a basic concept in liberation theology, then surely it is moral theology that has to concern itself with the praxis or practice of Christian life?

So this is a courageous book, but it is also balanced. It realizes what John Paul II, in his message to the bishops of Brazil, asked of liberation theology. This "Latin American approach" to moral theology is in harmony with earlier approaches: it does not break with the morality of the manuals, or with the "renewed morality" of the last few decades in the West, but integrates their valid insights while moving critically on from them through taking up the challenge posed to moral theology by the destitution of the greater part of the population of the Third World.

So the main postulates of the book are our common biblical heritage: the themes of covenant, Kingdom, God's call, following Christ, the virtues. The work is faithful to the social teaching of the church, and it is in moral theology that the homogeneity of the church's teaching on the social problems raised by injustice and oppression, yesterday and today, in the First World and the Third, can most clearly be seen. Catholic social teaching arose in Europe at the beginning of the industrial era, originally as an "inductive" fruit of indignant reflection on the social injustices suffered by the mass of workers. It, too, was misunderstood, and those who sought to apply it were stigmatized as "red priests." For his part, the present pope, in his encyclical *Laborem Exercens*, points to a conflictive world in which Christians must participate, not to exacerbate, but to help resolve its explosive tensions. Christian morality cannot be confined to "close relationships," the "I-thou" relationship; it has to embrace "distant relationships," to engage in the "macro-charity" which seeks to go to the structural roots of so much injustice. In this quest, inevitably, it comes up against the two world systems that seek to impose their "humanist morality": capitalism and Marxism.

A great advantage of this book is that it is not written in "theologese." It is accessible not only to specialists, but to any interested reader, who will find it a real inspiration to following Christ in the here and now of his or her actual situation.

Abbreviations and Short Forms

Documents of Vatican II. Translations are from Walter Abbott, ed., *The Documents of Vatican II*. Piscataway, N.J.: America Press, and London & Dublin: Geoffrey Chapman, 1966.

GS *Gaudium et Spes*. Pastoral Constitution on the Church in the Modern World.

LG *Lumen Gentium*. Dogmatic Constitution on the Church.

OT *Optatam Totius*. Decree on Priestly Formation.

PO *Presbyterorum Ordinis*. Decree on the Ministry and Life of Priests.

LE *Laborem Exercens*. Encyclical Letter of Pope John Paul II. Original in *Acta Apostolica Sedis* 76 (1984), 876–909.

OA *Octogesima Adveniens*. Apostolic Letter of Pope Paul VI to Cardinal Maurice Roy. For an English translation see *The Pope Speaks* 16 (1971), 137–64.

PP *Populorum Progressio*. Encyclical Letter of Pope Paul VI. Original in *Acta Apostolica Sedis* 53 (1971), 401–41.

Puebla Third General Conference of Latin American Bishops, held in Puebla, Mexico, in 1979. A translation of "The Final Document" can be found in John Eagleson and Philip Scharper, eds., *Puebla and Beyond*. Maryknoll, N.Y.: Orbis Books, 1979; also in *Puebla*. London & Slough: CIIR and St Paul Publications, 1980.

QA	*Quadragesimo Anno*. Encyclical Letter of Pope Pius XI. Original in *Acta Apostolica Sedis* 13 (1931), 177–228.
REB	*Revista Eclesiastica Brasileira*. Petrópolis, 1941ff.
RN	*Rerum Novarum*. Encyclical letter of Pope Leo XIII, 1891.

Introduction

The uncertainties experienced in all spheres of life today apply equally to theology. Here, however, our historical sense can help to attenuate the effects of present-day surprises, since there have certainly been equally uncertain times for theology, and chiefly for moral theology, in the past. Yet there is no doubt that the discomforts now come from an accelerated rate of change. Movements and counter-movements take place not over a long space of time, as they did in the past, but over a few decades or even a few years.

In the specific sphere of moral theology, several centuries of relative stability gave way to a sharp change between 1950 and 1970; this produced a new framework known as "renewed morality." Scarcely was this framework in place when another one emerged, stemming mainly from Latin America and with a markedly social accent. When this latest tendency appeared to be gaining ground, the need was felt to pause and assess the "gains and losses" of the last two decades, and the last few years in particular.

The present work, which has three parts, is an attempt to extract "things old and new" from a storehouse whose contents date back to their source, Jesus Christ, and have been added to since then during the course of the journey made by the community of faith. In dealing with a storehouse so great in extent and rich in content, and one in which so many have worked before us, humility forces us to say that this can be but an unfinished book; its chief claims are that it brings out the new without downgrading the old; that it puts forward a particular viewpoint without neglecting what is universal; that it emphasizes social aspects without leaving personal ones in the shade.

This type of work forces one to take account of the fact

that, in theological terms, few factors are more significant than historicity. The principle of historicity, which has nothing to do with "historicism," was one of the formative elements of Vatican II. This principle tells us that nothing is played out; everything changes, but within a measure of continuity. Although the short term shows cuts, breaks, violent shocks even, the long term clearly shows certain lines of continued creativity. This means that the principle of historicity brings out the reality of a process of change, however deep it might be, a process that re-posits old problems in a new way and assimilates new postulates, the better to demonstrate fidelity to the gospel.

Our first concern will be to delineate moral theology today in comparison with what it was before. There are deep tensions today, above all on the level of practice, but also on that of theory. On the practical level, the dead ends of moral theology today are characterized by immorality, by permissiveness and by amorality. On the reflective level, the dead end seems to be caused by the—not always peaceful—co-existence of three systems: that of the "manuals," the "renewed," and the Latin American or "liberative." The confrontation between these will occupy our first three chapters.

In chapter I, after portraying the current malaise, we go on to trace its historical roots. These act as reminders that, if we think we are working on a higher level today, this is only because others have begun the painful process of construction before us.

One of the floors of this edifice we call moral theology is made up of the neo-scholastic manuals. It would be rash as well as unjust to knock this down, since it contains load-bearing columns that support the upper floors. To leave it intact, on the other hand, would be to ignore the advances made in building technology. This floor needs extensive rebuilding without knocking the whole edifice out of true.

Another floor is made up of renewed morality. This uses a more advanced technology, but is now in need of refurbishment and needs some finishing of details. Some of its joists also need strengthening, others replacing. This will be the concern of chapter II.

The next floor was added in a somewhat unexpected fashion. What happened was that several (numerous) families arrived and demanded a place in the sun. Despite their decidedly provincial appearance and lack of resources, they insisted on sharing a building they claimed belonged to everyone. The stage the construction has now reached, and common sense, prevent us from calling this floor the top one, since it is entirely possible that we shall need to add more in the future. The difficulties involved in the construction have delayed the official opening. Perhaps the whole project will need refurbishing first, or even rebuilding. . . . But it would be an unforgivable waste simply to abandon it, now that so much sweat and toil has gone into its construction. The skeleton of this new floor, with some of its building materials, appears in chapter III. This brings us to the end of part one: Moral Theology Yesterday and Today.

Following this, in part two, we attempt to make our own contribution by providing the essential services to make the building work and re-cladding it to make it look more welcoming. It is, after all, in the moral theology building that Jesus' brothers and sisters seek shelter, hoping to feel at home in the Father's house. So this second part lays out the broad coordinates.

Whenever new approaches are tried, they produce a sense of shock. They can look like the result of a quest for "novelties," which either do not fit in with the inheritance held by the church, or seem to lack sufficient consistency in themselves. However, the strength of renewal can sometimes be found in just its rediscovery of rich veins forgotten or buried for ages. This applies to both the "renewed" model and the Latin American one: both, though in different ways, seek their basic inspiration in the "new and everlasting covenant" (chapter IV). The covenant indisputably carries a religious message, but it also carries a social message. Brought to life by the prophets, this message carries with it a powerful appeal to conversion.

God's purpose, at once religious and social, is not completely contained in the Old Testament. Very much to the contrary: if the New is hidden in the Old, it is in the light of the New that the Old reveals its full meaning. The New in history is Jesus Christ: God's purpose fully revealed (chapter V). The annunciation and implantation of the Kingdom were made not in words alone, but through the historical practice of Jesus himself. Summed up in the "great commandment," this practice was distinguished by its eminently liberative—in the full sense of the word—nature. The morality of following Jesus derives from his liberative and salvific practice.

Yet it is not easy to discern God's purposes in Jesus Christ. Conscience, both personal and social, has always been stressed as a privileged sensor in discerning God's saving plans. A new overall approach, besides bringing out other aspects of conscience, permits a richer theological understanding of moral conscience (chapter VI). A critical social conscience, enhanced through various forms of conscientization, certainly poses no threat either to traditional "Christian conscience" or to the irreplaceable role of the magisterium of the church. These are all elements which help toward a better understanding of complex historical and personal situations.

Part three focusses on new human beings in a new society. Following Christ is first and foremost a call from God to embrace God's historical purpose with all our might (chapter VII). A historical purpose appears originally linked not to individuals, but to the community; in this case, the ecclesial community in the first place. The community aspect, however, does not rule out the personal level: the human person also constitutes a source of morality. Values, laws and norms refer both to the community and to the human individual.

A positive response to God's call, which echoes in consciences too, is what distinguishes virtuous beings (chapter VIII). Virtue is the power of God showing forth in God's people, in the quest for liberation from sin. Though not so much appreciated today, treatises on the virtues contain riches not obvious at first sight. The problem is to define a virtuous being in a social context of injustice.

Strictly speaking, there should at this point be a treatment of the negative response to God's call: sin. But it would seem foolhardy to deal with a subject as vast as sin in one chapter. It needs a volume to itself.

The dream of building a new humanity, nourished throughout the centuries, finds new opportunities as well as challenges at the present time. It is an eminently biblical theme which has also become a central component of various ideologies. This means that it has to be cast as one of the objectives of moral theology, which seeks to serve a new humanity in a new world (chapter IX). This is where the ongoing struggle between grace and sin, between virtue and vice, reaches its foremost expression.

Social and economic "models" of this new humanity have also been made. Moral theology has to face up to both the capitalist and the Marxist models, since both carry a moral concept. This raises the question: How should moral theology be conceived so as to provide an alternative model? How does one take a Christian stance in the face of the different systems put forward? (chapter X).

Those are the broad lines of this book. At first sight they do not encompass—nor do they claim to—all the themes belonging to fundamental morality. A keen glance will, for example, point to the absence of natural law, natural rights, moral norms, and so on, which in fact have no separate chapter or section headings. But as realities they can be found throughout the work. They are appreciated and integrated within a more dynamic and structured framework. We have been less concerned with giving them headings than with bringing out their underlying influence and deep meaning.

We have tried, while bringing an ancient and new heritage up to date, to present it in a language that will enable moral theology to be accepted as part of the good news proclaimed by Jesus Christ. Just as Jesus Christ attracted rather than threatened, so too a moral theology that carries the sap of the gospel should attract rather than frighten.

The summary style is intentional, too; it stems from a pedagogical theory which holds that it is not necessary, and sometimes not appropriate, to spell out everything. Socrates found that no listener (or reader in this case) started out with nothing. On the contrary, every human being is the bearer of unsuspected riches, waiting for someone to uncover them. The Master's wisdom was the same: suggesting rather than spelling out, asking rather than answering.

PART ONE

MORAL THEOLOGY YESTERDAY AND TODAY

Chapter I

The Challenges to Moral Theology Today

Speaking of moral theology *today* is no easy task. New approaches are in evidence, but at the same time so are new obstacles and dead ends. We move in a climate of uncertainty, in which the questions raised need to be weighed with extreme care. And we need to start by making a sort of inventory, however summary, of both past and present themes. First, moral theology needs to be situated generically, with a look at its origins, its deepest meaning and its main basis. Then, we should approach the obstacles and dead ends on the practical level. Only then can we go on to set out a first position on the reflective level, from which three systems emerge, not always harmoniously co-existing.

1. HOW TO SITUATE MORAL THEOLOGY

Morals as a science, in the basic meaning of the word, has a long history. Though as a "theology" its cradle is in the scriptures, as a science of customs it goes back into the dimmest mist of time. All ancient peoples produced moral codes by which they ordered their behaviour and thought to enrich their lives. It was perhaps the Greeks who succeeded in giving the most complete expression to their moral heritage.

(a) Etymology and Original Meaning

The word "moral" comes directly from the Latin *mos-mores*. The Greeks preferred the term "ethics," which enshrines a depth of meaning not always kept in the term "morals."[1] *Ethos* refers to our dwelling, our village, our identity; it designates the force that maintains and nourishes the inner identity of a people. From there, the word derived another meaning—it is understood also as the basic identity of individuals.

Although the term "ethics" has traditionally been kept more to philosophy and specific codifications, while "morals" has been preferred in the theological field, the two, properly understood, are basically complementary. Both refer to the *humanum* and are at its service.

(b) Rough Definition

All definitions detract from the richness of a concept. But despite its intrinsic limitation, an initial definition can help to grasp something of the deepest meaning of that concept. So we might say that moral theology is: That part of theology which, in the light of *revelation* and *faith lived* in the church community, aims to point the way to the full humanization of persons and society, in the footsteps of Jesus Christ and his Kingdom.

As part of theology, moral theology has to be closely linked to its various branches: ecclesiology, christology, exegesis, dogmatics, fundamental theology, pastoral theology, and the like. As part of theology, also, it has to relate in a specific way to revelation—not to a revelation hovering in the mists of space and time, but to a revelation contained in the scriptures and integrated into the life of the community of faith.

The community of faith, for its part, is not made up either of just the "simple faithful," or of just the hierarchy. It is made up the "people of God," which contains members with differing functions within the same overall quest for fidelity to the Master.

What moral theology seeks is not primarily psychological or social integration; it seeks a *total integration*, both of persons considered as individual entities, and of society as a whole. This integration is possible only through maintaining the historical and trans-historical coordinates between the two categories. Leaving either out of account produces an imbalance which affects the person as much as society. This is to state that personal integration leads to the integration of society, and vice versa.

(c) Christ: The Supreme Source and Norm

Though moral theology has close ties to the human and social sciences,[2] it is not confined to them and their conclusions. Moral theology claims to be *normative*; it does not just describe human behaviour patterns, but points to an ideal to be followed which is also their motive force. This ideal was incarnated in Jesus Christ.

The Fathers of the church already pointed to Christ as the supreme norm of Christian behaviour.[3] Christ is at once the full revelation of the Father and the full revelation of humanity.[4] This simultaneous conjugation of divinity and humanity makes moral actions both tense and serene, just as Jesus' actions displayed both tension and serenity.

It was not only through his words, but also through his deeds that Jesus showed the way to his Father's house, which is also therefore the way to a human habitation. In this way, he embodied the deep sense of "*ethos*": the dwelling-place of the Father and of humankind. So persons find their deep identity only in the tense and hope-full journey that characterizes human life. With their arms outstretched to embrace both heaven an earth, themselves and each other, human beings glimpse—through faith—a Kingdom that is at once "amongst us" and still awaiting its full realization.

2. DEADS ENDS IN PRACTICE

Since the fifties there has been a rising chorus of talk about the *crisis* that is buffeting moral theology. The extent of the literature on this crisis is enough to show that there is a lot of truth in the talk: moral theology indeed faces many obstacles and even dead ends.[5] Some of these affect practice, some theory. Taken together, they give an impression of general malaise, typical of periods of crisis.

There are various possible ways of approaching these dead ends in practice. Depending on what point of view one adopts, they can be seen as a universal or a more limited phenomenon. Looked at from the Western world, the overall picture seems to be one of breakdown. This is seen in various ways.[6]

(a) Breakdown through Immorality

The clear impression derived from looking at moral behaviour through Western eyes is that there is a marked growth in immorality, affecting all levels of society and all forms of behaviour. There is much talk of the breakdown in sexual morality, immorality in public life and general lack of respect for accepted canons of good behaviour.

There is no point in being ingenuous. There does seem to be a quantitative increase in the amount of evil: suffice to think of the refined and brutal forms of violence at large in society. Nevertheless, it is very difficult to measure immorality from this angle. Not only is the overall population much greater than it was in previous ages, but what was formerly done in secret is now done in the open; what used to be restricted to the few is now available to the many.

Furthermore, while the mystery of evil is an undeniable fact, so is it that grace continues to operate. Above all, there is a deeper and more widespread sensitivity to injustice, to the violation of human rights, to the exploitation of the weakest members of society, and so on. If it is true that there are greater possibilities for doing evil now, it is equally true that there are greater possibilities for doing good. This being so, we ought perhaps to nuance the darkest prognoses somewhat—but here again without being ingenuous.

(b) Breakdown through Permissiveness

The view here is that we live in an ever more open and pluralist society, the negative side of which is that it is ever more "permissive" and tolerant. Permissiveness has spread throughout society, while tolerance has crept into the legal system. The publicity spread by the communications media has much to do with this spread of permissiveness—which does not mean their function in this respect is a negative one: the publicity given to social failings and all types of scandals can have the effect of provoking a healthy and mature reaction.

Permissiveness impinges most on the "weak": on children, adolescents, immature adults. This alone is enough to make it worrying. The solution would seem to lie less in a return to past values and repressiveness than in critical education enlightened by the broad principles of the gospel.

(c) Breakdown through Amorality

The most serious phenomenon is not immorality, or permissiveness, but amorality; the most worrying thing is the loss of a moral or ethical sense. What is at stake is the breakdown of moral codes themselves: it is one thing to ignore them in practice while acknowledging their validity in conscience; quite another to challenge them in both theory and practice.

Loss of moral sense belongs to our Western type of civilization, dominated by consumerism and by the appearance of massified humanity: without work, without purpose in life, without sense. Massification brings a decline in moral standards; it produces a levelling-down, with accompanying loss of personal identity.

Another aspect of our consumer society is its deterioration in human relationships. All we can think of is producing and consuming. Everything that is not productive or saleable is relegated to a lower level in our estimation. Hence the resulting brutalization which pervades the personal and social spheres of our existence.

Added to this is the tyranny of the word through propaganda. And a society which makes profit and competition its golden rules will always be a more violent society. All this results in a brutalizing of the spirit: people lose their capacity for response, their resonance, their wonder; only bodily and material aspects are admired. And so the degradation spreads to all sectors. We seem to live in a world where tenderness is the preserve of poets and ladies and gentlemen of leisure.

(d) A Change in Moral Valuation

The truth of the matter is that we have to recognize something more than a breakdown in moral values. There has also been a shift in our framework of valuation. Vatican II spoke of profound and rapid changes recoiling upon people's "manner of thinking and acting, with repercussions on family, social and religious life" (GS 4). What is happening amounts to a real cultural revolution. Underlying this change in estimation is a new interpretation of humankind and the world. Human beings no longer see themselves and the world around them as givens, as something finished, immovable in space and time. Everything now is governed by the principle of historicity, which introduces the variants proper to space and time. There is continuity, but there is also evolution. Could moral norms escape from this unscathed? Could it be that, rather than talking of moral breakdown, we should be talking of a new way of judging human behaviour?

(e) The People as Criterion

We have seen that analysis of practice varies considerably, depending on the actual situation of the analyst. Here we come up against the fact that an analysis made from the Third World will be different from an analysis made from the First World. The data may be more or less the same; their interpretation and significance, however, can vary considerably.

Speaking of "the people," let alone speaking in their name, is possible only when one belongs to the people, or at least lives with them. Here the difficulty lies in defining what one means by "people." Whether one regards them as those who live outside the framework of "enlightened" culture, or whether one sees them as those deprived of the benefits of society, what is certain is that the people are emerging as a decisive agent in the history of Latin America. This is one of the "discoveries" made by Third World theologians in the last twenty years.

The humble people are coming to the fore not only as the great majority among the population of Third World countries, but as bearers of surprising cultural, moral and evangelical values. Jesus' words, "I bless you, Father, because you have revealed these things to the little ones," become steadily more comprehensible. It is also easier to see who the "little ones" are, through their openness to the good news.

This gives rise to a very serious question for moral theology: How can we have a theology that ignores "God's favourites," as Pope John Paul II called them when he went to Puebla (see 1143)? Should they be considered mere recipients of a ready-made system? What is their contribution in terms of Christian life? This is not the place to enlarge on this question: we merely want to record the fact that the great majority of the population of Latin America live on the margins of progress, but not on the margins of the gospel.

Besides their popular wisdom, full of ambiguities no doubt, but also of evangelical good sense, our people certainly have something to say on the subject of moral behaviour.[7] They too see the breakdown of morality, but they also see the breakdown embodied in other situations and attitudes that easily pass unnoticed by those who do not live with them.

It is not easy to compile an inventory of the values of "the people" of the different countries of Latin America. The contributions of the different cultures, corresponding to different ethnic groups, are many and various. How could we fail, for example, to see moral values most apposite for our age in the community spirit of the Indians, in their way of living umbilically tied to the earth, in their respect for transcendence? Or how could we fail to see gospel values sprouting in the resistance put up by the blacks, in their contagious good humour, despite the discriminations to which they are subjected? How can we fail to see that their solidarity goes beyond bonds of colour and race?

(f) The Base Communities Show a Different Approach

Of course "our people" are not made up just of Indians or blacks, any more than they are of *mestizos*. In the same way the base communities are far from exhausting the numbers of those who practise a deep faith. They define themselves as the seeds of a new society, and do not claim to be any bigger than seeds.

It is, nevertheless, an observable and impressive fact that those who belong to these base communities, conscious of their dignity as people and of their mission in the church, often produce deeper and more universal moral insights than the learned.[8] Starting from the fact that our present society is nonviable, the base Christian communities allow us to glimpse a new horizon, on both evangelical and socio-political levels. Overcoming age-old dualistic barriers, they unite faith and social action, personal life and life in community, in a way far closer to the sources of Christianity than any found in learned treatises.

There is no point in trying to make the base communities into the only way of being church, let alone into substitutes for the magisterium, just as there is no point in idealizing everything that comes from the people, even from a poor and oppressed people. But surely it would be immoral to crush such a promising seed and steal the place Christ himself reserved for it in the building of his Kingdom? It is just by asking questions of this sort that one comes to see that a theological view that claims to be universal does not always capture reality in all its richness, and does not always catch the deepest meaning of that same reality. This will become clearer as we examine dead ends in theory.

3. DEAD ENDS IN THEORY

The present crisis does not affect practice only, but theory as well. Here it is caused basically by the uneasy co-existence between three different approaches to moral theology: that of the "manuals," the "renewed," and one stemming from Latin America. The first claims to be comprehensive; the second is an attempt to adapt to the modern world; the third arose as a response to the more specific challenges posed by one continent, but has wider implications.

The approach of the manuals might be said to represent an objective phase, the renewed approach a subjective phase, the Latin American approach a dialectical and social phase. The co-existence of these three approaches, with the conflicts it brings, affects individuals, communities and the church as a whole; the tense relationship between them makes itself felt on every level.

As stated in the Introduction, we propose to examine each of these three approaches in turn, bringing out their positive aspects, but also the doubts they raise.

(a) A Long and Stormy History

Our concern with the present, particularly with the present reality of Latin America, does not mean that we can dispense with an examination of the past, even the most distant past. It is impossible to do theology for today without at least a brief study of what has gone before and in different contexts. Today, living as we do in a time of tensions, it is even more important to see what happened at similar times in the past.[9] A historical overview helps us to understand the deep changes that now leave us hesitating between "perennial" and "new" values. Our present crisis situation is not the first in history, nor will it be the last—it may not even be the most profound.

Furthermore, if we are to understand what is happening in moral theology at present, we need to situate it in the overall context of the worldwide changes and questionings affecting economics, politics and all aspects of society, culture and religion. The obstacles facing moral theology, too, need to be placed within those affecting theology as a whole. The more clearly we can situate these obstacles, the more relative they will appear.

(i) The moral teaching of the Fathers.[10] The rich theology of the Fathers stems directly from the word of God in the scriptures and the life of the church at their time. Their treatises are not divided into the subject-headings we have today: systematic, dogmatic, moral and so on. They are more comprehensive and integrated. So there is no systematic treatment of moral theology from patristic times. Morality is treated as part of the proclamation of the good news, commented on and applied to Christian life. The moral teaching of this period seems to have three main characteristics:

—The *scriptures* are treated as the main source of moral guidance;

—The *originality* of Christian morality is stressed, with the accent laid on divine filiation, Christ as the supreme norm and the influence of the Holy Spirit;

—The best of *pagan thought* is taken over. There is presupposition that all, including the pagans, are carriers of "seeds of the Word" and in this sense tend toward the all-embracing Logos, Christ.[11]

(ii) The penitentiaries: early manuals.[12] These appeared at a time of general decline in religion, culture and society. The Roman Empire was breaking up and giving way to the Nordic peoples, unjustly called barbarians. The penitentiaries which proliferated from the fourth to the eleventh centuries were essentially practical books, without an explicit theology, designed exclusively for the use of confessors: they provided a

list of sins with the penance appropriate to each. There were many different penitentiaries: by St Columbanus, Reginon of Prüm and many more, but all contain the same type of "theology," formalistic and juridical in approach, with no account taken of motivation. Nevertheless, they served to clarify matters at a period when great thinkers appeared to be dormant, and when illiteracy or semi-literacy was on the increase even among the clergy. They provided a sort of prop, even if a precarious one, in a theologically impoverished age.

At the end of this period, *summas* for confessors began to make their appearance. They were rather more elaborate, but still kept to the same general lines as the penitentiaries.

(iii) The renaissance in moral theology in the twelfth and thirteenth centuries. The historical context is the renaissance of learning associated with the first universities (Paris, Oxford, Naples) and the appearance of evangelism.[13] The great figure of the renaissance in moral theology was St Thomas Aquinas. His *Summa Theologica* is divided into three parts: *exitus*—everything comes from God the creator; *redditus*—everything has to return to God, but human effort plays a part in this; and the mediation of Jesus Christ—everything returns to God through Christ.

The part taken as being moral theology is the second. However, it is important to note that it is set within a theology of creation and redemption. This means that, virtually for the first time, morality is treated as theology. The Fathers took the same approach, but less explicitly. This Thomist renewal, nevertheless, was insufficiently absorbed into living practice; the people generally adopted a system of *nominalism*, which stressed the specific, individual sphere: in terms of morals, it suggested that norms were arbitrarily laid down by God rather than stemming from God's overall saving plan.

(iv) Autonomy after Trent. The Council of Trent (1545—63) inspired the production in 1600 of the first manual specifically devoted to moral theology, the work of a Jesuit named Azor. This manual, in which morality was considered apart from systematic theology and holy scripture, effectively set moral theology apart as an autonomous discipline. It was to have great influence in succeeding centuries.

(v) The crisis of the seventeenth and eighteenth centuries: moral systems. Moral systems were an attempt to adapt morality to the new requirements of the world, arising from geographical and scientific discoveries. They sought solutions to the problems of conscience experienced by the faithful, disorientated by the "novelties" of the age: Do Indians have souls? Should their rights be respected? Can one charge interest? Are wars of conquest justified?

The main systems were the following:

—*Probabilism*: in moral questions where certainty is impossible, any solidly probable course may be followed even though an opposed course is or appears to be more probable;

—*Tutiorism*: the more certain or probable opinion is the one to be followed (with a presumption in favour of law rather than liberty);

—*Rigorism*: a more rigorous form of *tutiorism*; everything not allowed by the law is sin (reaching an extreme form as "absolute *tutiorism*" with the Jansenists, and condemned by the pope);

—*Laxism*: carries probabilism to the extreme; in a conflict between liberty and law, a slightly probable argument for liberty suffices to furnish a basis for action;

—*Equi-probabilism*: tries to steer a middle course between the extremes of rigorism and laxism. St Alphonsus Ligouri was the leading exponent of this school.

This period certainly presented a theological picture as confused as that of our own. The faithful felt hemmed in by irreconcilable positions, each usually taken up by some religious order or congregation, which increased their confusion. Whom were they to follow?

(b) The Neo-scholastic Manuals of the Eighteenth to Twentieth Centuries

This heading brings us into the world of moral theology today. The neo-scholastic manuals, which belong historically to the period from the eighteenth to the mid-twentieth centuries, but which have roots in much earlier periods, still impose their mentality today.

Though our basic concern here is a moral theology of universal import, we are bound to take account of the situation from which we write. The neo-scholastic manuals, transported directly from the colonial powers where they originated to the colonies, contain a theology basically attuned to the colonial enterprise. Dissonant voices, and even prophetic resistance, made themselves heard, particularly from the end of the eighteenth century, but, because these manuals stemmed generally from the bourgeois liberal ethos of the time, they failed to address themselves to very deep or worldwide questions. The approach of these manuals dominated in seminaries and in the thinking of the church-going faithful. Hence the importance of looking at their approach more closely, particularly as it was the expression of moral theology right up to the eve of Vatican II, and in some places even more recently.

(i) The moral values of the manuals. Even though later developments have revealed notable weaknesses in their approach, it would be lacking in objectivity not to recognize that they contained real values. These emerge when one examines the approaches taken by moral theology: objective, subjective and social. The manuals represent the objective approach. Though historically earlier than the others, this is not annulled by the later ones, even though these re-interpret the earlier one on the basis of new ground rules.

Among the values the manuals seek to implant, we might include: the quest for what is universal; the quest for what is perennial; the importance of action; the importance of the individual; the importance of law.

—*The quest for what is universal*: There is an intuition that regional and historical differences do not annul certain features common to all human beings. While God has a plan for every individual, every generation, every nation, God's primary purpose is addressed to the whole human race. The manuals seek out these universal postulates, laying particular stress on the concept of natural law. On the basis of this, they seek postulates going beyond all frontiers, even beyond the confines of Christianity itself.

—*The quest for what is perennial* is another constant preoccupation of the manuals. They certainly do not contain the same degree of consciousness of the impact made on theology by its historical, cultural and social context that one would expect to find today. They have some regard for this, however, if only in that they seek to distinguish what is perennial from other, transitory elements.

The quest for what is perennial led to a "perennial philosophy" and a "perennial theology." The foundations for these are sought in early authorities, but above all in the commandments, the "law of God," revelation and the natural law. One might dispute the use they make of these sources, but one equally has to admit that they are the right ones to go to.

—*The importance of action* is opposed to the exclusivity of *intention*. Throughout history the accent has swung from action to intention and back again, from theory to practice and back again. Embodying as they do the objective approach, the manuals place the stress on action, though in a somewhat limited sense. A morality based on this sense of action is certainly limited, especially when one takes account of the complexity of the subject who lies behind them. The manuals state, correctly, that behind every action lies a being (*agere sequitur esse*), though they tend to leave the being somewhat shadowy. Despite this, it is a good basic principle.

—*The importance of the individual* has a double aspect: while on the one hand it brings out that something unrepeatable and original is found in every person, on the other it can easily lapse into abstraction.

Today we lay great stress on community and social aspects of life; in recent decades the accent was more on the personal aspect, and before that on the purely individual. It is strongly characteristic of the manuals to give priority to the individual and private level. This premise cannot be lost sight of in the dialectic between the different approaches to moral theology; again, our task is a matter of re-elaborating on the basis of new perceptions, not of eliminating one factor.

—*Law* became an indispensable parameter for moral theology, especially when understood as the Law in the context of the covenant. Law has a pedagogical function and as such can be a major force in forming conscience. The problem raised by law was intimately linked to a particular period and concept in which objectivity was stressed within a pyramidal understanding. In this context, law becomes enmeshed in legalism, which was so strongly condemned by Christ and St Paul. Nevertheless, understood within its inherent limitation, law will always have its place in any system of moral theology.

(ii) Questionable aspects of the morality of the manuals.[14] A close look will show that their questionable aspects are, fundamentally, the same aspects picked out above as values. The fact is that the strengths and weaknesses of an approach can be very closely related. Carried too far, a strength can turn into a dangerous weapon. Seen in this light, read calmly and at a distance in time, the manuals undoubtedly present weaknesses. Of course the whole historical context in which they were produced has to be taken into account. So our objections are aimed not so much at the manuals themselves, which are products of their age, as at a certain mentality derived from them which still persists today. The chief weaknesses of their approach can be summed up under a few headings, all revelatory of a greater whole: a mentality, in effect. So we can pick out: a morality full of certainty, but not always critical; a morality marked by pessimism; a legalistic morality; a privatistic morality.

—*Uncritical certainty*. Transition periods are generally marked by great pluralism, and despite the riches inherent in pluralism, it also entails an uncomfortable degree of uncertainty. Periods of stability, on the other hand, tend to produce a lethargic certainty.

The aura of certainty transmitted by the manuals derives from the halo of sacrality with which they have been surrounded. Born of a sacral world, nourished by a particular sacralized and sacralizing theological vision, they emerge as the concrete, complete expression of that climate. The first manual, published in 1600, indeed bore the marks of sacrality in its very title: *Institutiones Sacrae Theologiae Moralis*. Now, what is sacred is placed above discussion, thereby becoming untouchable by subsequent criticism. The theology of the manuals is vertically structured and becomes a science reserved to confessors, unattainable by any more historical and critical type of reasoning. The results of this on the social, ecclesial and even personal level are obvious: institutions are not renewed, since they allow no questioning.

—*Pessimistic tone*. The sacralization of morality stemmed from a naturalistic cosmological vision. Its pessimism stems from a dualist anthropological viewpoint. Influenced as they were by a Platonic interpretation and by rigorist heretical movements, the manuals in turn nourished a negative view of humankind and the world. They viewed the world and human beings with mistrust. The world as a whole became synonymous with danger: hence the incentives to *fuga mundi*, flight from the world. Human beings, though bearing marks of the divine, are also burdened by the weight of their materiality. Hence the negative attitude taken to the body and sexuality. In this climate, the balance achieved by St Thomas was lost.

Regarded more as an occasion of sin than as a drive in the service of love, sexuality became the touchstone of problems of conscience. The treatment *De Sexto* was always the longest in the manuals, on a subject that both terrified and fascinated.

This obsession with sexual sins is not as harmless as it might appear. It performs an important ideological function, in the sense that it obscures more vital problems. Self-absorption blocks out concern for the problems of "the world" and reduces the whole of human behaviour to questions that favour a particular way of regarding and organizing society. That it is important to deal with sexuality, there can be no doubt: sexuality is a force that pervades all human relationships. But it all depends on the standpoint from which sexuality is approached.

—*The rule of legalism*. No one has been more incisive in condemning legalism than Christ himself. Yet legalism is such a central characteristic of the manuals that it can almost be called their hallmark. The morality of the manuals is a sort of strong arm of the *Codex Iuris Canonici*—as shown by the significant title of a classic work by Jone: *Moral Theology in the Light of Canon Law*.[15]

Against a backdrop of this sacral world-view and anthropological dualism, though disguised, the manuals were written under the rule of law. By forgetting the covenant, the natural framework of divine law, and by virtually equating the human-made laws with divine law, they made a positive value into an effectively negative one. Sometimes simple ecclesiastical, liturgical and even civil laws came to have an almost divine force. This failure to distinguish between levels not only hinders understanding of law; it can even de-moralize it. This is precisely one of the accusations Christ made against the legalism of the Pharisees.

This distortion makes everything appear perennial, universal, thereby stifling creativity and putting a brake on all evolution. Law, which should be a sign pointing out the road of life, becomes an instrument of sin and death, as St Paul called it (see Gal. 2:15ff; 3:21ff).

Legalism was greatly strengthened by the tendency, produced by casuistry, to make abstract norms something to be imposed. In evaluating problems, matters that deeply affected human behaviour and its significance were left out of account: personal, socio-cultural, economic, political, ideological, religious and other factors, for example. The solution to problems was sought on a more essentialist level, for which all that was needed was for norms to be applied objectively. Persons are then swallowed up by the established order, forced to subject themselves to what has been decided in the abstract on the level of principles. In this way, juridicism and casuistry themselves become important players in the process of subjecting consciences.

—*Privatizing morality*. Despite the inclusion of a section on "social morality," the manuals are dominated by a privatistic ethos: "Saving *one's* soul" becomes the regulatory principle around which the whole edifice is built. One should beware of dirtying one's hands with the "things of this world"—politics in particular is a very dangerous activity, held to be hardly worthy of a Christian!

Privatism is cultivated in a special way in terms of sin and conversion. Everything happens in the inner realm of "the heart": falling away and reconversion are something affecting the individual alone. Despite inveighing against Protestants for confessing their sins directly to God, Catholics too run the risk of embodying views that leave community and social dimensions out of account. What then becomes important is simply to convert individuals, who repent in the intimacy of their hearts—as though sin were confined to this inner dimension. The social dimension of sin is then conjured away. Of course it is wrong to say that sin is only social; but it is equally wrong to ignore its social dimension. Both extremes constitute grave faults in any moral system.

So the questionable aspects of the morality of the manuals do not derive from their insights, which can be valuable; they derive rather from concepts and practices that distort the features of moral theology as good news, leaving it to show only its threatening aspect. If this criticism seems unduly harsh, it can be mitigated by making two observations, already hinted at: one on historical context, the other on good sense.

There are of course considerations—many of them—that the manuals were unable to take into account. So our criticism is not directed so much at the manuals themselves, which replied to questions of their time in categories of their time. Our criticism is aimed at a mentality, still widely found, which insists on clinging to outdated considerations. It was not the manuals that were in error: those who continue to ignore the data of human and social sciences, let alone the theological data adduced to enrich the moral outlook of our day, are in error.

The second observation concerns a gift from God often found among the followers of Christ, and to a special degree in figures such as St Thomas Aquinas and St Alphonsus Ligouri: fortunately there have always been men and women of good sense, enlightened by the gospel. Fortunately too, this good sense has generally informed pastoral practice, ensuring that the letter does not kill the spirit.

(c) A Painful Confrontation

The "renewed" and "liberation" approaches will be examined in the succeeding two chapters, but first a confrontation—that among the traditional, renewed and liberative approaches—needs to be brought forward to set the scene of moral theology today. For a variety of reasons, this confrontation has been painful up till now, though if it is carried forward with serenity, its results can be beneficial. The confrontation has not been a matter of the traditionalists inveighing against those who seek to detail the reasons for changes of approach; nor has it been a matter of the adherents of the renewed or liberative approaches inveighing against the past as such. The purpose of the confrontation has just been to explain the reasons for the changes that have taken place, so that they can more easily be assimilated.

(i) The basis of renewed morality. As we have seen, morals are part of theology, and theology always refers to the life of the church. So renewed morality was not worked out either in the vacuum of an infantile debate about the past, or by simply going back over the field of morals alone. The motors of renewal were started by a whole new context of both church and theology. The impetus for renewed morality came not so much from Vatican II, which had little to say about moral theology, as from the whole church and theological setting that gave rise to Vatican II and developed with it.

Consideration of what is known as "the life of the church" revealed a growing concern with making a positive response to the challenges posed by the "modern world." For a variety of reasons the church and the modern world were once again drawing apart from each other to such an extent that not only was a fruitful dialogue between them difficult, but also the church saw the effectiveness of its own mission in the world threatened. Hence the gigantic effort made to open up paths of dialogue, without of course jettisoning the vital kernel of the message the church bears.

Theology as a whole felt in need of an *aggiornamento*, as an abundance of literature on the subject shows.[16] And within this wider context, moral theology saw the need for "new directions."[17] When the Council fathers threw out the preparatory schema *De Ordine Morali*, this was the signal that the new avenues being explored since the fifties were leading in the right direction.[18] In order to preserve the values of tradition, it had become necessary to go back to the sources, and going back to the sources had led to basic questioning of the system used in the manuals; fidelity to tradition involved discarding lesser traditions.

Vatican II, not in a few texts but in all its texts, not in its texts alone but in its whole context, in this way lent fresh impetus to efforts at surmounting a whole series of characteristics: eternalism—through the principle of historicity; dualist pessimism—through recovering confidence in the human race; terror of sin—through confidence in grace; legalism—through stressing the theme of the covenant; privatism—through assigning value to earthly realities. Underlying these efforts, there had of course been deep studies in biblical and patristic theology, as well as endeavours to assimilate the postulates of the human sciences.[19]

All this clearly did not evolve in a totally calm manner. There were tensions, and these came to the surface. They did not result from bad faith, but from the very sincerity of the quest for truth—on the part of representatives of both currents—which bruised not a few reputations. For everyone involved, it was a question of abandoning the safety of a sheltered anchorage and putting out to the high seas, with all the risks and discomfort involved in such a journey.

(ii) The basis of liberative morality. The theological debates between the adherents of the traditional approach and those of the renewed approach, which gathered force at speed, were interrupted after less than ten years by the arrival of a new approach from the Third World.

Vatican II had already noted that we were living in a time of accelerated historical change and rapid and deep transformations. Neither the world nor the church has stood still since then; on the contrary, the rate of change has increased. In this changed church context, expressed in the conferences of Medellín and Puebla, moral theology began to realize that not everything had yet found its proper place. If moral theology was to keep in step with the times, with the whole theological output coming from Latin America and with the developments taking place there within the church as a whole, it needed to make a more radical overhaul of its postulates.

Medellín and Puebla were like a seed of revolution planted in the church itself, in the sense that they brought a latent series of problems to the surface. Medellín and Puebla were two stages, a decade apart, but together formed part of a single process. Medellín was more influenced by theologians, and looked forward; Puebla was more influenced by bishops and tended more to confirmation of a course already undertaken: the course of liberation.

Both conferences had their point of departure in Vatican II

and were faithful to the Council. The final documents of both were approved by the Vatican. But both realized that, in order to be faithful to the insights of the Council, they needed to take greater account of actual facts. And one of the great insights of Vatican II was openness to the world in all its complexity: society, economics, politics, religions. Medellín and Puebla drew out the consequences of this Vatican II insight, and at the same time expressed it more clearly, through asking the basic question: To which world are we committing ourselves in the name of the gospel? The reply they gave to this question proved decisive for church praxis, and therefore for moral theology as well. The world to which the church is committed, in the name of the gospel, is not the world of progress, still less the world of the powerful. The church cannot ingenuously accept the world of progress as though it were a forerunner of the Kingdom. This progress is achieved, very largely, at the expense of the weakest, and through the sacrifice of many human values. The seeds of the Kingdom are hidden in the sub-world of the impoverished. They are the ones, Puebla says (1124), who will build a new history and a new society. And it is because they are Christ's favourites and the builders of a new history more attuned to the demands of the gospel that the church sees itself obliged to opt for them and to struggle with them for their integral liberation.

The adjective "preferential," added to the option for the impoverished, was not enough of a palliative to prevent skirmishes of all sorts. The fact is that this option has shaken various branches of theology, as it has disturbed the whole course taken by the church. For this very reason, it should come as no surprise that it has profoundly discomfited both the adherents of the manuals of moral theology and those of renewed morality. Both these approaches were formulated in a very different social setting, and both were attempts to respond to the challenges of a very different reality. Faced with the ever-increasing clamour rising up to heaven from the hearts of many lands, even the new formulations of renewed morality seemed to stop far short of the expectations aroused. Even though many of its postulates are deeply revitalizing, they do not seem to provide an adequate response to the cries of the poor who are suffering and crying out for greater justice, liberty and respect for their basic human rights (Puebla, 40ff). These postulates are whispers drowned out by a storm.

This is the source of the main criticisms addressed to renewed morality: that it is still very much focussed on the Western world, still very idealist, still very personalized, still socially conservative. These criticisms are not aimed primarily at renewed morality and the theologians who espouse it. Both should be appreciated for their undeniable achievements. No, the criticisms are addressed far more to those who live in the historical-social context of the Third World and yet fail to hear the evangelical demands that spring from this context. Simply trying to transpose a thought-pattern originating in the First World to the brutal reality of the Third and Fourth Worlds is like giving a sophisticated piece of electronic equipment to a shantytown dweller and expecting him to be able to use it. This is the nub of the question, and it is on this level that debate has to be joined.

Unfortunately, there are many vested interests at stake; there is a lot of questioning and very little serenity. Hence the difficulties in conducting a true dialogue, one which might open the way to mutual enrichment and, above all, sweep away the encumbrances preventing the construction of a more just society and a church still more attuned to the purposes of its Master.

Chapter II

Renewed Morality: One Way Forward

The movement of theological renewal begun in the fifties was clearly not confined to moral theology. Far from it; this renewal embraced the whole of theology, especially the areas of biblical and patristic studies, christology, ecclesiology and liturgy. Moral theology found its way back to the same fertile river that irrigated the theologically productive patristic and high scholastic periods. It became part, and a more organic part, of a new awakening of the whole life of the church.

Renewed morality found its way to Latin America through the works of Bernard Häring, one of its most distinguished exponents, followed by those of Marciano Vidal and others.[1] Their works have inspired, and still continue to inspire, ecclesiastical circles and the Catholic middle classes, especially those engaged in lay movements.

As anyone who follows theological literature through the reviews, especially European ones, will know, these two theologians are but representatives of an astonishingly fertile current. Literally thousands of articles testify to the new sap rising in moral theology, giving it a fresher, more cheerful and decidedly more evangelical look.[2] As the approach of the neo-scholastic manuals ran its course, that of renewed morality took its place as one alternative, pointing out the weak points of the morality of the manuals and establishing its own ground rules—which we shall examine a little further on, after studying the sociological context and principle of historicity underlying this new approach. It is not a monolithic approach, and we intend to pick out some of its central themes as proposed by its main authors.

1. THE SOCIOLOGICAL CONTEXT AND PRINCIPLE OF HISTORICITY

In the last section of the previous chapter we sketched out the ecclesial and theological context underlying the renewed approach. But we need to remember that it also has a social setting, and it is difficult to understand its main direction without examining this.

(a) From a Closed to an Open Society

The Industrial Revolution, beginning in England in the eighteenth century and reaching beyond Europe by the late nineteenth, was marked by a progressive change from a closed to an open society. This change has been most obvious in the Western countries, but can also be seen at work in the poor countries, though there it is slower and more localized.

A closed society has very definite features, which have an immediate repercussion on behaviour. These features are: homogeneity; a rural environment; predominantly internal influences; authority exercised by a minority, usually on the basis of age, experience or heredity; easily exercised external controls, through censorship or other pressures; predominance of group interests; primary loyalty given to institutions; stability; infrequent and shallow changes.

An open society, on the other hand, is characterized by: heterogeneity; pluralism; a predominantly urban population; largely external influences; division of powers; authority based on competence; internal means of control, such as conscience or persuasion; easy and varied means of communication; rapid and deep changes; variety and versatility.

These summary descriptions are not meant to imply a value judgment; it is too simplistic just to say that a closed society is better or worse than an open one. Security, continuity, mutual support, for example, are values inherent in some types of closed society. Furthermore, seen from inside a closed society, structures that seem intolerable to us may appear perfectly acceptable.

Whatever the rights and wrongs, the Industrial Revolution put an end to this type of closed society and produced a gradual shift to a more open one. This meant human beings beginning to experience a world in which movement became an increasingly dominant characteristic, in which the rate of change gathered pace. New pressures appeared and with them a continual need to adapt to new situations.

Morals, as sociological behaviour, equally shifted from age-old patterns. Even though moral theology is not based on sociological data, the fact of its being challenged and rejected in many aspects meant that it had to start questioning itself. The approach of the manuals may have responded to the needs of a closed society, but it certainly could not provide an adequate response to the challenges of an open society.

(b) The Impact of the Principle of Historicity[3]

We have used the term "historicity" several times already, and will do so many more times, since it is basic to an understanding of morality. So we need at this point to make a more detailed analysis of what it means and implies.

Human beings, one way or another, to a greater or lesser extent, have always seen themselves as beings-in-the-world, conditioned by time and space, and therefore as historical beings. Philosophy, from its earliest days, has always come up against the difficulty of determining the essence (nature) of things. Parmenides, for example, sought to define permanence, considering the static aspect of the world, stressing the identity of principles, essences. Later, Heraclitus saw everything under its aspect of becoming. We live in a world that is more becoming than being.

Despite the tension existing between these two modes of looking at the world, we can, at the risk of simplification, say that medieval philosophy gave more weight to being (*esse*) than to coming-to-be (*fieri*). If the Greeks managed to overcome the tension, integrating both lines of thought, this was certainly not true of late scholasticism, when *fieri* virtually disappeared into *esse*.

Contemporary thought, particularly since Hegel, has, one might say, rediscovered the historical dimension as basic to the human condition. All temporal reality is marked by this double aspect: an *esse*, which shows the continuity of the present with the past, and a *fieri*, a coming-to-be, which shows growth, development, within continuity. A person's own biological existence exemplifies this process: we renew all the tissue of our bodies every seven years, but this does not mean that we change our basic identity. I am not just what I am at this moment—I am also what I have been and what I will be; the future me is already a seed in the present me. The same can be said of a people: it carries its past in its present and is germinating the seed of its future.

The principle of historicity suggests that human beings need to be given a new physiognomy: what characterizes human beings—their "humanity"—cannot be considered a finished component, but rather a potentiality to be realized. Human beings are not, so to speak, themselves except insofar as they are in quest of their own identity, which has to be progressively achieved, starting from an initial datum and the circumstances surrounding this. They are beings who continually alter the world, society and themselves as well (GS 35; see LE 26).

(c) Impact on Theology

The impact of this element in contemporary historical thinking led many theologians to consider historicity as a basic category for theology itself.[4] If it is to be faithful to divine revelation, theology has to be tied to saving history, which has a past but also continues in the present. God was revealed in the past through historical events, the greatest of which was the incarnation of the Son. But this same God, who made the Son-event the norm for all others, is still being made manifest through present history. This is why Vatican II is so insistent on the need to be open and alert to the "signs of the times" (GS 11; see PO 9). Underlying this is a dynamic understanding of revelation.

Revelation comes to us in the first place, of course, from the scriptures, which makes them the obligatory reference point for any theology. But we have to remember that in many ways the scriptures themselves bear the marks of their times and of the people who wrote them. So if we are to be true to the deep meaning of revelation, we cannot be fundamentalist.

Theologians use the texts to try to discern their underlying meaning, and look to them for clues to the meaning of human existence itself. They do not do this on their own: they listen to tradition, their colleagues in faith and the magisterium. The principle of historicity also tells us that God did not speak only in the past, but continues speaking to us in many different ways today.

(d) Repercussions on Moral Theology

The principle of historicity is also of capital importance for moral theology. Accepting it has numerous consequences. Let us look at some of these, all of which are closely bound up with one another.

The first impinges directly on the very basis of moral theology. Accepting the principle of historicity means desacralizing theological constructs. They can no longer be the end of our quest; we need to find a new point of departure beyond them, in a deeper dimension. A solid point of departure has to be sought in the primordial fact, reiterated in different ways throughout the scriptures, that *God loves us and seeks our loving response*. Human beings are called to make this response and so to live in the realm of faith through the passion, death and resurrection of the Son of God.

So our faith in the God who loves us and who, through the only-begotten Son and numerous other interventions in history, invites us to live in the realm of faith, would then become the point of departure, the *proprium* or *esse* of moral theology. Human constructs would then become merely more or—sometimes—less successful efforts at expressing this fact and, by relating it to life at a given time, helping the faithful to respond to God's saving purpose. So no authors or books can be seen as untouchable. Hence the criticism made of neo-scholastic manuals.

Secondly, accepting the principle of historicity implies accepting a dynamic moral theology. This would be no longer a simple matter of applying principles, but an ever-renewed quest to remove the dross of history and so reveal the authentic face of the Other. The first postulates of a dynamic moral theology would be the idea of growth and a progressive understanding of the gospel message and of the ultimate meaning of the Christian presence in the world.

In the third place, historicity teaches us that moral theology too is inserted in history. It may contain a treasure, but is itself made of fragile clay and is not to be confused with the treasure within. Consequently, the renewal of moral theology is not just a fact to be recorded with a greater or lesser degree of disquiet; it also becomes a duty guaranteeing its fidelity.

(e) The Danger of Subjectivism

Fidelity to God's saving plan does not consist in pure and simple repetition of eternally valid principles, but in a constant seeking for a more adequate response to the appeals God is making to us *now*, at this actual moment. Put another way: moral theology—like all theology—is made up of an *esse*, given by the primordial fact of a God who loved us first and who summons us to live in the light of faith, and also of a *fieri*, provided by interpretation, by the response we try to make to God's loving summons. This double dimension always has to be respected in any production of a treatise of moral theology, so that it can never see itself as something definitive.

A common worry is whether this way of looking at moral theology does not lead to relativism, where there is no space for immutable norms and principles.[5] This is a valid concern, and one that is constantly being expressed. Certainly all human constructs are relativized, and very much so, but this does not mean calling into question the absoluteness of the mystery of God, who calls human creatures and awaits their creative response. Subjectivism or arbitrariness in handling the treasure of revelation is avoided by our paying attention to the calls God addresses to us today.

The danger of being subjective, and even arbitrary, is not confined to those who seek renewal. It also threatens those who inadvertently seek to confine the whole richness of the divine mystery within closed formulas. The purposes of renewing moral theology are precisely to avoid arbitrariness, to adopt an attitude of humble listening, and to be conscious of the limitations of one's position.

2. THE MAIN THRUST OF RENEWED MORALITY

Vatican II made few explicit references to moral theology, which has led some commentators to conclude—unjustly—that it made little contribution to renewal in this field.[6] Others find a double suggestion in the paucity of texts: first, that moral theology should seek inspiration in the whole message of the Council; second, that it is up to moral theologians themselves to pursue the course of renewal.

The few explicit texts do in fact establish some central guidelines for renewal: the exposition of moral theology is to be "scientific," and needs to be "more thoroughly nourished by scriptural teaching. It should show the nobility of the Christian vocation of the faithful, and their obligation to bring forth fruit in charity for the life of the world" (OT 16d).

(a) A Morality More Thoroughly Nourished by Scriptural Teaching

Even before the Council had declared that "sacred scripture . . . ought to be the soul of all theology" (OT 16b), and that moral theology should be more thoroughly nourished by it, theologians had seen the need to go back to scripture. This they had deduced from historical studies: in the past, in the golden periods of the Fathers and the scholastics, moral theology had been basically scriptural, whereas in the period of late scholasticism and the neo-scholastic manuals it had not. The manuals in particular were distinguished by their lack of scriptural basis. First attempts to put this right were made by Sailer and Hirscher in the last century, using biblical themes somewhat fundamentalistically and even romantically. This led to a phase in which moral expositions were juxtaposed with a brief biblical summary. Then came a period of integration, but it was not till Tillmann, followed by Häring, that a new phase of moral life was actually built on a scriptural foundation.[7]

But what does it mean to be more thoroughly nourished by scripture? Scripture is basically made up of the proclamation of the good news, which invites human beings to direct themselves toward an ideal that surpasses ordinary human perfection. This is the sense in which sacred scripture can be said to present a moral conception: it enshrines a doctrinal content and gives a direction to life.

This does not, however, mean that we can look to scripture for a theoretical framework of Christian morality, or expect it to have something to say about every human problem. However precious scriptural indications are, it is possible to point to a certain insufficiency of scripture in matters dealing with the concrete situations in which human beings find themselves.[8] The scriptures are not a recipe book, but they do contain the basic meaning of what it is to be human, since Christ is humanity in its fullness.

One thing is certain: basing moral theology on scripture does not mean piling up "proof texts," looking for texts to support pre-established theses. What it does mean, above all, is that morals should reflect the good news expressed in scripture—good news characterized not by "You must," but by "I have set you free."

Moral theology has to see the scriptures as its deepest well of inspiration. Here moralists will find indispensable sources in the numerous studies that exist on different aspects of how the Bible relates to being Christian. These deal with faith, hope, charity, mercy, love of God and of one's neighbour, justice, humility, pride, sin, suffering, and so on. Such studies serve to help our understanding of these realities, in the light of the Bible.[9] Their main value, however, lies on a different level: that of the meeting between, on the one hand, the history of salvation and the mystery of Christ and, on the other hand, our own questions and responses. This is something the renewed approach took very much to heart.

(b) A Christocentric Morality[10]

The covenant set forth by God in the Old Testament refers constantly forward to the great promise: Jesus Christ. It is in him and through him that the new and everlasting covenant is established. He is the new Law. Incarnate in Christ, at one and the same time and in the clearest way possible, are God's saving pro-posal and humankind's perfect and complete re-sponse.

This basic fact was emphasized by the Fathers and by the great masters of the Middle Ages (St Bonaventure, Duns Scotus, St Thomas Aquinas); it was also one of the great losses from the *Institutiones* of 1600 and the neo-scholastic manuals that derived from this and similar works. They lost sight of Christ-centredness as the central axis round which all life and theology revolve. And it was not till the thirties, with the biblical and liturgical renewal, that moral theology returned to a Christ-centred approach. Sailer, Hirscher and Tillmann were the great forerunners; the latter structured his manual around the call, "Follow me." Christocentrism also characterizes the work of Bernard Häring, and was stressed by Vatican II when it said that moral theology should show the nobility of the Christian vocation of the faithful.

What, then, is meant by the "Christian vocation of the faithful"? The call it refers to is in the first place a gratuitous call from God: God calls us to salvation and at the same time to a way of life corresponding to salvation—a way of life, that is, of perfect charity, such as Christ's own life was. This call carries a dynamism within it; God's call, issued once and for all, resounds ceaselessly through the action of the Holy Spirit. The quest for an ideal never fully realized is an integral part of the dynamism of God's call, which can be more fully understood in the light of a theology of "following," which we shall examine later.

(c) Bearing Fruit for the Life of the World

One of the weak points of the moral theology of the manuals was its emphasis on the individual element. With the development of the human and social sciences, this over-emphasis became untenable: Aristotle was right when he said that human beings can be perfected only in the *polis*. Human beings are matter and spirit, and as such live only to the extent that they co-exist with their like and with the whole of creation. The scriptures too show that God did not make a covenant with individuals, but with a people. Individual vocation has a community and social dimension.

This is the perspective from which Vatican II described bearing fruit for the life of the world as an essential component of Christian life. Christians bear fruit not for themselves, but for the church; not for the church only, but through the church for the whole of humanity. Christians have a real commitment to the world: this commitment springs from the dynamic of their faith, from creation and redemption and the resulting value of earthly realities.[11] "Earthly" here does not, of course, refer only to material creation; it is not just by cultivating their gardens that human beings become perfect, but by transforming both the created universe and the human community, in accordance with the creator's purpose.

Renewed morality did not draw out the full consequences of this rich filiation. It did, however, grasp the main implication: feared earthly realities, the most characteristic constructs of the whole melting pot of human activity, cease to appear as stumbling blocks and instead become the great opportunities for human beings, collaborating with God in creation. Though still left with an inherent ambiguity, the whole thrust of renewed morality brings out the positive character of earthly realities. Jesus Christ is the definitive installation of God's dwelling-place in the world. Christians, as leaven in the dough, have nothing to fear, since their history is presided over by the Lord of history.[12] So the Christian message does not turn human beings aside from the task of building the world, nor lead them to neglect the good of their fellow human beings, but rather obliges them more than ever "to measure up to these duties" (GS 43a). And more: the earthly activities which we are called on to undertake lead us to a wider conception in which our own personal lives are re-evaluated; we see human beings invited to form part of a great epic—the epic of the people of God who, led by the Lord of history, throw themselves into the audacious project of transforming the world. Their great opportunity does not lie in flight from the world, but in embracing the world, as Christ embraced it.

(d) From Pessimism to a Realistic Optimism

It would be ingenuous to attribute the anthropological shift in present-day theology to Vatican II. It was already present in sound theology.[13] Nevertheless, Vatican II certainly assimilated the main postulates of modern anthropology, as it did of what are known as the human sciences. Starting from a basic scriptural datum, that human beings are destined to become ever more the image of God, because they carry the "godlike seed which has been sown in them" (GS 3c; see 18b), Vatican II saw human beings as the centre and pivotal point of all created things—human beings not as ethereal, spiritualized beings, but as beings of flesh and blood, part of a people and inserted in a history.

While humankind has been disfigured by sin, it has also been renewed by Christ, who "restores the divine likeness" (GS 22b). And it is precisely in Christ, the perfect human being, that all men and women come to rediscover the greatness of their humanity. Sent as human to humankind, Christ indissolubly links the human to the divine, showing that there is no opposition between humanity and divinity. Nor is there any opposition, consequently, between time and eternity, body and soul, matter and spirit, human love and divine love, friendship with fellow human beings and friendship with God. They are different dimensions, but not opposing ones. It is in the light of this anthropology, based on a christology, that pessimist dualism has been banished from the framework of Christian theology.

The truth is that this Christ not only took on human flesh, but totally embraced all that is human: "He worked with human hands, he thought with a human mind, acted by human choice, and loved with a human heart" (GS 22b). This overcomes not only crass dualism, but also that refined sort which distrusts human beings and their achievements. It is through these that the world is humanized, and being humanized, in the deepest sense of the term, enters too into the sphere of the divine.

(e) Grace Is Stronger Than Sin

Grace and sin are the two basic postulates of the Christian understanding of life. They form the two poles of a dialectic that can never be transcended in our life on earth. What the morality of the manuals did was to inflate sin and "occasions of sin" to such an extent that living in a "state of grace" became pretty exceptional. Seen objectively and individually, sins, especially mortal sins, grew into an impressively long list, leaving little room for grace, which was likewise objectified and divided.

All the re-thinking that took place on the subject of sin in the post-conciliar period put it into its proper place.[14] Which means: while its power should not be minimized, neither should it be exaggerated. Seen in the light of faith, sin is a sort of shadow, constantly being shortened by the advance of the light.

This re-establishing of the dimensions of sin was brought about largely by stressing the overall context of a person's life, which is needed if we are to speak properly of sin.[15] However, that emphasis on the context of a person's life—if exaggerated—also has its limitations in this area: it too can highlight sin, as is shown by expressions like "situation of sin" and "structures of sin." But even liberation theology, which uses these terms, does so in a Pauline perspective: where sin abounds, grace superabounds.[16] If the social dimensions of sin are now stressed, this is done in the light of Christ who sets us free from all sin, in all its forms and dimensions. It is not sin that characterizes this period of history, so much as grace, which is being made evident in a multiplicity of ways.[17]

(f) From Legalism to the Release of Love

Despite remaining forgotten for many centuries, the covenant is one of the most essential biblical concepts for moral theology.[18] It will receive a whole chapter to itself for this reason later on, but for the moment we need to make a few observations pertinent to the main thrust of renewed morality.

In the Bible, the relationship between God and the chosen people is expressed through the covenant. It is the covenant that sets the tone for the commandments. These are not a series of Kantian categorical imperatives, but spring from a pact of love offered by God to the chosen people. Just as Thomism impoverished its master by reducing his moral teaching to the second part of the *Summa*, so the morality of the neo-scholastic manuals impoverished the biblical message by reducing the covenant to the ten commandments.

The covenant presupposes a God of love who offers an invitation to human beings, who offers to be their partner in building a history at once both divine and human, a God who treats human beings not as objects but as subjects, even going so far as to discuss the terms of the covenant with them (see Exod. 19:3ff). In the light of the covenant, even the morality of the Old Testament ceases to appear through the prism of legal rigidity and shines through that of the malleability of love.

Just because what was known as the morality of the Old Testament had not given up the whole storehouse of its riches, Christ was seen by many as another rabbi among rabbis. But once the category of the covenant had been given its rightful place, the full appeal of the beatitudes made itself felt.[19] In this way, opposition between Sinai and the Mount of the Sermon vanishes, with the latter shedding light on the former. The thunder and lightning of Sinai no longer inspire fear, but can be enthusiastically welcomed by those who receive them filtered through the spirit of the covenant and the beatitudes. Love takes the place of terror; the good news replaces threats; the spirit is set above the letter: this is the message of Moses interpreted by Christ, not by the Pharisees.

The demands made are no less for being dictated by love. On the contrary. Nevertheless, the atmosphere engendered is not only more authentic, but also more favourable, one in which God's plans can be embraced with greater enthusiasm.

3. OMISSIONS AND QUESTIONABLE ASPECTS OF RENEWED MORALITY

(a) The Real Achievements of Renewed Morality

Vatican II is undoubtedly a platform on which the universal church rests, a framework from which theology in general, and therefore moral theology too, cannot deviate. Many of the dead ends we face today can be explained only as failures to assimilate the message of the Council. This is as true for those who regard it as virtually outdated as it is for those who—without saying so openly—hold it responsible for the church deviating from its true path.

While maintaining the necessary distinction of levels, we need to stress that the theological insights of Vatican II are invaluable, and that the main lines of renewed morality cannot be cast aside. Just as Vatican II is the platform on which theology as a whole rests, so renewed morality is the indispensable point of reference for moral theology today.

Preserving the authentic values of the earlier approach,

recovering other values lost along the way, digging deeper into the original sources, renewed morality has come a long way in a short space of time. Starting by concentrating more on the defects of the earlier approach, it has moved on to a more constructive second phase. In this, it has produced its own internal critics, who point to different tendencies within a basic unity of approach. Some lay greater stress on theonomy, emphasizing transcendent aspects; others place the accent on autonomy, bringing out the human-being-as-image-of-God as the basis of morality.[20] Some stress normativity founded on "objective" criteria; others emphasize responsibility based on conscience. These different accents—signs, let it be said, of a healthy pluralism—both bring out internal differences and help in retaining a common viewpoint. Hence the impression that the renewed approach is all of a whole. In fact its main lines have been drawing together, giving the impression of a harmonious and virtually complete whole.

However complete, it has furnished many people with new answers to old problems, and if it has not provided all the answers, it has at least posed the problems in a more intelligible form. It has widened horizons; it has borne abundant fruit for the life of the world. For these reasons, despite the critical comments that follow, renewed morality deserves our respect, as do all efforts to re-vitalize the heart of the true Christian tradition.

(b) But . . . Doubts Creep In

The accelerating rate of change in contemporary history, as described by Vatican II (see GS 4–10), as well as the impetus provided by the Council itself, applied to Latin America by the Medellín and Puebla Conferences, provide the backdrop against which reservations about renewed morality are expressed. It has become a praiseworthy and fruitful attempt to respond to the challenges of the "modern world." It seems, nevertheless, not always to provide an answer to the cries rising up from the periphery of humanity, from those who still do not live in the "modern world." This is where the main problem with it lies.

The last twenty years have brought the sores of the Third and Fourth Worlds closer to the surface; they have forced us to take a more considered look at the contradictions presented by the world of today, where riches and poverty, abundance and need, progress and regression go side by side. A sophisticated electronic and supersonic world rubs shoulders with an anachronistic and worn-out one. The contrast is not only between different geographical areas, but is found equally within the same areas. Those who accuse the sixties of ingenuous optimism are not wrong: the modern world is not so marvellous, whether seen from the standpoint of politics, economics or religion. On the economic plane above all, the achievements hide a mass of suffering, resulting from the exploitation of the weak by the strong. The place where this can be seen at its starkest is Latin America.

Applied to the church, this means that while the church in the First World is dealing with challenges proper to a materially satisfied but religiously atrophied society, the church in the poor countries is going through a period of evangelical effervescence probably without parallel since the twelfth and thirteenth centuries.[21] In the poor countries the acuteness of the social, political and economic problems has posed an unparalleled challenge to the followers of Christ: either to take on, in the name of faith, a struggle spreading beyond the boundaries of the church itself, or to recognize that the salt has lost its savour, the yeast its power to raise.

It was through facing up to this overall challenge that many pastors and theologians first heard the mute cries arising from peoples who were at once starving and enslaved. The worst aspect was that the crisis reached scandalous proportions "in countries that call themselves Catholic" (Puebla 28).

It is within this context that the cycle undergone by the morality of renewal has been repeated in other latitudes and with other notes: first a more critical phase, then a more constructive one. To assess what is at stake, we need to look first at this critical phase in order better to understand the constructive phase later.

(c) A Morality Primarily Applicable to the First World

Nearly all Third World theologians were educated in Europe. Many of the younger ones (and the now middle-aged) were fired with enthusiasm by the renewal they found in progress there. All recognize that there can be no son without a father. But they also know that the son honours his father only by carrying the banner handed down to him onward, and in a creative manner, not slavishly following the path mapped out.

Furthermore, various distinguished theologians who belonged socially or geographically to the First World managed to see beyond its frontiers and appreciate the questions being raised in the Third World.[22] Again, let us state clearly that our criticisms are not aimed at those who live in a different setting; nor are they designed to demolish any individual positions. All they are aiming at is to point out certain omissions. If they have a target, it is those who have eyes but do not see, ears but do not hear, those who, like *nouveaux-riches*, turn their backs on their historical and cultural roots, putting on new clothes that do not suit them, throwing aside real gems to bedeck themselves in costume jewellery.

The main problem with renewed morality is that it raises to the first rank certain problems that, when confronted with others, deserve to be relegated to a lower rank. Of course they are human problems: so were those dealt with in the neo-scholastic manuals. Certain features are common to the whole of humanity. But there are also differences which should not be neglected.

Looked at from the perspective of these differences, renewed morality appears *progressive* rather than properly renewing. The questions it tackles undoubtedly affect all social classes and all parts of the world. But they do not do so with the same intensity. They are "vital" to those who live in a First World setting, less vital to those in the context of the underside of humanity.

Effectively, renewed morality still largely reflects problems that preoccupy people who enjoy a privileged economic, social and even religious status: genetic engineering, the arms race, suicide, euthanasia and so on. These are not really the moral problems that most affect the great majorities who live deprived of the benefits of a society of abundance.

The *manner* in which these problems are approached also gives rise to questioning, since it implies certain concessions that do not always seem justifiable. So, for example, if virtually everything was a sin in the morality of the manuals, renewed morality favours an "understanding" that sometimes threatens to compromise the gospel. So it argues, through recourse to the human sciences, that at the end of the day it can be possible to justify pre-matrimonial relations, masturbation, divorce and the like. It can even find rational justification for the arms race. Some social and psychological situations would justify certain attitudes; people can be seen as victims of circumstances over which their will, assaulted by doubts from all sides, has no control. We are not here trying to deny the strength of various sorts of conditioning, but just to plead for verification of their actual power and influence, and above all to question the point of departure, placed in the individual rather than in society as such. And understanding for difficult situations cannot be confused with concessions that cannot be upheld in the light of the gospel.

(d) Examples

To illustrate what we mean by a First World outlook that is grounded in personal terms, let us look at the prominence given to the question of euthanasia. Heated debates are held over whether a person's life should be prolonged for a little while longer or not. These take place without reference to the fact that the person in question is bound to be one of those who can spend time in hospital and benefit from the spectacular advances made in modern medicine. In Brazil, however, some forty million people never see a doctor in their lives, are born without help from one and die without help from one.[23] Their daily living is a process of being allowed to die. Of course individual life is an inestimable value: Then why not approach the problem in such a way as to bring out the living death that is the fate of millions?

Another example would be the question of "human rights," a term so hotly bandied about on all sides. A First World outlook sees these as the rights of citizens, that is, of those who enjoy legal recourse to the safeguard of their rights. A Third World outlook would lay the stress on those who have no means of safeguarding them.[24]

A look at the arms race suffices to show what the First World outlook means in social terms. Have nations not the right to invest fabulous sums to guarantee their security? How can "star wars" be immoral if it serves to defend the West against communist aggression?

These questions and others like them are obviously complex matters deserving of full study. But is it not a more pressing moral imperative to examine solutions for the masses who die every day because of their precarious living conditions? What we are questioning is not just the type of problem tackled, but the way in which it is approached, which sometimes seems to preclude a consistently evangelical viewpoint and practice.

(e) A Still Very Idealist Morality

Any moral theology has to aim at an ideal; if it is merely descriptive or defensive of certain situations, it is neither theology nor morals. And the Christian ideal is a very demanding one, as can be seen from the Sermon on the Mount: "You must therefore be perfect just as your heavenly Father is perfect" (Matt. 5:48). This is one of the greatest norms in all morality.

Nevertheless, Jesus himself warned against loading other people with burdens too heavy for them to carry. This means that, without in any way renouncing the ideal put forward by Christ, moral theology needs to be capable of taking account of the actual situations in which not only individuals, but also social classes and even whole peoples find themselves. Sometimes realities prevent the full realization of the Christian ideal.

The main thing to bear in mind is that God showed the chosen people a progressive pedagogy. Patriarchs and even prophets saw their words and actions condemned by some moral systems. Yet the whole of the Old Testament is the history of God's patience with human weakness and failures, even on the part of the chosen people. Truly this is a God rich in mercy.[25] The same could be said of the relationship between Christ and the apostles: they are sluggish of heart; they have difficulty in accepting certain facts, even going so far as to deny them. This does not make Christ give up or turn to condemnations. He is Masterly in the way he holds fast to two absolutes: the ideal and mercy.

Simply because it springs from a First World outlook, renewed morality addresses a type of man and woman who enjoys a privileged position in the economic, social, cultural and religious spheres. This emerges very clearly from the way it approaches family matters. The ideal it puts forward in family terms presupposes adequate income, a house with several rooms, good health, emotional stability and a lot of free time. The families of the impoverished have no hope of achieving any of these things. So the progressive approach comes to a dead end as far as they are concerned, through its failure to adopt a truly social outlook on human problems.

This last statement might appear to contradict what was said above with regard to "understanding" that threatens to compromise the gospel. The contradiction is only apparent: the parable of the talents tells us that much will be required of those to whom much has been given . . . and not the other way round.

(f) A Still Very Personalist Morality

Here again we are faced with an apparent contradiction. Surely one of the great achievements of renewed morality was precisely its incorporation of personalism? This is indeed one of the key elements that distinguish this approach: it starts with the subject, not with the object. Nevertheless, personalism taken to its ultimate consequences can produce an impoverishment: it is very good at dealing with immediate "I-thou" relationships; it can, however, be maintained only in a context of social reflection. This is not to deny the value of personalism, but to assign it its proper place.

Renewed morality, which is very good at assimilating the human sciences, especially psychology, seems less able to assimilate the social sciences. It has certainly not succeeded in assimilating them in a non-functionalist perspective. This means that what could have been one of its great strengths has become a possible weakness. So, for example, its failure to integrate social factors into its teaching on marriage and the family leads to "familyism," an attempt to understand and resolve problems in this area by reference only to home and family, without giving sufficient weight to economic, political, social, historical, cultural and even religious factors.

(g) A Still Socially Conservative Morality

The preceding sections show that, in several ways, renewed morality is more concerned with reform than with renewal. In social terms, it starts from a recognition of dysfunctions within existing systems. What it does not do is call them directly into question. This, at least, is true of its treatment of capitalism. In this sense it lags far behind documents of the official magisterium, such as the encyclicals *Populorum Progressio, Octogesima Adveniens* and *Laborem Exercens*.

This being so, what can renewed morality have to say about problems such as land redistribution in Third World countries, or the imbalance in international terms of trade? Its outlook, derived from the social setting it belongs to, is rather that of a world in which "things are as they should be," at least on the surface. However, one has to say that it would be worse if it took the attitude: "Do as we do and things will be better."

The renewed approach has unquestionably brought more gain than loss. It has disinterred riches lying buried at the bottom of the mine; it has introduced a sap capable of bringing fresh growth to many Christians; it has tried to respond to real questions raised by people living in the social sphere from which it originated.

More: it has provided a real way forward from the earlier approach. The latter, despite the values it brought out, left room for undue sacralization, refined dualism, something of an obsession with sin, legalism and legalistic privatism. This may be an exaggeration, but between them these qualities led to a logical conclusion: flight from the world and mistrust of earthly realities. The renewed approach, on the other hand, valued historicity, produced a realistic optimism, brought out the power of grace and the release of love. Through these, it led to a different logical conclusion: the way to be human lies not in flight but in engagement. It leads to embracing the world, as Christ did, and this is one of the central goals of moral theology.

Nevertheless, this approach seems not to have drawn the full consequences from its own postulates. A system can never *be* renewed; the most it can be is *on the way to renewal*. As a result, it needs to be open to developments that could not be foreseen at first, but which gradually come to be seen as necessary. So should we not be looking for other ways forward?

Chapter III

Latin American Approaches

Speaking of Latin American "approaches" might sound like a euphemism to avoid polemics surrounding liberation theology. But we are not concerned with polemics as such, only with the question of what is meant by liberation theology, and only insofar as it can help to show ways out of the dead ends we have found in moral theology. The choice of heading has been made to enable us to assess losses and gains in the quest for something more constructive. The choice of the plural is not gratuitous either, since there is little that is systematic in the field of Latin American moral theology; it is mapped out in a series of rough sketches rather than in a finished composition.

While seeking to avoid the rough waters of polemics, we cannot altogether avoid what produces them: cowardice has never been a moral virtue. And if the storm forces us to take certain precautions, it also gives us an opportunity to test the seaworthiness of our vessel, and even to set our course more surely. Besides, in theological matters, it is wise to bear in mind that very few deep questions have failed to rouse storms; it has been in the midst of storms that light has flashed on the horizons of faith and works. It is also true that, throughout history, good sense has always won through: if not in the short term, then at least in the long.

If we are to approach the question correctly, then the first thing needed is to pose the right questions and ask exactly what is at stake. The preceding chapters have referred to dead ends and crises in the past, but the fact is that the real crisis for theology is only just beginning. We are coming up to a crossroads, and the route we choose from there will determine at least the near future. So what is at stake in the whole polemic surrounding Latin American theological approaches, especially those classed as liberation theology?

Having cleared the floor, we need to move forward in the direction of the points of reference belonging to an approach in moral theology that corresponds to liberation theology; these points were implicitly set out at the end of the preceding chapter:

—What are the moral problems raised by the irruption of the poor?

—Are they problems that affect other social classes, or are they exclusive to a particular class?

Behind such questions lurks a bigger challenge, which exceeds the exclusive competence of theology: that of creating a new society. The problems of the poor are not, in fact, properly theirs: they are not the cause of their problems; they are the ones who suffer the consequences of them.

To have stated the problems, and to have set them in the context of the dream of a new society, is already something achieved. But it is not enough: we also need to indicate possible ways in which such a goal might possibly be reached, insofar as these ways are the proper subject of moral theology.

1. WHAT IS HAPPENING?

Never in recent history has theology had so much mud slung at it as in the years since 1984. This in itself has a thoroughly positive and even evangelizing aspect: theology is once again seen, as it was at the height of scholasticism, as a weighty science with something real to say about how human beings overcome their problems. It could even be an indication that the crisis about which so much has been said and written is actually an unusually deep one.

The word "crisis" is somewhat overworked. Even so, it is still the best word to describe situations and periods in history when confrontations and the basic doubts that stem from them have been most pronounced.[1] What is certain is that crisis can just as well have a negative outcome as a positive one; it can lead to irrecoverable losses as well as substantial gains: it all depends on the way it is "resolved." And if a crisis is to be resolved, the first stage in the process has to be to "situate" it correctly, either by comparing it with similar situations from the past, or by placing it in a wider present-day context.

(a) Some Past Crises

(i) In the apostolic church. The past, particularly that of the church, can look like a tranquil lake when seen from a distance. But the first signs of the crises that have in fact recurred in the church and in theology were already apparent in apostolic times. The narrative of Acts, with the different deeds attributed to Peter and to Paul, show undeniable tensions apparent in both the lives and the theological views of these two great pillars of the church. The questions of Judaizers and of the cult of idols (see 1 Cor. 8:1ff and 10:14ff) were not as peripheral as might appear from a distance. They raised basic problems—of theology, morality and pastoral practice. The proof of this is that they produced the need for the first Council, that of Jerusalem.

(ii) In the ancient church. The period known as that of the ancient church produced similar tensions. There are marked differences between St Augustine and St Jerome. Less well known, but no less deep, were the differences that arose between other major figures: Polycrates and St Victor (over the celebration of Easter); St Stephen and St Cyprian (over the question of the *lapsi*—those who had fallen away from the practice of the faith); St Damasus and St Basil (over trinitarian matters).[2] Curiously enough, nearly all these major figures are canonized saints.

(iii) In high scholasticism. The strictly theological polemics of high scholasticism were even more numerous. The famous "disputations" were not just verbal duels between intellectuals, but produced real battles between proponents of different understandings of subjects as basic as creation, redemption, sin, grace, repentance, the Eucharist, and so on. Though St Thomas was eventually officially endorsed, he too saw many of his theses questioned.

In the more strictly moral field, the seventeenth and eighteenth centuries produced real storms over basic points of moral theology.[3] Opposing positions were taken up by distinguished theologians or "schools," with veritable armies lining up behind them.

(iv) Other crises. Other examples could be adduced: the battles over various heresies in the early centuries, the Protestant Reformation, the modernist crisis. Those given, however, are sufficient to point up certain common factors in theological crises.

In the first place, provided they are well "resolved," crises lead to greater clarity in expressing problems. But if they are badly resolved or artificially covered over, they produce at best theological impoverishment, and at worst irreconcilable splits. A good resolution of a crisis requires the observance of certain minimal ethical norms in dealing with adversaries.[4]

Then, coincidentally or not, it is always the periods of well-resolved crises that show the greatest theological and pastoral richness. More tranquil periods generally run out in a lack of vitality shown in repetitive treatises and unmotivated pastoral practice.

(b) The Setting of the Present Crisis

The present crisis is very complex, on account of both the depth and breadth of the questions it covers. This makes it difficult to characterize, but some main features can be picked out. The first thing to make clear is that it is not a conflict between one type of theological approach and the faith of the church. We need to keep the distinction between faith and theology. The conflict is between "two ways of understanding the same faith, between two theologies . . . and the ecclesial experiences underlying them."[5]

The salient features are: (i) reading of reality; (ii) methodology; (iii) conception of God; (iv) conception of the church; (v) anthropological conception; (vi) conception of theology and morals. Whole books could be written about each of these, but here we want just to take them as reference points for establishing the context of the crisis.

(i) Reading of reality. Epistemology is, undoubtedly, a difficult subject and one charged with centuries of debate. How far and how can we succeed in grasping ever-changing reality? And

in what sense is reading of reality a touchstone for theology in general and moral theology in particular? Reading reality "situates" theology within a definite framework.

In the Latin American framework, there might be said to be three basic types of theological reflection: popular, pastoral and professional.[6] These three are unified by the same history-transforming faith. The first is found in the midst of the simple people, above all in the base communities, where the situation of oppression is felt most keenly and at the same time the gospel is breathed most freely. Here perception of reality is provided virtually spontaneously by the gospel-life binomial. The people intuit rather than reason logically.

The second, pastoral, type is found, as its name implies, among those trained as pastors and other agents. Reading of reality is also provided here by the gospel-life binomial, but through a more elaborate and organic mode of perception. There is more "reading" than pure intuition, with a certain technical knowledge added to good understanding of the gospel, though perhaps not over much concern for linking reality with rigorously "scientific" data.

The third type is the professional, where reading of reality has to be carried out with more care: the data of human and social sciences have to be taken into account along with intuition and pastoral experience.[7] This does not mean that the first two types of reading are less valid, or that there is any opposition between the three types. On the contrary, one feeds into the other, all in the service of understanding and practising the gospel.

All three levels need to take care to avoid an ingenuous or functionalist understanding of reality. Ingenuous understanding fails to see what lies beneath the surface; it easily assimilates the interpretation provided by the dominant ideology. Functionalist understanding, though more embracing, fails to see all details and the underlying roots of a question. Ingenuous perception seeks to solve a problem by throwing aid at it; functionalist perception for its part goes no further than reformism. The critical reading required by liberation theology, on the other hand, demands a practice of "deep and daring" transformations consistent with its perception of the deepest roots of reality. Applied to the reality of oppression, these roots show sin engraved on an "iniquitous" socio-economic system (see PP 26; Puebla 29–30).

Finally, none of these types of theology can rest content with a reading of reality that stays on the purely sociological level. While reading of reality is only the first step in the triple process "see-judge-act," in theological matters the data of faith and of Christian practice always have to be taken into account, while primacy of value always has to be given to the word of God.

(ii) Theological methodology. The second critical point is closely identified with the first: this is the question of method. The theology of the manuals, which represents the phase of the object, follows a starkly deductive methodology. It starts from the data of revelation and from tradition in order to arrive at concrete norms. In this respect, renewed theology, which represents the phase of the subject, has a different vision: it favours a more, though not entirely, inductive method. An example of this can be found in *Gaudium et Spes* itself: the first chapters *describe* the state of the world of today, and only later does it go on to set forth the Christian message and practice.

Liberation theology, which came about in the social phase, did not create its methodology *ex nihilo*. This might be seen as a development of the inductive method, but, since liberation theology sees itself as a new way of understanding and doing theology in the face of a specific situation, it is not surprising that it should insist on the originality of its methodology.[8]

This Latin American method, which finds its roots in the "see-judge-act" process implicit in *Rerum Novarum* and explicit in *Mater et Magistra* (see no. 232), has specific characteristics:

—In seeing as much as in judging and acting, it adopts the perspective of the poor. This is not the place to argue the legitimacy of this preferential option of the poor (for this, see Puebla 1134, 1141, 1145), but it is worth just noting that it has a theological, christological, eschatological, apostolic and ecclesiological rationale.[9] Even allowing that its stress is on a "situated" reading of the word of God, a reading that proceeds from particular situations and contexts, there is no doubt that it is an evangelical option. The option for the poor cannot concern itself just with the economically poor: we need to move beyond a class concept of the oppressed which relegates them to the socio-economically poor alone; we need to broaden the picture, though not to the point where its edges become blurred. The centre will always be occupied by those whose impoverishment is "the product of economic, social, and political situations and structures" (Puebla 30).

Neither can taking the viewpoint of the poor as our primary one mean abandoning the priviledged minorities. It means rather offering them another line of vision which will integrate them too in a gospel perspective. In the end, after all, since it is an option based on the gospel, it is not optional in the sense of being a choice: all Christians have to take it up as best they can, and liberation theology cannot ignore those who seek to live according to the gospel but have not yet understood its full implications.

—The Latin American approach, like that of *Laborem Exercens*, takes social conflictivity seriously (see LE 16). Accepting the conflictive dimension in society as a point of departure does not mean exacerbating it, but detecting it and denouncing it so as the better to overcome it. In this way morality performs one of its main tasks: to enable persons and society to be fully themselves. Clearly, a morality worked out from the perspective of the impoverished and recognizing the conflictivity in society will not be to everyone's liking: it disconcerts, changes a routine approach, alters behaviour patterns, displaces. But we must bear in mind that a morality that does not question is neither theological nor evangelical.

—There is an undeniable accent on practice. This is not really such a novelty: the church's social teaching always stresses that words are not enough but that we must "commit ourselves through action" (OA 48). What is particular to this approach is the perception that Christian practice leads to a better understanding of the word of God itself, and that the Word which became flesh launches a new practice. So we can speak of the "circular relationship" between theory and practice.[10] Perhaps we could even, more accurately, speak of a spiral movement between Christian word and practice, in which understanding of the word and Christian practice enrich one another. And precisely because it is "circular" or "spiral," the stress on practice, which is decisive in moral theology, does not reduce the whole of theology to a morality, but links morals more closely with the rest of the theological framework, thereby avoiding the schizophrenia of an "autonomous" science.

—There is equal stress laid on the social dimension. This is not seen as the only angle from which to understand and transform human reality, but as a more all-embracing viewpoint from which to understand properly and transform the whole and the parts. Faith has undeniable socio-political implications; otherwise charity and justice would not be the keys to the implantation of the Kingdom.

(iii) God. Inevitably, the question of God lies at the heart of any true theology. But the fact is that the God of the Israelites was not quite the same as the god of the Egyptians or the Babylonians. In the same way, calling on God in the world today does not have quite the same meaning for all those who call themselves theists. And one can refine this by asking whether it means quite the same thing for all those who call themselves Christians: the polemic surrounding secularization and the "death of God" suggests that it does not. This shows once more the truth of what medieval theology said: theo-logy is always stammering about and from a greater reality which we call God.

Conflicts between different theological conceptions show that underlying them are different understandings of God. This is possible within one faith because of the multiform riches of the mystery of God. So the death of God and the problem of atheism can be burning questions in the First World, while they are of only secondary interest in the Latin American context. In Latin America, the urgency of social problems means that emphasis is placed far more on christology and ecclesiology than on theodicy as such. Rather than asking whether God exists and who God is, liberation theologians ask what repercussions God has on the concrete existence of people and society.[11] Hence their insistence on the God of life, the God who is made present in history, the God whose favourites are the poor.[12]

(iv) The church. We should not be surprised that there are different understandings of the church: they follow from different understandings of God and the resulting pastoral practices. While the ecclesiology of the First World tends to

concentrate far more on internal problems, the church in the Third World finds itself challenged mainly by problems that seem to come from outside it, but which nonetheless profoundly affect its mission and force it to give new life to forgotten aspects of its deepest identity. Being faithful to its saving mission makes it act differently, and also produces a different understanding of itself. At stake, of course, are not two churches, but two ecclesiologies. The same church of Christ, placed in different situations, takes on different connotations, in a pluriformity which can be enriching. It is a matter of incarnation.

(v) Anthropology. The anthropology underlying any theology is another point of friction. Theology always postulates an anthropology. All Christian theologies have common presuppositions, such as Christ as the perfect model, human beings as the image of God, openness to transcendence, and so on, but there are also different emphases, stemming from different needs. It is not surprising that First World theology should reflect First World reality, addressing people who are divided and anguished, but also privileged in a number of ways. While they may feel an inner insecurity, they affirm themselves through a whole series of guarantees afforded them by the context in which they live, above all through their undeniable achievements in the fields of science and technology. They are people who carry the signs of their success around with them, and their ethical preoccupations are those of a liberal, wealthy society.[13]

Liberation theology and the moral theology that corresponds to it are concerned with "non-persons,"[14] human beings disfigured by sufferings imposed on them not through their condition as creatures, but through the situation of destitution of which they are victims. The faces that appear here are ravaged and suffering; as Puebla describes them, they are "the faces of young children, struck down by poverty before they are born . . .; of young people, who are disoriented because they cannot find their place in society . . .; of the indigenous peoples, and frequently of the Afro-Americans as well; living marginalized lives in inhuman situations, they can be considered the poorest of the poor . . .; of the peasants . . . they live in exile . . .; of labourers . . . frequently ill paid . . .; of the underemployed and the unemployed . . .; of marginalized and overcrowded urban dwellers . . .; of old people, who are growing more numerous every day . . ." (32–9).

(vi) Theology. While theology stemming from a First World context tends to concentrate on individuals, theology born of a Third World context tends always to consider persons in an indissoluble relationship with society. And the society they are bound to is not only one of inequalities, but of conflicts virtually inherent in the type of social structure it presents.

All these aspects show that the three schools of moral theology examined are indicative of far deeper differences. Each one carries its own overtones, though these are not necessarily mutually exclusive.

2. BASES OF A LATIN AMERICAN MORAL THEOLOGY

We have already seen, in the last section of chapter I, that the Latin American approach is not the product of theological speculations, but of a whole body of church practice. We have just seen that the confrontation between the three approaches goes beyond them in themselves: there is a whole historical, cultural, ecclesial and theological world called into question. The two earlier approaches, despite their undoubted virtues, do not seem to provide an adequate response to the challenges thrown up by the sub-world of the impoverished. And we need to remember that this sub-world is much bigger than the "modern world."

At the outset, we need to recognize that the Latin American approach is still in a fairly embryonic stage.[15] While bulky volumes have been produced in the philosophical field,[16] in that of moral theology we have articles rather than complete books, with only a few exceptions.[17] Indeed, "the poverty of theological/moral reflection" and "fragmentary reflections" are descriptions that have been applied to it, and rightly so.[18]

What we are seeking to do here is to broaden the horizon and set out bases on which subsequent chapters can be built. Starting from the impoverished as new social agents, we need first to enunciate their main problems. These will in turn lead us to a wider challenge: the building of a new society and the ways that might lead toward it.

(a) The Impoverished as New Social Agents

The incursion of the poor into theological and ecclesial consciousness is not really a new phenomenon; it has taken place in previous eras.[19] The novelty now is in the strength, intensity and breadth of the phenomenon. Such a development has come about because the "modern world" with its resources and apparent abundance has transformed the destitution imposed on so many millions of human beings into a scandal to the Christian conscience.

The repercussion of this phenomenon on the different schools of moral theology was only a matter of time. The Latin American approach has for some time been arguing for a shift not only in the object, but in the subject of moral theology. Of course both subject and object concern human beings, created in the image and likeness of God. They concern *all* human beings, but even this is very general and will fail to do justice to the great majority of the children of God. Left on the fringes of society, they will also be left on the fringes of theology if their specific problems are not brought deliberately to the forefront.

The "object" that needs to be brought to the forefront, as a matter of simple justice, is the integration of the marginalized into a community so organized that they can become protagonists of a new history, one more in accordance with God's plan. As a result, the "subjects" that need to be brought to the forefront are these same marginalized people with their specific problems.[20] The Medellín and Puebla documents both make these the special object of their attention, as new social subjects.

What do we mean by a "social subject"? "In speaking of a *social subject* we mean not individuals considered as such, but inasmuch as they form groups or social classes, taking on, carrying out a decisive function, a primordial role, at a certain moment in the life of the church."[21] One of the achievements of moral theology done from a Latin American perspective is to have perceived this new social subject of the church and of moral theology.

Speaking of a "new social subject" means admitting a shift in the centre of interest: one particular social grouping becomes the chief partner of the church and of moral theology in place of another. If the church and moral theology are to be consistent with their declared preferential option for the poor, they have to listen much more to the questions, concerns and interests of a previously "forgotten" social group. While the questions that emerged previously came mainly from the "well-off," it is now necessary that room be made for questions that come from the rest of humanity.

(b) The Impoverished and Their Problems

We have already stressed that the problems reflected by the morality of the manuals and by renewed morality are human problems, and as such affect the whole of humankind. Nevertheless, they do not affect everyone in the same way and to the same extent. It is not a matter of devising one moral theology for the impoverished and another for the more fortunate. It is a question of redressing the balance, bringing the problems of the impoverished to the fore as well, making sure that all moral problems are approached in a fairer way. This means not rejecting the valid intuitions of the morality of the manuals and of renewed morality, but basically re-working them, in such a way that their most evangelical aspects can be brought out. This means that the more fortunate are not left out—but are deeply challenged.[22]

Some of the basic problems that affect the impoverished are not exclusive to them: the breakdown of family life, drugs and alcoholism are problems common to all "worlds," even though their immediate causes may not be the same in each. Neither lack nor plenty seems to favour human integration. Other problems are more specific and affect the impoverished layers of society more deeply. They are all linked to the basic issue of survival. Puebla lists them: hunger, disease, lack of education, the struggle for a piece of land, for a roof over one's head—for a minimum of human dignity, in short.

Hunger, which afflicts two thirds of humanity, is always and everywhere an affront to human dignity. But how much more humiliating it is when, in one assessment, the "modern world" is capable of feeding not just its present five billion inhabitants, but fifty billion.[23] The resources employed in the manufacture and maintenance of armaments would alone be sufficient to do away with hunger completely. This without mentioning the resources wasted in a thousand and one ways in a consumer society. This is the moral iniquity of hunger.

Disease has been shown to relate to the relative income of a country or region.[24] No one denies that some diseases are simply a fact of the human condition. But these are incomparably less numerous than those that afflict the poorest regions. In Brazil, for example, it is estimated that eighty million people are verminous, eight million suffer from malaria, the same number from chronic ulcers, millions from leprosy . . . all diseases that can easily be controlled and which are closely tied to living conditions.[25]

Between 20 and 40 percent of the population of the Third World are illiterate or nearly illiterate. In times gone by, when survival depended more on brute strength than on the use of intelligence, illiteracy could be tolerated, and its spread was understandable in view of the structural impossibility of providing basic education for everyone. But now, with the increase in the numbers of "lettered," being illiterate means being marginalized, in both work and social spheres.

Unemployment, it is true, does not affect the poorest layers of society alone. Even developed countries have an average of 10 percent of the workforce unemployed. It is the implacable logic of the market place. But in developed countries the unemployed can fall back on their savings or on social welfare, while those in the poorest countries and regions have neither of these to support them.

The struggle for land is as dramatic in the cities of the Third World as it is in the countryside. In countries like Brazil, lack of available and affordable land is a consequence of speculation in land and property values.[26] There can be no other explanation in a country with such a relatively low population density. Lack of housing, which affects millions of people in Latin America, is another structural problem that leaves masses of people literally living in the streets.

These are just some of the problems that most typically affect the impoverished. When we realize that they are all interrelated, we come to see that we are dealing with a phenomenon that affects the very "human-ness" of human beings. They are moral problems for two reasons. The first concerns their causes: these cannot be said to be natural, in view of the degree of technical and scientific development reached by the world today. The second concerns their effects: they cause a feeling of despair which normally goes with the lack of basic conditions necessary for survival. This does not explain everything, for human life is a complex business, and the mystery of evil in the world cannot be attributed solely to external causes. But it does explain a lot, and means that the usual explanations miss the point. This is precisely why the problems of the impoverished challenge both the order of importance normally given to moral questions, and also the way in which they are approached. Though behaviour does not determine moral notions, it cannot be ignored either, especially in its deepest causes.

(c) The Challenge of Building a New Society

The morality of the manuals specialized in resolving cases, with individuals as its horizon. Renewed morality broadened this horizon, basing itself on human, and to some extent social, sciences. But, for reasons already explained, neither system gave enough space to the social level. Both are in effect micro-moralities, even if broadened.

For reasons likewise given earlier, the liberation model of morality lays stress on the social element: not as an exclusive angle from which to approach what it means to be human, but as the basic perspective which leads also to a better understanding of the individual and personal spheres. Without denying personal responsibility, it sees individuals as forming part of a greater whole and their behaviour properly understood as stemming from this greater whole.

This strong accent on society as a moral category is not exactly something new. Rather the contrary: when the Old Testament states that "the people" have sinned and that "the people" need to be converted, it is using the same basic viewpoint.

The same is true of what is called the social teaching of the church. It starts from the presupposition that some problems originate in society and have to be faced by society as a whole. The Latin American approaches are merely trying to explain and particularize what the magisterium teaches on a general level. In his *Octogesima Adveniens*, Paul VI stressed this dimension when he stated that it was up to Christian communities, in communion with the hierarchy, to analyze their own situations and discern the choices they must make, the commitments they need to enter into, "so that social changes may be brought about" (OA 4). His analysis leads to an unequivocal conclusion that existing socio-economic and political systems have exhausted their possibilities (OA 30ff, 45). Though this is not the place for a more detailed examination of this complicated question, it is worth recalling some of the recent pronouncements of the magisterium on the subject.

After preaching the need for "daring and deeply innovatory changes" (PP 32), Paul VI went on to state that war against poverty, though urgent and necessary, was not enough: "It is a matter of building a world in which all people . . . can live a fully human life, free from the slaveries inflicted on them by other people and by a poorly tamed nature; a world in which freedom is not an empty word and in which the poor Lazarus can sit at the rich man's table" (PP 47).

No less insistently, Pope John Paul II has, from the outset of his pontificate, continually preached the creation of a *more just world*, described in these terms: "Making this world more just means, among other things, ensuring that there are no children who do not have enough to eat . . .; that there are no young people without adequate education, that there are no peasants without land . . .; that there are no workers ill treated or deprived of their rights; that there are no systems which allow the exploitation of man by man or by the state. . . ."[27] And referring specifically to the situation in Latin America, the pope said that "bold and truly innovative changes are needed to overcome the grave injustices inherited from the past . . .." Latin America must "claim its share of responsibility for building a *new world order*"[28]

Puebla refers back to Medellín's statement that "a muted cry wells up from millions of human beings, pleading with their pastors for a liberation that is nowhere to be found in their case" (Puebla 87), and Puebla commits itself to an ambitious project: "To evangelize in order to contribute to the construction of a new society that is more fraternal and just" (12).

What seems to be above debate is that existing society is not in accordance with Christian aspirations and that this same society is itself the cause of many moral wrongs. It is true that in relation to a new society, we have a better idea of what we do not want than of what we do. But perhaps that objection that very little positive is put forward hides an ideological reasoning: that since we have so little idea of what we do want, might it not be better to remain content with what we have got?

But then again we can ask: Should we preserve a tree that gives such fruits? There can be discussion about what other sort of tree should be planted, and how it should be planted, but what is certain is that it will never be donated by those who have vested interests in existing society. It is also true that moral theology should concentrate its efforts more on overall problems than on particular solutions.

(d) Education for the Practice of Justice and Love

Of course, a new society cannot be built on moral norms; we need to avoid "voluntarism." Society has mechanisms which normally even contradict moral norms. Nevertheless, because it operates on the level of conscience, moral education can have an effect on society. Its influence can be positive or negative, a force for change or a force for conservatism. It is in this sense that education for the practice of justice and love can be put forward as a way to usher in the creation of a new society.

Since Medellín, the church of Latin America has opted decisively for four basic courses of conversion: conversion to the people, conversion to the poor, conversion to base communities, conversion to the liberative process. Naturally all four presuppose the most basic conversion of all: to God. These conversions must have direct repercussions on moral formation, which is still seen as the church's basic activity in society. But it is not any process of formation that can respond to the church's new direction. Medellín showed that education can serve the *status quo* as one ingredient in a society that promotes injustice, just as much as it can serve integral liberation.

On the level of the universal church too, since the 1971 Synod, education for justice has been singled out as one of the main contributors to the building of a new society. It was a First

World theologian who wrote: "Genuine Christians . . . cannot limit themselves to carrying out their just duties, but must engage themselves seriously on behalf of their oppressed brothers and sisters, of all those who suffer injustice."[29]

Puebla prefers to speak of "evangelizing education," but understands it in the sense of "liberating education." It notes that the elites, who are small in number, have all the resources of modern culture at their command, while the great mass of the people are still illiterate or semi-literate; that the prevailing educational system, instead of leading to a radical change of economic, social and political structures, works rather to reinforce the mechanisms of oppression. Hence its conclusion: education is authentic only if it includes training in the process of transforming one's region, one's country, one's continent. It is authentic only if it foments the exercise of a critical function, if it forms standards that will "enable people to create a new society that is truly fraternal and participative" (1029).

This is also the basic postulate of a liberating moral education. Moral education cannot revolve around itself, around minor intra-systemic matters, around the petty interests of individuals or groups. It must not lose sight of the interests of the Kingdom, founded on justice and love. Only thus will it escape from a harmful narcissism and re-situate personal problems. People, as well as institutions, can be saved only by going out from themselves.

If it is conducted in the light of the gospel, however, liberating moral education will be distinguished from one that teaches bourgeois freedoms. It will be more like a process of unwinding, saving energies for the great battle. And this great battle is fought by Christ himself, who relieves us of unnecessary burdens in order to release our energies for service to the cause of the Kingdom.

Moral education for the practice of justice and love will not be any less demanding. On the contrary, it will place people in situations from which there is no easy way out: social, ideological and political conflicts. But it is precisely in these that peple discover their deepest identity: through conflict and confrontation they find themselves following the Master in the great adventure of the Kingdom.

3. MAJOR QUESTIONS

A balanced critical appreciation of Latin American approaches leads to two conclusions: that there is still a long way to go, and that these approaches open up new horizons. As one sympathetic critic has observed, liberation ethics "contain, in germ, all the criteria of Christian orthopraxis." And he adds: "They also carry with them an enormous potential of ethical/religious symbols, capable of bringing new vitality to our jaded theological/moral thinking."[30] Both the potential and the gaps have already been alluded to here. But some questions need further examination. These are: the epistemological status of the morality of liberation, its establishing of criteria, its specific content and its dialogue with the modern world.

(a) Epistemological Status

The history of moral theology is divided into periods when it has maintained close links with theology as a whole, and periods when it has broken these links and become "autonomous." This history also shows that the high points are the times when the links are maintained; the low points the times when they are cut. There is undoubtedly a need to avoid both schizophrenia and loss of proper identity. The morality of liberation, as it has emerged in Latin America, is making an attempt—not always understood—to maintain a dialectic between morality and theology without drawing the boundary between them too carefully. This creative balance promotes the cross-fertilization between the two poles of the dialectic.

(b) Establishing Criteria

It is obvious that the basic criterion, the *norma normans*, is the following of Jesus Christ. All other criteria have to be established in relation to it. This does not mean that criteria drawn from revelation, conscience, the magisterium and so on, are left out of account. Their role is precisely to shed light on what the *specific* following of Christ entails. It is just that the epistemology and other presuppositions of the Latin American approach lead inevitably to a different hermeneutic of this patrimony.

(c) Specific Content

"Basically, the content of liberation ethics may be summed up as the affirmation of the *criterion of Christian orthopraxis*," and "what gives authenticity to Christian praxis is its *liberating character*."[31] This summary may seem to say very little, and that in the most general terms. But once one realizes that behind it lies the whole Christian patrimony viewed from new postulates, what looks little explodes with the power of the leaven in the mass or the mustard seed. Seen in this light, not only is the approach to moral problems broadened and deepened, but the problems themselves have to be reclassified in order of importance.

(d) Dialogue with the Modern World

Finally, there is the question of dialogue with intramundane moral reasoning. In effect, the dialogue has changed with the change of "social subject." It is certainly not the reasoning of the modern world or of the Enlightenment that will fertilize theology in general, and much less moral theology: the values of the gospel do not seem to be hiding there. The values of the modern world so well described by Vatican II, can and should be redeemed, but from the standpoint of the impoverished. Jesus' prayer, "I bless you, Father, for revealing these things not to the wise . . . but to little ones," takes on a new specificity. The wise can contribute to building a new world, but only to the degree in which their lights are enlightened by *the* Light. And this presupposes abandoning the Promethean temptation currently being pursued by the modern world and "modern man" in their quest for autonomy.

"Latin American Approaches" was a deliberate title; there is still a long way to go and there are still many gaps to be filled: in epistemological terms, in methodological terms, in terms of theology, anthropology, ecclesiology. We must not forget that this whole huge endeavour is very young and has few resources behind it. But, in view of "our jaded theological/moral thinking," there is no doubt that these alternative approaches have to be tried. Not to destroy the edifice built up with so much care over the centuries, but to save it and give it new life. Furthermore, how can we follow the poor Christ without providing an edifice in which the millions of his poor brothers and sisters can find shelter?

These first three chapters have not been an answer to the questions raised by Latin American approaches to morality. They have just tried to open up a space in which basic aspects of fundamental morality can now be developed.

PART TWO

THE MAIN POSTULATES

Chapter IV

The Covenant: Revelation of God's Purpose

The main purpose of any theology is to uncover God's purpose in relation to humanity and to a particular historical period. Throughout history the methods used in this uncovering have varied, as have the results of the quest, but theology has always been concerned with knowing the divine purpose, and moral theology with making its incarnation feasible.

Talk of "renewal" or "new quests" often gives the impression of something that has never happened before. Yet sometimes novelty consists simply in rediscovering an ancient and hidden thread. This is what has happened with the covenant. Though it is a central biblical concept, it remained virtually ignored for centuries. One of the merits of renewed morality, with its accent on returning to sources, has been to bring the covenant to the fore as a basic category not only for biblical morality, but for any moral theology. A mass of studies made over the past twenty years has laid fresh stress on important parts of the rich theology of the covenant, examining its basic context and content, bringing out its specific implications for theological thought.

For a series of reasons already examined, however, renewed morality would seem not to have dug to the bottom of this particular mine. It has seen a lot, but not explained everything. It has shed light on the covenant as a religious programme; it has shown the part played by the prophets; it has pointed the way to a fruitful theology of conversion. But it has still focused on the religious aspect and the personal dimension, leaving the social and political aspects, which are in fact closely linked to the religious, in the shade. This chapter seeks to examine the main characteristics of the covenant that were brought out by renewed morality, while bringing into the light what it left in the shade.

1. THE RELIGIOUS DIMENSION OF THE COVENANT

The covenant undoubtedly belongs to the sphere of salvation. It is the start of God's saving plan which reaches its culmination in Christ, the embodiment of the "new and eternal covenant." It is also clear that the covenant constitutes a gift from God. Chronologically, the first step stemming from this gift is the building of a people who will really be the people *of* God. As its celebrates the covenant ever anew, this people feels its belonging to God revivified and finds the strength to carry out an undertaking in history, an undertaking inspired by God which God's people are given the task of carrying out in historical terms.

(a) The Covenant as a Basic Religious Category

Without the category of covenant, the Old Testament becomes virtually unintelligible. The same is true of the "Kingdom of God" in the New Testament. And while the expression "Kingdom of God" occurs 123 times in the New Testament, the term *berith* (Greek *diatheke*), translated as covenant or alliance, occurs no less than 286 times in the Old.

(i) Several meanings. The word *berith* can be interpreted in a number of different ways.[1] Each of the interpretations, however, always includes a religious character, and a connotation of moral commitment when describing the covenant in Israel.

There are basically two models of covenant in the Old Testament: the priestly one (from the sixth century B.C.) and the Deuteronomic one (from the seventh century B.C.). The first emphasizes a one-sided character: practically everything is reduced to a solemn promise made by God. The second stresses the bilateral, though still unequal, relationship between God and God's people: the covenant is God's free and gratuitous initiative, but involves a definite human response. This is brought out clearly in the oft repeated formula: "You will be *my* people and I shall be *your* God."

There are also several descriptions of covenant,[2] the principal ones being of the covenants made with Noah (Gen. 9:1–17), with Abraham (Gen. 17), and on Sinai, the great covenant (Exod. 19:20; 24). All these show a different conception both of God and of human beings. But God is always a transcendent being who nevertheless turns to humanity; human beings are always weak, but are transformed into something like partners of God. Also, in all the descriptions, though it is made through a central personage, the covenant is sealed in community terms: it is with the people of God. Furthermore, the covenant implies the idea of a *way*: the human response to it is embodied in a dynamic process.

(ii) Originality. Neither the literary genre nor the content is in itself exclusive to Israel. Something similar can be found throughout the Middle East.[3] As far as the literary genre is concerned, the usual pattern consists of a historical prologue, in which the contracting parties are identified, the terms of the mutual commitment, the evocation of witnesses, blessings and curses, and a solemn reading of the pact, which has to be renewed periodically. All these elements can be found in both the biblical covenant and in non-biblical examples. Neither is the content, the ten commandments in the case of Sinai, really exclusive, if one takes account of the Babylonian commandments[4] and those found in the Book of the Dead.[5]

Despite these similarities, the covenant between God and God's people in the Bible does show traces of undoubted originality: it accentuates God's initiative; it has a dialogal character, which is brought out in the course of time; it is concerned with worship, the community, history.[6] Its gratuitous nature is brought out in the "credo of Israel" (Deut. 26:5–9); its community and dialogal character is revealed in the episode of "negotiation" established on Sinai (Exod. 24:1–8); its historical aspect is brought out through three basic points of reference: creation, Christ, consummation; its relation to worship shows both in its periodic renewals, and in the invective of the prophets against an empty ritual divorced from history and from the actual life of the people.

(b) The God of Israel

The conception a people has of God is a decisive factor in its history, the more so when its religion becomes that of a particular people. The gods worshipped in Egypt and by the various peoples who inhabited the lands of Canaan were organized into a certain hierarchy, with greater and lesser gods. This “theology” transposed to heaven what happened on earth, and vice-versa: there was an aristocracy and an impoverished and uneducated people. Using the services of religion, the aristocracy monopolized worship, learning and possessions. A historical situation was sacralized through myths linked to creation, making the actual situation something willed and maintained by the gods.

In Israel, in this as in so many other fields, there was a clean break with prevailing concepts, which explains the originality and strength of the Israelite people. The God of Israel was one, and stood at the origin of all peoples and all things. From his universal fatherhood, an equally universal brotherhood and sisterhood stemmed logically. As became clearer in later stages, this theodicy provided the roots for Israel’s historical progress.

One of the distinguishing features of this theology is the sovereignty of God, who is not to be confused with any creature. But equally significant is that the “I am who *am*” is presented as “Yahweh your God who brought you out of the land of Egypt, out of the house of slavery” (Exod. 20:2; Deut. 5:6). Though distinct from history, the God of Israel is a God who is concerned with it, and who constantly intervenes in it.

Yahweh’s interventions in history, nevertheless, are not neutral, in the sense of being indiscriminately for some or for others: he shows a clear preference for the weakest. This is shown already by his choice of a people: he did not choose the Egyptians or the Babylonians, either of whom would apparently have been better fitted to carry out his plans. He chose those who were not even a people: “Yahweh has bound himself to you and has chosen you, not because you are the most numerous among all the peoples (on the contrary, you are the least)” (Deut. 7:7). This concern for the weak, who are given many names, is worked out in many ways: sometimes through recommendations, sometimes through institutions.[7]

(c) The People of God

The relationship between Yahweh and his people is unique. At the same time as being a relationship founded on fear, it is founded on love. Hence the images of father-children, bridegroom-bride, shepherd-sheep, and the like. But its deepest mark seems to be the fact of the people becoming the personal property (*segullah*) of Yahweh, precisely on account of the covenant (see Judg. 5:11). Despite successive historical dominations (by the Arameans, the Egyptians, the Babylonians, the Persians, the Greeks, the Romans), the consciousness of being the people *of* God is never extinguished, and lies at the root of all their achievements and restorations. This is all the more remarkable in view of the fact that the origins of Israel seem to lie in a mixture of clans and tribes. What came to unite them—besides their faith itself—was their common condition as exploited and oppressed. The deepest links between them were of faith and historical condition.

Sociologically speaking, the building blocks of the people were the tribe, the family and the household (see Judg. 7:16–18). This social structure produced the earliest concept of what it means to be a human being. Isolated individuals, closed in on themselves, are not recognized; personal characteristics and rights are acquired through belonging to a household, a family, a tribe, and finally to the people of the covenant.

The Israelites' concept of what constituted a *neighbour* sprang from the structure of the patriarchal household and their designation as people *of* God. Consequently, at the same time as respect for father and mother is enjoined, so is respect for the rights of one's neighbours (Lev. 19:3–18). This respect for one's neighbour, enunciated by Leviticus as: "Do not oppress your neighbour or rob him" (19:13), "do not pervert justice" (19:15), "love your neighbour as yourself" (19:18), is anchored in the twin grounds of justice and love. The people *of* God cannot be other than a people *of* brothers and sisters. The decalogue is structured around this: four commandments relating to God, followed by six relating to one's neighbour.

2. THE COVENANT AS A POLITICAL AND SOCIAL PROGRAMME

The eminently religious nature of the covenant has led to its political and social dimensions being pushed into the shadows. There are few hints of these in renewed morality,[8] understandably in view of the fact that its tonic note is the rediscovery of a personalist morality. But once the social aspect is taken as a key to the personal dimension too, then traces of a social and political purpose, intimately linked to the religious purpose, begin to emerge.[9] In this case, not only do the social and political dimensions not overshadow the religious dimension; they make it plainer, the religious and political dimensions emerging as two sides of the same coin. Here there is no doubt that the Latin American approach finds solid biblical and theological foundations for what might at first sight appear surprising.

(a) The Task of the People: A Different Society

Of course the covenant is a gift, and the first mission of the people of God consists in keeping their faith in God alive and spreading it. Nevertheless, looked at more closely, this first mission is closely bound up with their historical purpose. It is through this historical purpose, the building of a different society, that the people of God can live as such and demonstrate the existence of their God to others. So the gift points to a task.

This different society had its origin implanted at one and the same time through a historical experience and through the covenant. The historical experience goes back to the context out of which Israel arose and took its life, particularly the painful experience in Egypt. It was an experience of slavery and liberation. The people learned through their own experience that slavery comes through making persons into gods, and that liberation comes through recognition of one God, above everyone. Slavery comes from divinizing sacralized structures; liberation through recognizing that God alone is sacred and perfect. Slavery comes from society being organized in social and political layers which are discriminatory by nature; liberation through a society that is participatory at all levels. Slavery comes from distortion of justice and the law; liberation through proper respect for both: justice and law are a sort of refrain running through the whole dream of building a society of brothers and sisters, as they were the basis of the restoration preached by the prophets, as we shall see below.

This different society takes its shape from the covenant. The ten commandments are of decisive importance in terms of building a new society. They must not, however, be seen just as words spoken; they have practical application in everyday personal life and in society and politics. The ten commandments focus on two dimensions in life: The first is our relationship with God, the God of life: while other gods could be used to justify all sorts of discrimination, the God of life is guarantor of a society dedicated to the life of all its members. God is the life in which God's people, and all creatures, share. The second dimension has to be that of human life itself: respect for the origin of life (father and mother), for life itself (not to kill), for sexual generation (no adultery), for material sustenance (no thieving the product of another's work), for the dignity and good name of others (not bearing false witness), for "otherness" in itself (not coveting another's "goods").

(b) The Structure of a New Society[10]

Though the general lines of a new society have already been indicated, it is worth examining them in more detail so as to appreciate their implications. The key word in all its dimensions is "participation." This society will be different from others by the degree to which it is participative at all levels.

(i) Religious participation. The life promoted by this new society should include a different religious conception from those of other peoples. This does not just mean having one God, but affects the way religion is practised as well.

Though the central importance of the Temple of Jerusalem needs to be recognized, its meaning could be, and in fact was, debased. This debasement emerges from Jesus' conversation with the woman of Samaria, which also brings out the true significance the Temple should have: a symbolic place for the worship of God in Spirit and Truth, not the centralization of ritual worship.

Heads of family should play a leading role in worship, as in all other aspects related to religious life. The function of the Levites was not just to perform the ritual, but also to interpret the will of Yahweh and to stimulate the people in their mission. Significantly, the Levites were not allowed to own land, in contrast to the custom among other peoples. The centralization of worship in Israel was very closely linked to the danger of idolatry.

The differences become more marked when we look at the content of worship. In Egypt and elsewhere, myths were propounded, and these had an ideological function: to maintain the *status quo* and prevent change. Israel's worship told of Yahweh's great deeds on behalf of his people, particularly his freeing them from the slavery of Egypt. The chants told of the wonderful works Yahweh wrought in their midst; worship was at once celebration and reinforcement of the people's commitment to God's purpose. While in the other nations rites were mingled with magic powers designed to force favours out of their gods, in Israel the rites were designed to reactivate the people's determination to adhere to God's plan.

(ii) Participation in politics and administration. Concentration of power is nearly always closely linked to concentration of knowledge. The Pharaonic school was not devoted to the democratization of knowledge; on the contrary, its objective was to form and strengthen an elite which was to rule over the ignorant masses. In Israel, a new simplified literacy campaign, backed by a network of "schools" spread throughout the country, served to provide basic education for all members of God's people.

In contrast to the leadership concentrated in the hands of Pharaoh and the aristocracy of Egypt, Israel instituted a whole variety of degrees of leadership. On Jethro's advice, Moses initiated the office of lesser leaders. The Judges, in their turn, were not permanent, but were appointed as needs arose. Even women had a voice, as shown by Moses' sister, Miriam. The Assembly of Elders provided the tribal structure with a forum in which participation extended from families and clans to tribes and the central government, and its regular meetings rendered participation effective at all levels.

Even the armed forces were controlled. Instead of a professional army, always tempted to use its force, all able-bodied men from all the tribes were summoned to bear arms against enemies. Once the war was over, they went back to their usual occupations (Judg. 6ff). This defensive system broke down only in the time of the Kings, with familiar results.

The Law too, precisely through being anchored in the ten commandments, ceased to be an instrument for the protection of the ruler and the nobility, and became one that served the whole community.

(iii) Economic participation. Political and administrative decentralization is possible only through economic decentralization. The latter begins in the ways in which work and the distribution of production are envisaged. All great empires have been built on exploitation of the work of others. Experience under the Egyptian empire, allied to the wisdom that came from the covenant, made Israel follow a different path. No one had the right to seize land, which was divided among the tribes and thence among clans and families. The Israelite productive system was designed to make concentration of land ownership in the hands of a few practically impossible. Four basic institutions upheld economic participation: the sabbath, the sabbatical year or year of forgiveness, the jubilee year and the triennial tithe.

The sabbath, as an important part of the covenant, had a primarily religious character, but without a dichotomy between its religious and social aspects, which were harmoniously related. The day set apart for celebrating the wonders of God was also the symbol and practical expression of a different society: "For six days you shall work but on the seventh you shall rest, so that your ox and your donkey may also rest and the son of your slave girl and the stranger as well may have a breathing space" (Exod. 23:12). The context is illuminating: those who held small tracts of land were dominated by those who held large tracts, and the former were literally forced to sell their labour in order to survive. But at least on one day of the week there was no place for slaves or slave labour.

The sabbath—and later Sunday—became a sort of foretaste of the time when no one would any longer be anyone else's slave, and all would enjoy the full freedom of children of God.

The year of forgiveness still further accentuated the relation between religious and political-social dimensions. The land was worked for six years, but every seventh year it was to lie fallow, and the poor could eat what it produced spontaneously (Exod. 23:10–11). Furthermore, all debts were to be pardoned, and those who refused to lend to those in need on the eve of the year of forgiveness were condemned as harbouring perverse thoughts in their heart (Deut. 15:1–3; 7–9).

The jubilee year was still more profoundly revolutionary; every fiftieth year (i.e. after "seven sabbaths of seven years"), all land was to revert to its original owners, as laid down in Leviticus 25:10. If put into effect, which seems not to have happened, it would simply have prevented any large accumulation of land, since lands were only "lent" and not definitely made over to new owners.

Finally, the tithes of every third year's harvest were to be taken to the city and stored there—again a way of ensuring economic participation: "Then the Levite among you who has no inheritance of his own, and the foreigner, the orphan and the widow who live in your cities may come and eat, and be satisfied" (Deut: 14:28).

(c) The Evangelizing Impact of the Covenant

Consciousness of being a chosen people eventually led Israel to an equivocal nationalist view of itself. But here too there is an evangelizing aspect of the covenant at work: other peoples were to come to know the God of Israel through God's people. The great instrument of evangelization, therefore, appears linked to the carrying out of God's purpose in history. So blessings and curses are always conditional, as for example: "If you obey in truth the voice of Yahweh, your God, *practising* and observing all the commandments . . ., Yahweh your God shall raise you high above all the nations of the earth. . . . But if you do not obey the voice of Yahweh, your God, and do not take care to practise all his commandments and norms . . ., all these curses shall come upon you" (Deut: 28:1–2; 15).

The link between fulfilling the Law and the social and political programme becomes clearer when one bears in mind what breaking the covenant meant. It was only later, after the Babylonian exile, that personal responsibility began to emerge.[11] The earlier stress is on the people sinning and the people being converted. The covenant is broken in the context of human relations: the people breaks with its God when it breaks its promises and breaks with those to whom it owes obligations. It breaks with God when it fails to respect the Law and does not protect the oppressed, do justice to orphans and defend widows (see Isa. 1:16–17). It breaks with God when it becomes oppressor and violator of the rights of the poor (see Hos. 5:11–15). On the other hand, it fulfills the demands of the covenant when it makes justice rule in the assemblies, respects the Law, protects the oppressed, breaks the fetters of injustice, unfastens the thongs of the yoke, sets the oppressed free, shares food with the hungry, gives shelter to the needy, clothes the naked and does not turn its face away from its own kin (see Isa. 58:5–7). In other words, the moral norms are bound up with the historical programme as much as with the religious one. What is asked of the people is not just a profession of faith, but the working out of this faith in historical terms.

This accent comes through in the various praises of the Law: How are the neighbouring peoples to know that a different God rules in Israel? The reply is suggested in Deuteronomy 6:6–8: "If you observe and practise [these laws], other peoples will come to regard you as wise and intelligent. When they come to know of all these laws, they will say, 'There is no people as wise and as intelligent as this great nation.' For in truth is there a nation as great as ours, whose gods are as near to it as Yahweh, our God, is to us whenever we call upon him?" The Law and the commandments were of course given to enable the people to survive and reach the promised land (see Deut. 1); but it is equally true that God's purpose would be actually put into practice through the people acting as the vehicle destined to bring light to other nations.

3. THE PROPHETS REINVIGORATE THE PROGRAMME

The utopic character of God's historical programme does nothing to diminish it; just as the fact that it has never been fully put into effect does nothing to diminish it. One could even say that the continual breaks with the covenant suggest that something new needed to arise in the history of the chosen people. The prophets, while trying to inject new life into the old covenant, also point to its opening out into another covenant, through the Messiah.

(a) Frequent Breaks

Great plans often give rise to great disillusionments. The presence of grace usually goes hand in hand with the presence of sin. While the covenant was revealed in Israel, it was also in Israel that it was frequently broken. And this happened right from the start: remember the episode of the golden calf (Exod. 32); Moses had not even come down from the mountain before the people had already broken the covenant in advance!

All the breaks from all periods would be too much to list here. Suffice to take the eighth century B.C. to feel the full force of the drama—the century of the great breaks and of the rise of the great prophets, the golden age of prophecy, in fact.[12] And what the prophets did was to re-integrate the religious dimension of the covenant with its socio-political dimension.

Strictly speaking, one should distinguish between the histories of the two kingdoms, Judah and Israel; but the problems in each were basically the same, though they occurred at slightly different times.

In many ways, the eighth century was a brilliant period: there was rapid economic growth, and therefore political development. The conquests of Jeroboam and Josiah brought the two kingdoms into the ring of major economic currents of the period. Isaiah described the time in these words: "Their land full of silver and gold, there is no end to their treasures" (2:7). And the other prophets confirmed this state of affairs before going on to criticize it. But, as usually happens in times of great prosperity, contrasts in society became more acute. On one side was a bourgeoisie sunk in luxury and with an unbridled appetite for power, a society of abundance dominated by rich landowners and great merchants; on the other, the great mass of the people, made up of peasants, shepherds, small traders, artisans, unskilled labourers, slaves. . . .

(b)The Nature of the Breaks

The way the prophets of the eighth century acted can be seen from the objects of their criticisms. Besides more general denunciations, they aimed at specific targets. So Hosea, for example, attacks the ruling classes of Samaria (see 4:1; 7:1); Amos inveighs above all against those who "trample on the needy to do away with the weak of the land" (8:4–8). Micah and Isaiah also aim at particular abuses; the former rails against the rich, "those who plot wickedness. . . . If they covet fields, they seize them. Do they like houses? They take them" (2:1–12; cf 3:1–4; 3:9–12); the latter denounces those who "join house to house, who add field to field, till no room remains and you are left to dwell alone in the midst of the land" (5:8–10). The direction of their attack can be better appreciated by dividing it into three areas: money, power, worship.

Economic exploitation makes victims of the foreigners and orphans, who find themselves delivered to the violence of the powerful (Amos 3:9–10), who build with the blood of the victims (Mic. 3:10). Micah's language is the strongest of all: "You eat my people's flesh and tear their bones to pieces; you chop them up like meat for the pan and share them like flesh for the pot" (3:3).

The harshest criticism is addressed to those who use the laws and political power to cover over their abuses. Judges are so corrupt that they will acquit the guilty for a bribe and condemn the innocent (Isa. 1:23; 5:23). They enact unjust laws to deprive the poor of access to justice and defraud the weak of their rights (Isa. 10:1–4). They are even capable of allowing the poor to be sold "for a pair of sandals" (Amos 2:6; 8:6).

Religious ritual and accoutrements are equally capable of providing cover for this whole gamut of moral and social degradation. The separation of religion from justice prompts Isaiah to anger: "The number of your endless sacrifices—What do I care about them?. . . . Your hands are bloody. . . . Remove the evil of your deed out of my sight. Put an end to your wickedness and learn to do good. Seek justice, give hope to the oppressed; give the fatherless their rights and defend the widow" (Isa. 1:10–17). The only form of worship that pleases Yahweh is that which accords with the ways of justice and the Law: "See the fast that pleases me: To break the fetters of injustice and unfasten the thongs of the yoke, to set the oppressed free. . . . Fast by sharing your food with the hungry, bring to your house the unsheltered needy, clothe the man you see naked. . . ." (Isa. 58:6).

(c) Reconciliation through Justice and Law

The prophets are certainly violent in their attacks. They see that what is at stake is not simply the breakup of society, but God's plan, from which the people are turning away in practice through the way they relate both to God and to one another. The purpose of the prophets' attacks is not to destroy the existing system, however, but to call it to conversion. And the sign of conversion is not "tearing one's garments," but re-embracing the covenant with all that it implies in religious and socio-political terms.

The prophets cannot accept the inequality and exploitation implanted in society, since these completely undermine the covenant. The covenant demands equality among all and participation by all, at all levels. How can this requirement be presented in an approachably simple form, while retaining the force of the ten commandments? This is where the two concepts of justice and law (righteousness, equity) come in (see Amos 5:24; Isa. 11:4; Jer. 22:3, 15; 23:5; Ezek. 18:5–21).

The prophets, though, understand well that these concepts can also be invoked by those who violate their deepest sense. Because it is not a question of any justice and any law: when they are manipulated by the ruling classes, justice and law can become dangerous weapons. The justice and law preached by the prophets are the justice and righteousness of God, intimately linked to *hesed*, the solidarity among human beings which has its roots in the God who wishes that all should live. This justice and law take the rights of the poor as their starting-point, unlike the justice and law practised by the powerful of Israel (see Amos

2:7ff); they look after the poor because they are poor (Deut. 24:14); they take care of the weak—the widows and orphans (Deut. 24:17; Ezek. 23:9; Isa. 10:1–3).

The justice and law that form the central path back to the covenant go way beyond official texts, which can easily be used to defend rights acquired through force and wealth. They are the central route back because they re-vitalize solidarity in practice, ensuring the common good and the salvation of the whole people. Only they can bring in a new world: one of peace (Hos. 2:20), where strangers dwell together in harmony (Isa. 11:6–8), where there is no more premature death and suffering (Isa. 65:18–19; Jer. 31:13). The first hints of this new society can already be detected by looking at the poor and oppressed placing their trust in God, trusting in God to make justice reign. It is through their hope that people begin to guess at something new that is to come (Isa. 52:13), when the Messiah will appear on the horizon (Mic. 4:4; Zech. 9:10).

So the ideal of reconciliation to the covenant through justice and the Law is achieved through a long process and points toward a still more decisive actuation on God's part. Before this comes about, the ways have to be prepared: "Render true judgment, be kind and merciful to each other. Do not oppress the widow or the orphan, the alien or the poor; do not plot evil in your heart against one another" (Zech. 7:9–10).

4. THE IMPLICATIONS FOR MORAL THEOLOGY

The past forty years have been a time of intense search for a way out of the dead ends in which moral theology had become entangled. Many ways were tried and many paths opened. Both renewed morality and the Latin American model have come a long way. While retaining their identities, they have exchanged views, and now present a more encouraging picture.

Despite all the progress made, however, some basic problems remain. Some of these are: how to devise a moral theology that, without sacrificing anything of what can be called the Christian ideal, can yet give convincing replies to the challenges thrown up by an ever-changing reality; how to find a satisfactory balance between personal and social responsibility; how to give due weight to both the religious and the socio-political dimensions.

(a) The Polarity between the Ideal and Everyday Life

One of the basic challenges to moral theology is how to maintain the polarity that always exists between the ideal and everyday life. Obviously the ideal cannot be sacrificed for the sake of the changes that affect society and personal circumstances. The ideal of Christ is perennial. And yet the rigidity found in many neo-scholastic manuals is not a satisfactory response. They present an ideal in such a way that God shows only one face: that of the harsh judge, unmoved by human drama, always ready to punish those who infringe unchanging, divine laws.

Duty for its own sake, or founded on extrinsic criteria, seems to make little impression on our contemporaries. Today, even Christians are more inclined to look for an inner and outer coherence, integrating the historical viewpoint and keeping a certain flexibility in regard to historical developments and the circumstances that affect people. The liberal approach, however, which ends by conforming the Christian programme to "the world" in the Johannine sense, can look attractive at first, but eventually fails to satisfy the deepest human longings. In the end, it is a hollow creed.

This basic problem cannot, clearly, be solved within the strict limits of a morality of the covenant as found in the Old Testament, which itself looked forward to a fuller revelation in Jesus Christ. Nevertheless, it can afford important insights into a way forward. God's purposes cannot be put forward juridically and impersonally: to do so makes the ten commandments into simple edicts, unshaped by the climate in which they arose. But once they are put into the context of a pact, in which God's "partners" see them as arrows pointing the way forward in a project in which they are participating, then they take on another aspect. They are no longer arbitrary demands, nor even demands made from outside; they are not coldly juridical impositions. They contain an invitation to human beings to take part in a great endeavour, not as robotic executors of it, but as characters deeply involved in its fulfillment. The motive force of moral obligation then no longer resides in duty, but in the fascination exercised by the project. The Kantian imperative has nothing to do with Christianity.

Furthermore, one of the characteristics of the morality of the covenant is a degree of flexibility present from the beginning in the biblical understanding of the route to be followed. There is a goal to be reached, but through a historical process—and this applies on the personal level as well as on the social. The God of the covenant is not an implacable Jupiter, ever ready to punish God's "partners" for the least infraction. This God is truly patient and rich in mercy, and is shown as such in the Old Testament. This is the only way to understand figures such as Abraham, Moses and Elias, and the only way to understand how the people's continual breaks with the covenant are followed by as many reconciliations.

(b) The Polarity between Personal and Social Spheres

As long as morality addresses itself to the personal sphere alone, it remains a micro-morality, incapable of affecting wider structures. God's programme in the covenant is not, in the first place, one for individuals; it is a programme for a people. Even the leaders of the people, however important they may have been in history, are basically no more than intermediaries. The breaks and reconciliations are also seen in terms of a people.

On the other hand, if morality takes account of the social sphere alone, it breaks down, simply because there is no social sphere without individuals. There is no such thing as a historical undertaking in the abstract; it is made up of the persons who support it. The most idealistic social structures cannot function in defence of life without the support of individuals.

The morality of the covenant has at once a personal dimension and a community, social dimension. This does not mean that the social one is the sum total of the wishes of the persons involved; it means that persons acquire status and find their place to the extent that they become part of a people and attuned to a common purpose. As isolated individuals, they remain sterile. This is why one can speak of a "corporative" personality, in which responsibility falls as much on the community as on individuals.[13] It is impossible for each individual to journey alone within a covenant framework. Salvation is conditional on adherence to a common purpose. Each person becomes "someone" only insofar as he or she is affiliated to a family, a clan, a tribe, a people. In this way, we can move beyond both individualism and massification.

So the morality of the covenant shows the way forward from the person-society dichotomy. What is kept is a polarity, which can generate energy for both individuals and society; eliminating either pole would leave both inert.

(c) The Polarity between Religious and Political Dimensions

Attempts to link religion and politics are often branded as neo-clericalism. Indeed, whenever religion tries to take over politics, or politics tries to absorb religion, the result is either neo-clericalism or a sort of intra-historical messianism. But attempts to build a society with two perfect, completely autonomous spheres also prove unproductive. It would seem that politics lacks the mystic power to forge ahead without religion, while religion without a political dimension tends to produce alienation.

Secularizing movements claim to build a new society without God, while sacralizing movements have the ultimate vision of a theocracy. Though Israel might at first sight be defined as a theocratic society, it was in fact a tense but very vital articulation of the religious and political dimensions. To call it a purely religious endeavour does not fit the historical facts; neither does calling it a purely political one.

Here again, the morality of the covenant shows the gods of other nations incapable of forming a society that could be divine and human at the same time. They would sometimes pull too hard toward heaven, sometimes too hard toward earth. But the God of Israel is a God who transcends history while at the same time acting on the historical level. There is no dichotomy here, no mixture. The impasse is overcome through maintaining both dimensions in a state of tension, in which religion and politics keep their autonomy while cross-fertilizing one another. Religion provides the mystical dimension; politics anchors it in reality.

The linkage between religious and political dimensions is found in the basic conception underlying the morality of the covenant. Seen as a whole, this points to the contrast between morality of the Egyptians (and other neighbouring peoples) and that of Israel's time in the desert. The morality transmitted by nations that manipulate religion in favour of a socio-political system of domination can appear coherent at first glance: it has laws, norms, values, justifications; it can even come to form a "moral conscience." Yet when confronted with the morality of the desert, that of the ten commandments, it is shown up for what it basically is: a morality of domination and in the service of domination. Contrasted with this, the morality of the desert appears for what it is: a morality of full liberation, in both the religious and the political senses of the word, a morality serving the growth of persons and society.

It is interesting to note that the same parallel can be presented in terms of the New Testament. The Pharisees displayed a coherent morality, but one that Christ and later St Paul rejected. Its coherence was only on the surface, under which lurked justification for every sort of wickedness, personal as well as social, religious as much as political.

The covenant comes through as the basic category in Israel's understanding of itself as a people and of its mission. It is also the key category for understanding the morality underlying this perception. The deeply religious nature of the covenant brings a different understanding of both God and the type of society to be built as witness to the covenant. The richness of this theology consists not only in the way it structures the religious dimension, or the socio-political dimension, but in its articulation of both at once. The participation it brings in the economic, political and religious spheres is the fruit of a theological understanding. In the same way, its basic concepts of justice and law are not merely sociological; they are profoundly theological.

Because of all the different strands the idea of the covenant brings together in such a rich way, moral theology—whether of the renewed or liberative pattern—cannot but make use of this concept. But the Old Testament covenant did not end with itself; it found its full expression only in Jesus Christ, in whom God's purpose was revealed in all its fullness.

Chapter V

Jesus Christ: God's Purpose Fulfilled

For decades now, people have been saying that moral theology needs to be more christocentric, and pioneering work has been done to make it so. But as with so many other aspects, the full riches of a christocentric moral theology have been apparent to only a few. It both elucidates and deepens the theology of the covenant; it leads on from it and introduces new basic elements.

The main focus of the christocentric approach in liberation theology has been the theme of the Kingdom of God, which is clearly the nucleus of Christ's life and message. The proclamation and implantation of the Kingdom form the body of the way he carried out his mission and fulfilled the Father's purpose. The fact that the expression "Kingdom of God" occurs 123 times in the New Testament is sufficient to show that it must also be a key theme for moral theology.

The Kingdom of God takes on more definite features when one looks at the way Jesus acted in history, the manner in which he faced up to the challenges he met. His attitude is at the same time historically situated and normative for all times, and since he is the supreme norm of moral theology, his attitude is decisive. His practice not only confirmed his words, but also showed the way for his followers.

This practice had love at its centre. This is the new commandment and the primordial commandment, revealing the deep meaning of all the others and forming the source of all the others. But "love" is a multi-faceted word, and we need to examine the type of love Jesus practised and enjoined on his followers. The Kingdom, Jesus' practice and his love all lead naturally to the question of what is meant by "following" Jesus. This has long been a common theme, but its meaning has been enriched in recent theological reflection. We need to enquire what following Jesus meant for his contemporaries and what it means for Christians today, in general and in specific situations.

So we need to ask four questions: How did Jesus face up to the challenges he met? What did he mean by love? What did following him mean then? What does it mean today? The answers to these questions should give an indication of the lines a more christocentric moral theology has to follow. So they lead to the heart of all moral theology.

1. THE KINGDOM OF GOD AND ITS IMPLICATIONS

Despite bitter historical experiences, the idea of kingship continued to represent a utopic hope of better days to come for Israel. The historical failures did not serve to blot out the hope that God would never finally abandon the chosen people. So, by beginning his public ministry by proclaiming the Kingdom (Mark 1:15 and parallels), Jesus touched on a burning question, one calculated to arouse unusual interest.[1]

It is true that people understood this proclamation in different ways according to their expectations: some understood it in the sense of "restoration" (Acts 1:6); others seemed to see it as indicating that God would play a more active role in this Kingdom (Isa. 40:9ff; Ezek. 34:11). Despite this, the proclamation went to the heart of everyone's hopes and archetypal dreams.[2]

With Jesus, the double aspect of proclamation and practice was to show that the Kingdom surpassed not only Israel's expectations, but also any other cultural form in which these expectations had been couched. What Jesus announced and brought in was something that went way beyond anything that either existed or could be imagined.

But how does one characterize this Kingdom? Why does it need a complete change of heart, a total conversion? For whom is it good news? These are the main questions that need to be asked in this context. Examining them will lead us into an understanding of the reality of the Kingdom, and reveal some deep implications for the basic Christian attitude.

(a) What Does the Kingdom Consist Of?

Put like this, it is a rash question, and by no means an easy one to answer. Many interpretations have been put forward: some stress the eschatological and spiritual sense, some the political and social; some emphasize the "already" aspect, others the "not yet." All these emphases have their justifications; answering the above question depends on linking these emphases.

There can be no doubt that Jesus went beyond all exclusions. So the Kingdom he proclaimed exists on the eschatological and spiritual level, and on the socio-political; it is both "already" and "not yet." The Kingdom of God cannot be placed in any particular setting: it embraces everyone and everything—the world, individuals, society; the whole of reality is destined to be transformed by God.[3]

Nor can there be any doubt that because it is the Kingdom *of* God, it stresses the divine actuation, and therefore gratuitousness. If it is God who reigns, the transcendental and religious dimensions, as well as the eschatological, must be there. And yet, if God reigns in the midst of humankind, it is also clear that the divine actuation will infuse all aspects of what being human implies, and will be carried out with the cooperation of men and women. There is perhaps a parallel here with what we said of the old covenant: it articulated the religious dimension with the socio-political, taking the latter term in its fullest sense.

The Kingdom of God points to a new manner of being and of relating: in relation to God and God's purposes in the first place. The Kingdom is accepted only by those who open themselves out in the direction of the Father and his historical purposes. But at the same time, the Kingdom is accepted only by those who open out equally toward one another, seeing one another as brothers and sisters because they have a Father in common, and extending this approach to the whole of creation. All this is embraced by an expression which has theological, socio-political and even cosmic implications. Christ proclaims and seeks to establish a new type of relationship embracing everything.

(b) Why a Change of Heart?

The presupposition of the Kingdom is that something has to be changed in the human sphere. Otherwise we should not be faced with a proclamation. This change cannot come about without the whole of human existence being profoundly shaken, since what is proclaimed is a *new* reality and a *new* set of relationships. The proclamation of the Kingdom provokes a crisis on both social and personal levels; accepting it means breaking with the old order in both.

History shows that when men and women rule without regard for the divine purposes, injustice, violence and all sorts of evils reign in the world. If God reigns, even though dependent on human collaboration, the overall picture is reversed: then peace, justice and all that can be called good reign. The proclamation of the Kingdom awakens echoes of the narrative in the first chapters of Genesis: a new creation has to follow the old.

The Kingdom is the way what will be fully realized beyond human history is put into practice, though partially, within that history. It is thus a utopia, but one that is beginning to come about. Since it has a historical aspect, it is not static, but dynamic; it grows like the mustard seed (Matt. 13:31ff); it spreads like yeast in the dough (Matt. 13:22ff).

Though the Kingdom aims at reconciliation, and total reconciliation,[4] this cannot be realized without traumas. There are many contrary interests and expectations. In order to implant a "new order," Jesus had to challenge the old order. Likewise, those who welcome the "new" will have to expect resistance from those who cling to the "old." This is the context in which Jesus saying that he came to bring "rather division" (Luke 12:51–2) and that the Kingdom of heaven "has been subjected to violence" (Matt. 11:12) has to be understood. And this is the context in which Christ himself paid with his life for what he preached and did. What he in fact proclaimed was the subversion of the old order on all levels (Luke 23:2).

The new order proclaimed and ushered in by Jesus echoes the main lines of the prophets, with God's justice as its central theme. This is not the justice of the "teachers of the Law" (Matt. 5:20), which, even when not unjust, seldom went beyond the distributive level and finally left things much as they were. This is God's justice, and God's justice does not consist in giving all persons their just deserts, but in opening up human beings to a new condition. God's justice is an essentially salvific activity, through which the good things promised by God are offered.[5] The term recovers all the Old Testament richness of a God who rescues God's people from all sorts of slavery. But it also goes beyond this: God has to create conditions in which victims of human "justice" are compensated, in which captives are set free, the good news is preached to the poor, and the benefits of the sabbatical and jubilee years are made permanent (Luke 4:18ff). In this sense, justice can be called the genetic value of the Kingdom,[6] since it is the motive force for a truly new situation, different from what Jesus found in his day—and from what we find in ours.

(c) Who the Kingdom Is For

Jesus addresses the call to seek the Kingdom and its justice to everyone, beyond the confines of Israel (Luke 13:29), beyond all geographical boundaries, but also beyond all social boundaries. But while it is true that the Kingdom is "available" to everyone, there is one basic and radical requirement: being converted. Conversion (*metanoia*) is above all "turning to," giving one's deep assent. Faced with the call to the Kingdom, however, people find themselves in different situations, so its implications vary. Those faced with the challenge of the Kingdom can be divided into three groups: those excluded according to the Law of the scribes and Pharisees, those who oppose it, and those who take up the call and follow.

The news was really good and new for those who were arbitrarily excluded, and these certainly made up the majority of the population. They included the poor, the unlettered, those afflicted by any sort of sickness. The connection of poverty/suffering with *sin* (John 9:2, 24, 34) turned them into *accursed*, in the literal sense of the word. For them there was no hope, neither on earth nor in heaven. Hence the shock produced by the beatitudes and Jesus' actions: *theirs* is the Kingdom of heaven; God's power is exercised on *their* behalf. The condition is that they believe this unheard-of pronouncement, which went beyond anything in established theology.

The second group is composed of those who refuse to accept the Kingdom as good news. They are those who actively resist it, though not necessarily as direct opposition to God, and sometimes even invoking the name of God in support of their resistance. Led by the scribes and Pharisees, they feel the full impact of the Kingdom, but in a negative sense: they would have to make a radical change not only in their thought patterns, but also in their whole way of behaviour. Their conversion would indeed imply a total break with the existing order. In this sense, the proclamation of the Kingdom was perceived by them as a threat, already expressed by John the Baptist (Luke 3:9) and reiterated by Christ (Luke 13:9). From beginning to end, the Gospels are permeated by the mortal conflict between them and Jesus.

The third group are the "followers." What is meant by following Christ will be examined in section 4 of this chapter. Suffice, therefore, to say here that the requirement for them is of an ever deeper and more joyful adherence to the coming of the Kingdom.

So the Kingdom implies a profound shift in human relationships, involving all conditions and classes of men and women. Jesus' actions, examined in the following section, particularly when contrasted with the dominant practices of the time, make this even clearer. His actions confirmed and illustrated his teaching.

2. JESUS' ACTIONS

Jesus did not merely announce something surprisingly new. Through his words and actions, he also ushered in a whole new pattern of behaving and being. These not only left a deep mark on his surroundings and period, but spread and survive far beyond them.

His whole approach, in words and actions, is the decisive factor in finding out what "following" him implies. To understand it, we need first to situate it in its historical context. This will also show how it differed from that of other groups active in his time. The difference between his actions and those of others of the time stemmed from the fact that he was a different person, and motivated by a different impulse. The difference can be summed up by saying that his attitude was one of sovereign freedom. Though he acted from within and on a specific reality, Jesus cannot be equated with any other group active at the time: his "inspiration" was different. Even the "liberation" he proclaimed as the kernel of his message had no parallel in any other human undertaking. So the imminent coming of the Kingdom and its radical nature formed a message that both fascinated people and left them perplexed.

(a) A Context of Tensions

It is obviously impossible to reconstruct the context in which Jesus acted in a few lines, particularly if we are attempting an interpretation as well as a description. We can only refer to fuller accounts,[7] and concentrate on the main lines.

The frustrations of centuries of expectations rebuffed by harsh setbacks had culminated in military occupation by the Romans. This occupation brought major changes in the economic and political spheres, and in social and religious life. Though the retention of local authorities provided an appearance of normality, the Romans' subtle tactics eventually undermined all national aspirations: the technique of *divide et impera* was here employed with consummate effectiveness.

The internal structure of the nation was complex, with a number of different and well-defined groupings. There were the Pharisees, distinguished by their strict observance of the Law, which gave them an ascendancy over the common people, whom they despised for their ignorance and "impiety." Then there were the scribes, or doctors of the Law: though less cohesive as a group, their position as teachers of the sacred sciences gave them great influence. The Essenes lived a strict life in community, and had broken away from the pattern of religious life based on the Temple. The Zealots were always involved in movements of armed insurrection, and formed the group most marked by an immediate political and religious messianism. All these groups were trying to impose their viewpoints and enlarge their sphere of influence.

This complex structure remained fairly well defined till the Roman invasion, but rapidly fell apart under this new threat.

The threat posed by the invaders affected all levels of life, but finally boiled down to the question of what attitude should be taken toward them. The political and religious leaders eventually aligned themselves with the interests of the Roman Empire, but not everyone followed them in this. The big landowners and wealthy merchants also found a *modus vivendi* with the invaders. But tensions mounted around the position of smallholders, who were reduced to wage-earners employed by those who had found favour with the Romans. The usurpation of their land was not merely a material deprivation, but seen as actual sacrilege by those who regarded it as their promised land. And all felt the burden of more or less arbitrary taxes, varying according to the whim of the hated tax-collectors.

All this, allied to a closed system of ideological control, made the basic unity of the nation fragment in all directions. Rivalry between the various groups, heightened by the need to adopt a particular approach to the Romans, produced a state of permanent tension. Then the pervading divisions—between rich and poor, collaborators and resistance, influential people and the despised masses—were complicated by the appearance of a new element: Jesus of Nazareth.

(b) A Different "Praxis"

"Praxis" has been defined as: "An activity that transforms a historical reality. A synthesis of actions and words, the term *praxis* means an action carried out in all freedom, and one that faces up to, re-directs and transforms a given reality." It was through such a praxis that Jesus revealed his mission and put it into practice.

This praxis, however, was not performed in the abstract. Jesus came into an existing interplay of powers, a society full of tensions and conflicts, to which he had to define his approach. He did not just emerge from the midst of this confusion, however: to carry out his mission, he had to take up a definite position in relation to the various groups and interests with which he found himself confronted.

So, despite being a skilled worker (Matt. 13:54–5), he made himself poor and a spokesman for the aspirations of the poor. Excluded on "moral grounds," the poor now become the messengers of the Kingdom (Luke 7:22). Most of Jesus' miracles were performed for them and in their midst. The corollary of this is that Jesus spoke harsh words and adopted harsh attitudes to the rich. He did not exclude them, but tried to open their eyes by showing them their riches as a virtually insuperable obstacle to entry into the Kingdom (Matt. 19:23–4; Mark 10:23; Luke 18:22–4). He pointed out that riches usually make their possessor uncaring for the needy (Luke 12:21–33; 6:19–20). He set before them the counter-propositions of the Beatitudes (Luke 6:24). In the same way, he worried the powerful by recognizing one power only: that of service (Luke 22:25–7). All this was to create an initial distancing from them, and, as a result, an initial area of conflict.

Jesus also kept a distance between himself and the various organized groups. So, though he adopted the lifestyle of the teachers of the Law, he did not spare them comprehensive and radical criticism: that they arrogate the keys of sacred learning to themselves (Luke 11:47–52), but pervert the deepest meaning of the Law by turning it into a new tool of discrimination instead of placing it at the service of the people. Following the prophetic line, he saw the Law as perverted whenever it was not used to protect the stranger, the orphan, the widow and the oppressed. The Law should be the foundation of a truly different society, one built in response to the covenant: a fundamentally participative and non-discriminatory society.

In the same way, though he had positive contacts with the Pharisees (Luke 7:36ff; 11:37ff; 14:1–6), he showed that zeal for the Law was not shown by adding six thousand new precepts, nor by observing its letter, but that the Law is at the service of the practice of love and justice: they pay tithes on everything, but fail to fulfill what is most important in the Law (Matt. 23:23).

Jesus equally distanced himself from the Essenes, in that, instead of steering clear of the weak, the sick and outcasts, he acted in their midst and on their behalf. Evil, for him, came from what is inside a person, not from externals (Mark 7:18–23). Unlike the Essenes, furthermore, he refused to become imbued with their pessimism in the face of the forces of evil, but placed himself in a position to mount an attack on them on all fronts.

Finally, Jesus did not share the revolutionary zeal of the Zealots, neither their violence nor their plan to restore the Temple. Jesus' liberative programme went beyond the confines of Israel and his religious programme extended beyond the Temple (Matt. 21:12–17). By distancing himself in these ways from the various interpreters of "the Law and the prophets," Jesus did not set himself up in opposition to the old covenant; he took up its deepest meaning and shed new light on it. In this way he incarnates the "new and everlasting covenant."

(c) A Different Person, with a Different Programme

Jesus' praxis relates to the mystery of his person. He is not someone who looks for a "political" solution to problems, but a person clearly defined in his own right and totally attuned to his undertaking. He cannot be reduced to objective categories or fitted into any particular scheme. His divine-human nature places him beyond categorization. Yet there is one characteristic in him that outshines all others, and has been recognized as such by many theologians, [8] that of his sovereign freedom.

Without acting provocatively, Jesus refused to bow to either family pressures (Mark 3:31–5), or to religious powers (John 18:19ff), or to the civil authorities (Luke 13:31–3), or even to those who threatened him with death. His sovereign freedom appears in his interpretation of the Law and tradition, and in his attitude to social and religious preconceptions. Hence his supping with tax-collectors, dealing with the sick, conversing with Samaritans and with foreigners. . . . He does not look to appearances, but shows God's way of acting with everyone. In short:

> The freedom of Jesus, which was inspired by the Father's will to save, found a way through social conflict without using euphemisms or evasions and without ever surrendering his sense of the other or his concern for individuals in their concrete situations. The practice of the kingdom supported this freedom of Jesus that was dedicated to creating the human conditions needed for a creative life and a life free of the bonds that limit it to the past and prevent its full development.[9]

This is the route to a better understanding of his purpose: he did not just exercise sovereign freedom in his life, but opened up a perspective of true liberation. Starting with the programmatic discourse (Luke 4:18–19), it is clear that his proclamation and establishment of the Kingdom point the way to a programme of liberation. Although this programme had been outlined in the Old Testament, the programme Jesus sets out differs from that in many respects and goes beyond it in all: liberation is now not just of one people, but of all the oppressed of all nations; liberation is now not achieved through miraculous deeds, nor by charismatic leaders, but by the new people of God, chosen from among all nations and from among those least equipped by human standards; liberation is not limited to a particular period, but becomes a challenge for all times; liberation from sin no longer ends on the socio-political level, but takes on a soteriological and therefore trans-historical character. Henceforth, socio-political liberation draws its force from soteriological liberation.

In some ways one can say that Israel's hopes for deliverance, as they were held out in Jesus' time, were opposed to the reality of the liberation he pursued: "The liberation of Christ is a new creation, totally unforeseen by the Israelites of the times and by their likes of all times."[10] Jesus was not seeking to create a nation like all others; rather, in accordance with the true purpose of the covenant, to create new human relationships: human beings open to God and therefore to one another.

3. LOVE AS LIBERATING PRACTICE

There is nothing easier for Christians to accept than that love of God and of one's neighbour constitutes the greatest commandment. Originally stated by Leviticus (19:18), repeated by Christ as the new and great commandment, love of neighbour should be above discussion. Yet this is not the case. The commandment is accepted in its general sense, but discussion abounds about what it means in practice. Even Vatican II regarded "love" as a very fluid concept.[11]

In connection with the "liberation model" of moral behaviour, the problem becomes more acute. What does it mean in practice to love as Jesus loved? What does it mean to talk of love as "liberating practice"? We can perhaps pick out three aspects that show the various faces of love in practice, and at the same time illustrate the mounting difficulties as one approaches the socio-political plane; the three aspects are love in close relationships, love in distant relationships, love in the context of social and political tensions—the field in which tensions are at their greatest.

(a) Love in Close Relationships

Love in close relationships, in the I-thou relationship, plays a dominant part in all treatises of moral theology. The renewed approach pays more attention to it than previous models. Its characteristics are set out in various terms: service, giving, forgiveness. . . .

Despite this, experience shows that it is not at all easy to love in the Christian sense; it is rather a great and constant challenge, even on the interpersonal level. Loving means always recognizing and accepting otherness. In all love there are always two worlds that first collide before meeting. Many factors are at work behind each of these worlds: historical, racial, educational, religious, social, political, ideological. . . . If love in practice were something spontaneous and easy to experience, there would be no need for it to be a commandment, let alone one equal to the first, to love God.

It is perhaps worth recalling Freud's theory here: that *eros* and *thanatos* are the two basic impulses in human beings. *Eros* represents openness, desire to communicate, joy, life, the impulse to encounter another and thereby overcome solitude. *Eros* gives us the power to overcome the first great temptation: to sterility, self-absorption, selfishness. Yet at the same time we feel the contrary impulse: to self, to isolation, to sadness, death, alienation. . . . While *eros* impels toward the "life" resulting from communion, *thanatos* pulls toward the "death" resulting from solitude. Christian love is built on the ambivalence between basic impulses: giving on one side, taking on the other.

Still on this interpersonal level, there is another difficulty: Do we just give or do we help develop? Even the sternest critics of aid admit that there are desperate situations requiring immediate relief.[12] One cannot leave someone homeless or starving while waiting for a better society. There are situations of spiritual or material need that call for immediate aid. And yet love in practice cannot stop at this first step; a second step is needed: going in search of better conditions for those concerned. This means that love reaches its fullness when it moves in a liberating direction in all senses.

The most painful test for interpersonal love is when one is faced with an "enemy." Strictly speaking, according to St Luke, this is the test of true Christian love (6:27ff). This is where the novelty of the commandment really shows. The old saying, "Hate sin but love the sinner," points in the right direction, but does not solve everything. There are many types of "enemy," some seeking our life, some our death. Furthermore, to love persons sometimes demands bitter remedies. Christ himself spoke and acted harshly to his "enemies," as we have seen. But his "Father, forgive them" showed that he was not an enemy to his enemies. In everyday life, it needs a deeply evangelical spirit to guide us in practical love of our enemies.

(b) Love in Distant Relationships

These are those that involve society and politics. Politics and society are more than the sum total of the individuals in them. So they need a different "psychology," since relationships in them are different. Though what was said about the two basic impulses is still valid, the scale is different, as though seen through a magnifying glass. There is a sort of chain reaction forcing the personal rationale to give way to another, the social rationale.

A Christian tendency to aversion to thinking on the socio-political level has long since given way to an understanding that love has to be effective on this level if it is to fulfill its true potential. Groups of Christians, though still a minority, began to put this into effect long before Marx.[13] This understanding has been reinforced and broadened in the social teaching of the church over the past century, though not without more or less overt resistance from within Christianity itself, where some sectors still see more virtue in interpersonal than in social love.

Two documents from recent teaching, one by Pope Paul VI

and one by Pope John Paul II, are worth mentioning in this respect. In his encyclical *Octogesima Adveniens*, Paul VI wrote: "Taking politics seriously, on its various levels—local, regional, national and world-wide—means affirming the duty of men and women to recognize the actual reality and value of the freedom of choice put before them, in order together to try to work for the good of their city, their nation, and all humankind. Politics is a demanding way—though not the only one—of living the Christian commitment, in the service of others" (OA 46). John Paul II, in his Letter to the Brazilian Bishops, again stressed the link between this dimension and that of salvation and integral liberation, in conformity with the evangelizing mission of the church. In doing so, he endorsed the pastoral direction taken by the Brazilian Bishops' Conference over the past years.

In the theological field too, the political dimension of faith, seen as a consequence of love in practice, has been far more widely discussed in the last few decades.[14] It is indeed the touchstone of various theologies of earthly realities, particularly of political and liberation theology. It was its efforts at analyzing love in conflictive situations that led the latter into no small difficulties.

(c) Love in Conflictive Relationships

As a matter of principle, and in general terms, few today deny that there is a link between Christian love and the area of society and politics. And this area is mined with more or less open conflicts and tensions. This brings us up against the main difficulty: If love is to become liberating practice, in the strictly socio-political sense, how does one love in the midst of these tensions and conflicts? And worse still: How does one operate as a Christian in a situation of real class struggle?

This is one of the most difficult questions facing both theologians and people trying to live an ordinary Christian life. Things would be easier if the world were a different place! But life in society and in politics shows us, and frequent papal documents endorse the fact, that we live in an unreconciled world. Here we can only scratch the surface of the problem, but there is no point in discussing love as liberating practice without examining it at least briefly.

The first thing to establish is that the conflicts in the world are many and various, and susceptible of differing interpretations. Sociological theories tend to divide into three schools:[15] on one side is the Marxist interpretation, which sees conflicts as the driving force of history; on the other, there are those who see harmony as the normal condition and conflicts as pathologies on the personal or social levels; in the middle are those who see a dialectical tension between conflictive and harmonious tendencies in society. But all theorists agree in defining conflicts as situations in which antagonistic interests exist, represented by opposing groups, each trying to impose its own point of view or interest on the others. Hence the ideological charge that usually underlies conflicts.

Referring again to the documents that make up the "social teaching of the church," we can separate various aspects of conflicts. First, their origins are extremely varied and this leads to different areas of conflict: socio-economic (cf LE 11), racial, ideological, over land, between generations, within families. . . . Accepting the existence of conflicts (cf QA 82, 83, 115; LE 11) can lead to different attitudes to them: encouraging them, stifling them, channelling them. This last is of course the proper course for Christians. One can also recognize that, providing the opposing parties in a conflict keep a basic attitude of respect for their opponents, it can serve a positive purpose by leading to a more just outcome.

The real problem arises when conflicts are brought about by institutionalized situations of injustice. The imperatives of justice, closely allied to those of love, do not permit passivity in response to these situations. This would amount to complacency in the face of sin. So *Laborem Exercens* has this to say about the world of work: calling all Christians and the whole church to support workers' solidarity movements, it observes that such movements arise "against the degradation of man as the subject of work and against the excessive and concomitant exploitation in the realm of profits" (LE 8). And it goes on to say that the church's official teaching, from *Rerum Novarum* on, has been that *social morality* has justified resistance to the injustice "crying to heaven for vengeance" which has characterized rapid industrialization. This is not merely to recognize a conflict of interests between capital and labour, but to support resistance against an unjust system. In its no. 20, it justifies the struggle against injustice in that it is a struggle *not against others*, but *for justice*. This is the essence of the Christian position in the face of structural conflicts: the struggle is *for* justice and therefore cannot be motivated by hatred, and has to watch the means used to overcome structural conflicts.

Again, we can remind ourselves that Christ himself did not run from conflicts, but faced up to them in order to remain faithful to his mission. The implantation of a *new* order of relationships came into conflict with the old. The interests of the Kingdom were opposed to those of existing groups.

4. FOLLOWING JESUS CHRIST

Following Christ is one of the central themes of the gospel, so it is not surprising that it should re-surface at different times with new vigour. The vigour the theme displays at any one time, one might say, determines the vigour of theology itself at the time. The Fathers dealt with it, so did high scholasticism; it was taken up again by the Tubingen school in the middle of the last century, disappeared with the neo-scholastic manuals, and was reinvigorated by the renewed school of moral theology, particularly in the work of its great pioneer, Bernard Häring.[16] As with so many other themes, it was not invented by Latin American theology, but this has tried to steer it in new directions.

The first way to approach it is through the riches of the gospel texts, which show us not only what it meant for Christ's first disciples, but also bring out the most decisive perennial aspects of the theme. Yet, however great the riches to be found in the Bible, they become theoretical unless they are brought face to face with today's realities. We need to see whether changing historical circumstances make it possible to imitate the disciples, or whether we need a creative re-production of their following of Christ if we are to face the challenges of our day.

Our day, however, presents a multiplicity of aspects, each demanding a specific response within an overall general attitude.

How do we follow Christ in a situation of destitution and oppression? What demands does following him make of us in such a situation? For the Third World, these are the most pertinent and vital questions, for which the aspects examined in the last section have prepared the ground, since it is in the light of the Kingdom, of Jesus' actions and of love as liberating practice that following Christ takes on a specific character.

(a) ". . . And Followed Him"

In the course of his life, Jesus met thousands of people. He called them all to accept the Kingdom. He benefitted many in the most immediate fashion. Some he called directly to follow him—see Mark 1:16–20 and parallels; this call was so decisive that it did not allow for long deliberations (Luke 9:57–61): those who accepted the call left everything and followed him. The call was not only incisive, but decisive: "whoever has put his hand to the plough and looks back is not fit for the kingdom of God" (v. 61).

The immediacy of the call to follow comports a basic requirement of conversion to the Kingdom, but also brings in a new type of relationship between Jesus and his immediate followers: a relationship of absolute faith and trust, which leads them to embrace Jesus' way of life. Besides the special position and duties that the call brings (Mark 3:14 and par.), there are also another series of demands, involving breaks. So the disciples have to break their family ties, as Jesus had done (Luke 14:23); they have to break with their occupation and normal way of life (Mark 1:17–18), with material goods (Luke 18:18), and with all ambition (Mark 10:43ff).

The radical nature of these breaks, which will lead to total lack of material comforts ("nowhere to lay his head"—Luke 9:57), forbids any romantic image of the consequences: Jesus makes clear that the way is even that of the cross (Mark 8:14 and par.). And another series of demands reinforces the deep, complete transformation required: they have to become like little children (Matt. 18:3), always be reconciled with one another (Matt. 5:28), always tell the truth (Matt. 5:37), and so on.

All these demands would be disheartening if they led nowhere. But as they are open gates into the Kingdom, they take on a positive role: they make the heralds of the Kingdom into completely free men and women, really capable of giving themselves totally to their great mission. Their special link with Christ is a staff for their hard journey.

(b) Following Christ Today

There is no doubt that the call to follow Jesus is addressed to everyone. Nor is there any doubt that the corresponding demands are addressed to all who are called. There are those who would point to a difference between the Twelve and the rest of his followers, referring to a *way of life*. The Twelve would be called to a stricter following, and this distinction would be carried down to today. But even those who hold this point of view would not say that there are two classes of followers.[17]

There are, however, other considerations. Once Jesus had returned to the Father, even the way the Twelve followed him had to change, since it was no longer possible to follow him physically: "Where I am going, you cannot come" (John 13:33). Neither can Jesus' actions as he performed them in his life on earth be repeated. The question posed is whether Jesus left behind him at least some sort of route map to guide his disciples and his followers of all times. The reply to this is strongly affirmative and points to a double avenue: one more formal, on the lines of a sort of imitation; the other more actual, in the sense of taking the same historical road as Jesus.

Formal following is characterized by the attempt to imitate the virtues of the Master in a personal relationship with God and one's neighbour, seen in connection with what we have called close relationships. This sort of following has its place in an evangelical outlook. But it becomes problematical if it leads to a Christianity lived on the margins of history and without a commitment to its transformation. And it would become contradictory in its own terms if it meant compromising with downright anti-evangelical situations: Christian internally, but anti-Christian in personal and social relationships.

Actual following, on the other hand, means taking the historical road mapped out by Jesus: "I am the way" (John 14:6). This is Jesus' praxis on his journey to the Father, the inner meaning of his words and actions which must be revived and incarnated. This meaning is like a light for the road and a perennial source of inspiration and new embodiments. This is where the "logic of a practice"[18] provides the basic guidelines for a true following. These do not amount to a detailed action programme, nor a blueprint to be followed in all circumstances. They provide a basic agenda requiring a creative fidelity capable of enshrining the deep meaning of Jesus' actions and teaching.

This "logic of practice" can be worked out in four main directions: religious, ethical-social, political and economic. The mainspring of Jesus' way is of course the religious dimension. His communion with the Father led him always to do the will of the one who sent him (John 6:38). His actions were founded in prayer (Mark 1:35 and par.). It was on the basis of this deep communion that Jesus criticized formal religion (Matt. 32:1–36) for not leading to a practice consistent with the Father's purposes. To this, he opposed, through his way of life, a religion open to the real needs of others, a religion based on mercy (John 8:10–11; Matt. 18:12–14; Luke 15:11–32; Mark 6:34). This is also a religion that breaks out of the closed circle of close relationships, moving to the distant relationships of the ethical-social sphere: precisely where the demands of the Kingdom are set.

The logic of this practice cannot stop short of the political and economic spheres either. Against divisions, domination and structured violence, Jesus set service based on a fundamental equality. Against accumulation of wealth, he put forward the need to share and an attitude of communion with the poor (Luke 16:19–31; 19:1–10). Against the selfish projects of the old humanity, he proposed the building of the new humanity.

(c) Following Christ in Critical Situations

There is no need to play down the fact that following Jesus' historical practice shows the way, all over the world, to liberation from sin, personal as well as social. Yet this soteriological aspect, however decisive, cannot in turn obscure the "unprecedented challenge" (the words are from the Vatican's *Instruction on Christian Freedom and Liberation*) presented by the destitution and oppression prevalent in the Third World. This requires not only a liberative theology and practice, but a type of following of Christ that carries out the ethical-social, political and economic agenda left by Christ himself.

This will involve different connotations in the following of Christ, precisely because it is being done in a Third World context. Both old and new understandings of what it means to follow Christ have to take on new forms, with fresh emphasis and urgency—the preceding sections on "Jesus' actions" and "love as liberating practice" provide the basic elements of a *true* following of Christ, which need to be adapted to fit particular situations.

In such circumstances, true following demands an efficacy transcending the simple establishment of facts or simple compassion, or even love in its close relationships. All these are presupposed, but need to be re-structured to meet the pressing nature of the situation. Changing the mechanisms that generate inhuman conditions ceases to be a socio-political objective and becomes simply an ethical imperative. The seriousness of the problem makes what would normally be regarded as the object of Christian generosity into an ethical demand.

In short, following Christ in critical situations is not a different form of following, but one more consonant with Christ's own practice in relation to the world in which he lived. It is not contradicting his heritage or setting up a new one in its place; it is simply drawing the full consequences from it.

Chapter VI

"Conscientization" and Conscience: Between Humanity and Divinity

Writing on conscience is a rash undertaking, especially when one is trying to be brief. It is a basic reality, and one which has prompted a mass of studies over the centuries, impossible to summarize here. Their sum total fails to exhaust the subject—as one author remarked, a book devoted to it might be entitled *Conscience, the Great Unknown.*[1] For our purposes here, the essential aspect is that conscience is fundamental to discerning God's purposes in Jesus Christ.

Even acknowledging the complexity of their approaches, all studies made before the advent of processes of "conscientization"[2] can be called "calm." The debate really became complicated with the coming of psychological and then sociological studies, which is where we need to start.

The object of our enquiry, though, is not just conscience but what is meant by the *moral* conscience. So, having set the more general scene and examined what different schools have to say, we need to immerse ourselves in this concept, which hovers somewhere between humanity and divinity. A theological approach should give most weight to the Christian heritage of thought, while at the same time borrowing insights from psychological and sociological approaches. This is still going to leave many grey areas, the more so the closer we come to actual life. Without wishing to resort to casuistry, some practical questions need to be asked, such as: Is it really possible to speak of forming conscience? What might we mean by a "Christian conscience"? What is the role of the magisterium in relation to personal, ecclesial and social conscience?

1. CONSCIENTIZATION AND ETHICAL CONSIDERATIONS

(a) Context and Evolution

Conscientization has become known in the English-speaking world mainly through the work of Paulo Freire. It could have arisen only in the Third World with its illiterate masses, though it has important implications for the First. It starts as an educational endeavour, setting out to achieve something that defied earlier conventional educational methods: the achievement of wide-scale literacy. But its premise is that this neither can nor should be achieved without at the same time awakening a new social consciousness in those receiving "basic education," a consciousness that would lead to deep changes in persons and in society itself. It was thus from the start a "liberating" undertaking.

At the outset it became clear that a new social consciousness could be developed only as a community process. Only a consciousness of solidarity, and held in solidarity, offered opportunities of providing a springboard for deep changes in the political, economic, social and religious fields. This was the "liberative" aim, but conscientization was also at the start used to further "conservative" aims as well: the integration of the marginalized masses into existing society, in such a way that they would come to "know their place" in it, rather than act as "subjects" in a process of transformation, as the liberative model proposed.

The two currents could not exist peacefully side by side, and their conflict had a markedly ideological basis. Hence the question posed to the church: How could conscientization be carried out without ideological imposition? In Brazil, the concept of "basic education" had been endorsed by the Bishops'

Conference, so the church was directly involved. Also, conscientization necessarily involves the process of "organic pastoral practice": evangelization and development. So without losing sight of its aim of evangelization, the church was drawn through conscientization into the whole process of the great struggles for the liberation of the poor.[3]

(b) Ethical Implications

The process of conscientization involves different levels of consciousness. Originally a pedagogical process with political and social implications, it inevitably affected individual and community value systems as well. It is not a partial, but an all-embracing process. Being all-embracing, it plays not only on a socially naive consciousness, but also on a theologically naive one. Its aim of producing a truly critical awareness in sociological terms can hardly fail to produce a truly critical awareness in theological terms as well. Both critical awareness and moral conscience tend to break out of the areas theoretically reserved for their field of action, to invade other areas. This leads to the question of how to preserve the inviolability of the hidden nucleus we call conscience.

There is also an ethical dimension to the role of "agents of conscientization." If they are working to further conservative aims, the manipulation they perform is easy enough to see: they are simply acting as elites who see it as their task to change the consciousness of the people. But the "liberative" agents claim that the people themselves are the real agents of conscientization, so if there is manipulation here, it is more subtle. Even liberative agents will admit that they have to have some influence, so this is where the serious ethical questions arise: is not all conscientization basically a form of manipulation? Is there one form of conscientization that can be more acceptable than another?

Within the liberative approach, distinctions are made. Some see conscientization as simply "humanizing." There would not seem to be much of an ethical problem here, but it is still a process of "bringing to." Paulo Freire himself stresses the "dialogical" character of the process, to which the people bring their values. But the agent still plays an important part. Others, concentrating more on the social effects, see the agent as someone who explains only, with the oppressed people as the true subjects of action. All these avoid the *dirigisme* of the conservative model, but all still affirm that the "conscientizer" has to correct falsified consciousness.[4] This they refer to as "naive," "magical," "a-historical." Even with their valuation of popular wisdom, there is always the danger of conscientization being an *external activation of sleeping forces*. What comes out is what should "suit" the people. There is no denying the fact that: "There is no completely non-directive and totally free pedagogical action." So the question is not "whether to influence or not. The question is *how* to influence, and in what direction to influence."[5]

One of the most plausible ways of avoiding manipulation is through a true "exchange of knowledge,"[6] in which all learn, all influence each other, all liberate themselves. The people are liberated from their "naive" consciousness and the agents from their "distorted"—by the social milieu from which they come—consciousness. The role of the "conscientizers" would be to *transmit* information of interest to the people (their history, for example); to *help* the people with their needs (technical assistance, legal advice, and the like); to *report* the progress already made by the people; to *enable* the people to organize in appropriate ways. The role of the people is equally indispensable: to reveal their *life*, their *practice*, their *sense of reality*, the *ethical and religious values* to which they cling, despite everything.[7]

One has to bear in mind that conscientization schemes are worked out not by bishops or theologians, but by specialists in the social sciences. As such, it is not their duty to consider the implications for evangelization. But the pastoral agents, priests, religious and theologians who become involved in the process do have to bear in mind the wider considerations that correspond to their calling, and which at the same time respond to a more all-embracing view of human nature and the divine purpose.

So the very concept of a new society raises the questions of the values to be promoted in it and the means to be used to bring it into being. On the question of values, in particular, it is important to bear in mind that no society will ever be truly human without openness to transcendence and all that this implies in terms of a final point of reference surpassing everything and everyone, which cannot be manipulated. This is what we call the dimension of mystery, touched by grace—and by the sin that is present in all human undertakings. It is on this level that pastors involved in conscientization should operate: strengthened by the charism of administrators of the mysteries of God revealed in Jesus Christ, they must make the constant effort to hand on the good news *as Jesus did*; this means presenting the Father's proposal in its entirety, but without sacrificing respect for persons.

Finally, we need to bear in mind that it is not just a question of changing the "system." The true change—*metanoia*—is within persons as well as within society and politics. This is the level on which an irreducible space belongs to what we call *Christian conscience*, which will be examined in the following sections. Educational and "conscientizing" schemes can open doors for true evangelization, but cannot take its place.

2. CONSCIENCE AS NUCLEUS AND SANCTUARY OF THE HUMAN PERSON

Our reflections so far have been sociological, with a consideration of the ethical and theological implications. The question of conscience can also be approached through the human sciences, particularly that of psychology.[8] This approach distinguishes, more or less convincingly, the various types and levels of conscience. It shows that conscience, far from being a static reality, is a dynamic one, whether it is examined as a personal matter, a social one, or with or without its theological implications: conscience always undergoes a series of influences both internal and external.

If we take this approach, it is important not to lose sight of two things. The first is that "moral conscience is not a sort of separate conscience. . . . There is but one conscience, which shows itself in different ways and on various levels."[9] The second is that, though there is a constant interaction between these different ways and various levels, one cannot make pure and simple transpositions from one to another. Psychological and sociological approaches can shed light on properly theological considerations, but cannot take their place. In this section we intend to use data from other sciences, but without confusing them with theological considerations. This means examining conscience under three aspects: that of human realities, that of the underlying reality behind everything, and that of the depths of the human psyche.

(a) Conscience as Total Openness

Our sociological observations show how far personal conscience is linked to the overall environment. To a large extent, we *are* our relationships and see ourselves in them: political, social, economic, environmental, religious. . . . Our personalization is achieved in the interaction between the "I" and the "not-I," and in this we discover not only who we are but also who we *ought to be*. This being the case, true conscience is never shut in on itself, and this applies especially to what we call moral conscience. This is always a *cum-scientia*, a wisdom that grows precisely through opening out to all that is apparently external to it, but that permeates it to a greater or lesser extent.

This perception is already present in the Greek word *syn-eidesis*, used in the Bible and particularly by St Paul, and meaning "seeing with," or "knowing with."[10] This is the process by which human beings gradually appropriate the *values* proper to a culture, a people, a religion. So conscience is intimately linked to what is generally called "ethos": the deep identity of human beings, discovered and developed in the "home" (Greek *ethos*) of all.

Yet, just as "ethos" originally referred to the deep convictions and values of a people, so "knowing with" always refers to something greater than itself. In Christian theological terms this deep tendency is called love. Love is the primary vocation of all human beings and the only way they become fully human: we are made to love; we discover who we are through loving; through loving, we discover who we should be and what we should be like. This is the level on which the double commandment of love applies: of our neighbour and of God. The mark of union between this double dimension is Jesus Christ, the only being to live this double dimension without division and in all its fullness.

So the ultimate growth of moral conscience is into Christ and the mission he took on: to bring in the Kingdom.

The Kingdom, as described earlier,[11] is not something external to human beings: every dimension of human existence is shot through with it, and it embraces them all without being confused with any of them. The result of this is that human beings respond fully to the basic call of their conscience only to the extent that they insert themselves deeply into the historical-saving movement whose high point is Christ.

This being the case, the basic "education" of Christian moral conscience is not to make it morally perfect, but to make it part of saving history through following Christ. This is the process that unveils our full humanity, and it is in this process that humanity and divinity touch one another. The link between humanity and divinity is what can be called the moral conscience. This is not a closing in on oneself, but an openness to the specific calls made by God in Jesus Christ.

(b) Conscience as Openness to Transcendence

The total openness described above begins with the mediations, not so much of the various sciences, as of embodiments of humanity. Yet these mediations, as the term suggests, "lie between" two realities that are both close and distinct: human reality and divine reality. What the scientific view discovers is important, since it sheds light on one of these realities, one end of the bridge: humanity. But it needs the theological view to light up the whole bridge, and to show what lies on its far side, in the very depths of humanity.

Primitive peoples saw human conscience as something extending beyond itself. Gods, furies and other mythological beings are less indicative of a naive perception than of a perception seeing something beyond ordinary material life.[12] In much the same way, when the Old Testament seeks to express the depths of human nature, it speaks of the "heart,"[13] meaning what lies at the vital centre of humanity but is outside immediate perception. The heart feeds life and to a certain extent is synonymous with it. It works in silence, virtually unperceived. Divinity operates in much the same way: it feeds humanity, but is hidden behind it.

The presence of the divine shows in that inexplicable

something that every human being meets at the dawn of conscious life. Very slowly, gradually, obscurely and vaguely at first, we come to know that we exist, that we are someone and that we can and must *become*: we begin to perceive our responsibility for our own destiny and for that of the world around us. This is the dawning of conscience.

This conscience, however, is not created at the time we become conscious of it. Psychological, moral, social and religious conscience are all existing realities which we come to discover. And it is here, at the root of what is properly human, that we have to look for God and God's active presence. God does not merely reveal a set of things that human beings should do or not do, but "creates" conscience itself as a power and light making our response to God's call possible. Our appreciation of this gift and call which pre-exist in us marks the beginning of our journey toward self-fulfillment and becoming protagonists of our own history.

This divine presence at the origin of conscience, commonly called "the voice of God,"[14] is not something magical, outside the limits of what is human. On the contrary, it presupposes our moral discernment: "Put everything to the test and hold fast to what is good" (1 Thess. 5:21). This is the key to the notion of conscience in the New Testament.[15] It is the practical ability to make a responsible moral decision. Discovering God's will in an actual situation presupposes a search anchored in faith, in human reasoning and in experience.[16]

This power of discernment is certainly nourished by adequate knowledge of the gospel and the practice of following Christ in the life of the church and the community of faith. And yet the most extraordinary aspect of conscience comes to the fore precisely when these dimensions are not obviously present. Each and every human being, by the fact of being human, carries in herself or himself the seeds of divinity: "In the depths of his conscience, man detects a law which he does not impose upon himself, but which holds him to obedience" (GS 16a).

(c) Conscience as Openness to Oneself

One of the best definitions of conscience is that it is "the most within us, the depth of each individual human being—does not whose voice echoes in his depths" (GS 16b).

This definition does not of course deny human responsibility in any way, or curtail the infinite variety of humankind. It simply indicates what might be called "radical conscience," or what is found in the depths of human beings. It is as it were the sum total of what constitutes human beings and what they work at becoming throughout their lives.

What terms like "core" and "sanctuary" denominate is how deep what we call moral conscience lies. All living beings have their own law inscribed in them: the law of their development and fulfillment. It is this inner dynamism that constitutes their being: what they have been, what they are, what they are becoming and what they will be. This dynamism forms the deepest level of human reality, the originality of our being. For this very reason, refusing to obey this dynamism would mean refusing oneself and hindering one's own development.

Among all created beings, human beings are the only ones who have the power to choose between accepting or rejecting this formative dynamism. All other beings are subject to a natural determinism from which they cannot escape. All other beings, however autonomous, are not conscious of this fact, nor are they capable of rejecting or accepting their own determinism. Human beings, on the other hand, "take cognizance" of what they are and what becomes of them.

Conscience is, therefore, in the first place, the capacity we have for standing back from ourselves and from our surroundings, so as to take progressive cognizance of what we are and what our possibilities and limitations are. The medieval schoolmen called conscience a human faculty, but it is more than that: it embraces the whole, the totality of humanity. Conscience can be defined as human beings themselves, seen as their inner core. It is human beings themselves realizing that they exist and that they are called to develop in a particular direction.

"Realizing that they exist" belongs to the psychological level; adding "that they are called to develop in a particular direction" brings us on to the theological level; it concerns vocation, the divine call to take part in God's plan.

The threefold dimension—what surrounds us, the divinity

secret core and sanctuary of a man. There he is alone with God, mean that one can be separated from the others on the level of daily human existence. They act simultaneously, ebbing and flowing in an endless dialectical process. So conscience is not a person's solitude, but the connection resulting from openness in a number of different directions.

3. SOME CLARIFICATIONS

Detailed treatises on conscience show that in ordinary life nothing is simple. Conscience in some way escapes us, being what we are. This produces a number of questions:

—If conscience is something given from the start, what can "forming" a conscience mean, and what are the risks inherent in such a process?

—How far can moral law determine personal conscience, or the conscience of a society?

—What role can the magisterium play in forming conscience, particularly in conflictive situations?

We have already touched on these questions to some extent, but their importance means that they require further clarification.

(a) What "Forming" Conscience Means

We have seen that conscience is what is deepest and most original in us, so that it could be called our basic identity. Hence the questions: If it is our very identity, can it, strictly speaking, be "formed"? If so how, and with what caveats?

At one extreme, these questions touch on what might be called the originality of each human being. God's power is revealed not in serial creation but precisely in the great diversity of creation. Though we all have common features that identify us as "human," we each also have unrepeatable personal features. Only each individual can ask: Who am I? Why do I exist? Where am I going? At the other extreme, these questions concern my "circumstances": my background, my social, political, economic, cultural and religious influences. In other words, originality begins to be "shaped" by numerous factors, mostly independent of the individual. It is in the dialectic between originality and environment—"nature and nurture"—that conscience is formed.

Alongside both originality and environment, there is usually an educative "formation," put in motion by both family and society, and religious education fits into this context. Therefore, so does the possibility of either a liberative or a manipulative education.

Liberative education starts from the premise that people, groups, and nations are the prime agents of their own education. Hence its basic attitude of respect for the fundamental identity of all, for their background culture, their characteristics, their origins. It fits the old saying that "education is a drawing-out, not a putting-in"; the educator is rather a "caller-forth," summoning, challenging, encouraging the "educatees" to develop in a manner consistent with their calling. It is a matter of invitation: proposition, not imposition.

An authoritarian educational approach, on the other hand, starts from the premise that it must "im-plant" at all costs, even dragging out what was there in the first place to put something supposedly better in its place. Here the educatees know "nothing"; it is accepted that they neither can nor should do anything of their own initiative. They are not subjects, but objects indeed. There are no propositions, only impositions; no questions, only statements; no invitations, only orders.

The first approach is typified by Socrates, with his "maieutic" process, in which the answer is never given in advance, but elements are provided from which an answer can be found. The second is the draconian approach, that of the lawgiver who knows and imposes everything, without distinction of ability or circumstance.

These two opposite educational concepts have an obvious parallel in religious and moral teaching. But here the matter is further complicated, since what is being "taught" is not just a body of acquired knowledge, but the content of revelation itself. How can this content be handed on without being manipulated? Perhaps a comparison with the types of religious and moral education offered at the time of Christ will help to show the answer: one school represented by the Pharisees, the experts in revealing the Law of Moses; the other was Christ himself, bringing the fullness of revelation. The Pharisees sought zealously to hand on the facts they had been taught, but did so in an authoritarian, inhuman and therefore arbitrary manner. Christ, on the other hand, enlightened, uncovered, fascinated, while being every bit as perfectionist in his own educational technique. Two pedagogical methods of implanting a theoretically identical message: one is threatening, bureaucratic, inflexible; the other is encouraging, experiential, comprehensive in the deepest sense of the word. One embodies a sort of repetitive fideism, the other a divinely creative fidelity. The formation of Christian conscience can follow only the model set by Christ: otherwise, it becomes de-formation.

(b) Conscience and Moral Codes[17]

One way of forming conscience is through moral codes. The correlation between the two is presented sometimes in opposing terms, sometimes in conforming ones. For the liberal outlook, moral codes have nothing to do with conscience: they kill both conscience and freedom, and therefore do away with responsibility too, so that no one who preaches moral responsibility can put forward a morality based on codes. But for the "rigourist" outlook, codes represent the objective criterion of morality, while conscience is the subjective criterion; conforming the two means that right conscience will always concur with objective moral codes.

Both points of view seem too simplistic. Opposition between conscience and code is either artifical or the result of a misunderstanding, generally the latter, which means that we need a better definition of both conscience and moral codes. True conscience can never be identified with subjectivism: it is the product of a tireless search, a constant *dia-logue*, in the sense suggested by the word's derivation from the Greek *dia-legein*, meaning to "read through," to recall through discourse, to reflect inwardly and so assimilate what comes from outside. So the process of forming a conscience always consists of a creative process in which various elements are weighed, reflected on and assimilated.

Furthermore, true moral codes cannot be confused with their formulation. Formulations always bear the marks of the person who establishes them, whereas the actual code refers back to a deeper source. True moral codes are not external but signs of something deep within human beings; they are true only insofar as they express human values. Moral values, especially when understood as evangelical values, are indeed normative in the real sense of the word: moral codes or laws are more or less binding according to their faithfulness or otherwise to what are recognized as values.

The formulation of moral laws goes through a process rather like translating from one language to another: there is a "source-code" and an "end-code," and good translation requires mastery of both. In terms of moral values, there is only one master and one good translator/interpreter: Jesus Christ. He not only masters both codes—the human and the divine—but *is* both. So other interpreters formulate moral codes well or badly depending on how far they allow themselves to be filled with the Spirit of Christ, on how far they are in communion with the true interpreter of moral values.

A final comparison may help to illustrate this better. This is a comparison drawn from the code of the covenant: the Pharisees confused the covenant with the ten commandments, and so betrayed its deep meaning; Christ placed the ten commandments in the context of the new and everlasting covenant, thereby re-situating the laws contained in the ten commandments and giving them their true meaning. This is why he could make the startling judgment: "The sabbath was made for man and not man for the sabbath."

To sum up: the source of the moral law and of conscience is one and the same: at root God and God's purposes. Human beings, faced with their deepest conscience, recognize that they are not the creators of moral values, that their creation is not something they can pronounce on. Yet they also know that their primary task consists in uncovering values that are sometimes hidden behind codes. This being so, then moral laws will be helping them to act in accordance with their own conscience and in accordance with the divine purposes as these concern them personally and as they concern the whole of humanity. When this happens, it abolishes both artificial opposition between conscience and moral law and equally artificial and unproductive conformism between the two, giving rise to a true conscience within a morality of responsibility. This morality reflects both the divine purposes and the appeals of conscience, since ultimately they are the same.

(c) Conscience and The Magisterium

There is no space here for a full consideration of the magisterium of the Catholic Church. Moral theology has to take many things for granted, and here we take for granted what is generally known about the magisterium: that there are ordinary and extra-ordinary levels; that there are papal and episcopal dimensions (the latter involving each bishop in communion with the pope and his brothers in the episcopate); that it involves internal and external assent. These distinctions are vitally important if we are to avoid a series of problems. Given these presuppositions, we can examine the role of conscience in relation to certain situations and real or apparent difficulties.

The magisterium is, undoubtedly, one of the gifts of the Spirit granted to the church of Christ. Given the task of encouraging the faithful in their following of Christ, and shedding light on an often dark road, the magisterium can be likened to a great lantern carried in weak hands. The paradox is that its functions become more problematical the more they are needed, and this paradox is most marked in times of deep change. In one way, the magisterium sheds light; in another, it raises questions. In one way it sets minds at rest; in another it disturbs and challenges.

It is not a matter of making superficial distinctions between those who are docile to the voice of the magisterium and those who are not. This would make it difficult to understand the way Paul contradicted Peter "to his face" and other historical events. But even presupposing good will and a sincere quest for the truth in all concerned, tensions between conscience and the magisterium can still arise. Their solution has to be found in what enables development to take place in both the magisterium and conscience: the gospel.

Such questions are also more easily resolved when their terms are well defined at the outset. The magisterium is not something that hovers over the church and church life. To the contrary, it can be understood properly only within the dynamic of a church on its march through history. It is thus a function within the church and within the world and history. As a function within the church, the magisterium has to be articulated with the *sensus fidelium*; as a function within the world, it has to take account of what is good and true in the world; as a function in history, it is inseparable from the experience of humankind.

Then, the magisterium is above all a service in the search for understanding of the will of God and putting this into effect in history. In this sense, the magisterium is always at the service of conscience and seeks to help the faithful to be faithful to their own conscience.

This being so, tensions between conscience and magisterium cannot be regarded as something normal and everyday. They arise rather in extreme situations, in which conscience and the magisterium, each keeping its basic point of reference in the gospel, are operating on the level of specific embodiment of gospel truths. The judgment of conscience looks more to specific actions, that of the magisterium is more concerned with principles. The judgment of conscience represents a practical verdict on what should be done and what should be avoided; the magisterium presents what should be done in an ideal and evangelical fashion. So, once again, conflicts properly so called, besides being relatively rare, do not prevent both parties to them from sharing the same fundamental reference point.

But when tensions do arise, despite everything, the first need is to examine the underlying reasons for them. Very often, tensions stem from a false understanding of the content and significance of the magisterium's teachings. Not everything that is said to be the teaching of the church is so in fact, just as not everything that is said to belong to freedom of conscience does so in fact. A truly critical spirit of faith can prevent many conflicts.

The distance between the "simple faithful" and those who exercise a magisterial function can also underlie many misunderstandings. No one can love what he or she does not know. Here rapprochement and genuine exchanges among the whole people of God—theologians, members of the hierarchy and the ordinary faithful—have removed many barriers and laid many ghosts to rest. Real dialogue is one of the most important forms mutual charity can take, and, like charity, can cover a multitude of sins.

Conscience is at once what there is most human and most divine in us. Hence the need to strip off its masks and let its true depths emerge. Chapter 25 of St Matthew's Gospel shows what the final criteria by which God judges are. Here we have tried to show both the depth of human conscience and its dignity: it is something to be respected by all, even when objectively judged to be in error with regard to moral laws.

The manuals introduced a range of distinctions with regard to conscience: right or erroneous, sure or doubtful, healthy or scrupulous. The process of conscientization shows that there are still other aspects that need to be taken into account: naive, magical, fanatical, emerging, transitive-naive, transitive, transitive-critical. And moral theology can still add: personal, community and social, ecclesial.

One certainty stands out among so many distinctions: from all points of view, the pursuit of a matured conscience in the bosom of the community is an ideal to be pursued at all times. And the church as a whole has to lend its service to this pursuit. What is certain is that the desired objective of a new humanity, which requires the deep transformation of all human structures, has to be pursued on the level of conscience: this the antenna that seeks out true and false embodiments of God's purposes through Jesus Christ.

PART THREE

NEW HUMAN BEINGS IN A NEW SOCIETY

Chapter VII

God's Call and Human Response

The proper response Christians owe to God's call is the life they lead and the human society they help to build, doing what is good, just and right and producing the true fruits of the Spirit (see Gal. 5:22). God, creator of all that exists, did not just launch human beings into the universe only to stand back as a disinterested spectator. The Epistle to the Hebrews begins by telling us that God in the past spoke to our ancestors through the prophets in many different ways, but "in our times" through the Son, who has been appointed heir of all things and through whom all was created (1:1–2). God's Word is efficacious, working, creating, making all things new through the Spirit. As the proverb says, "God writes straight with crooked lines," or, as sometimes happens, God writes crooked with lines we see as straight. It is through God's breath of life that the whole of creation, "subjected to frustration," will be "freed from this fate of death" (Rom. 8:19–21). It is to freedom that human beings are called.

Through the mystery of the incarnation, which began with the birth of Jesus, the Word of God took human shape and took on the human conditions of the time and environment in which Jesus lived. Christians continue to pray in the words that Jesus taught: Our Father . . . thy will be done, on earth as in heaven. But this will, sometimes so hard to decipher, was focussed in the person of Christ and in what he performed in our midst, as mediation of truth and way of life (see John 14:6). Insofar as Christian communities discover and accept who the Lord Jesus is, they also discover the Father and his will, which is none other than our sanctification (John 8:19; 19:9; 1 Thess. 4:3). The more Christians together live the Spirit of Jesus and follow the example Jesus left, the better they show in this world the true face of the God who is freedom and love, "from [whose] fullness we have all received favour upon favour" (John 1:16).

In general terms, what human beings have to do in response to God's call consists of three aspects of the same basic "way"—the way to bring about Christian community: grateful fidelity to God's word; conversion through growing faith in the gospel; the missionary commitment Christians undertake in the world of today, all according to their place in it and the talents they have received.

1. GRATEFUL FIDELITY

In the eschatological prospective Jesus opened up in the parable of the talents, the stress falls on those employees whose reward will be great because they have shown themselves faithful in small things (Matt. 25:14–30). In the light of faith, human life begins with the love that God first showed us and continues to show us (1 John 4:10, 19). Human response to this love cannot be just a *coup de foudre* or a passing passion. Its mark has to be persevering faithfulness, since "whoever stands firm to the end will be saved" (Matt. 10:21; 24:13).

(a) Basic Readiness

At first glance, response to Jesus' call and adherence to his plan of life seem disarmingly simple: Jesus calls and Christians simply say "Yes." Christian literature from all periods is full of fine pages on holy obedience and the readiness to hear and listen to what the Lord says. Life opens out to listening. In the Old Testament, each renewal of the covenant with Yahweh, celebrated by the people of Israel, and many prophetic exhortations and prayers by the Psalmists follow the same line. In expressions of gratitude to the God who set his people free, the people respond with submission to the Lord's commandments as their guide in this world. The basic formula is Samuel's "Speak, Lord; your servant is listening" (1 Sam. 3:10).

Jesus was distinguished by a readiness to listen and to do the will of the Father, so that St John has him say: "My food is to do the will of the One who sent me and to carry out his work" (4:34).

Perhaps the response of Jesus' first disciples had something of this direct simplicity about it, though we should not underestimate the burden of courage and sacrifice laid on them by the decision to leave their families and occupations. Nevertheless, they did not always find it easy to understand the mission of this Jesus who was to be handed over to death. After the resurrection too, difficulties in understanding God's will showed themselves in the church: it was debates among Christians that brought about the First Council of Jerusalem (Acts 15) and caused most of the apostolic letters to the various communities to be written. The Christian people did not set out on their journey through life with a detailed map in their hands showing them every path to follow once and for all.

(b) Obstacles

The people always begin their histories and stories of Jesus with the words: "When Jesus walked on earth." So they refer clearly to a past event, since Jesus no longer walks among us, inviting disciples to walk with him and share his life, listen to his preaching and observe the signs he worked, as the evangelists testify. Furthermore, perhaps because of the time lapse, life at that period looks simpler, lacking the complications and problems that beset us in today's complex world. In a simple world, the Lord's law and listening to his voice can be simple too. In complex present-day society, with its horizons spread across the globe and out into space, the means of listening also become more complex, and it is harder for us to decipher the messages relayed to our innermost being.

More than ever, the Tower of Babel described in Genesis 11 serves as a symbol for the confusion of ideas and contrasting plurality of attitudes that mark the modern world. And even the first Christians found serious obstacles to living their faith in the society of their time, as the Acts of the Apostles and their letters show. While some of society's customs and codes of behaviour could easily be adopted by the disciples of Christ, others had to be repelled and banished from their lives at whatever cost (see 1 Corinthians, etc.).

At the present time, the question of how to live in the world and build a human society faithful to the word of the Lord has become considerably more complicated. The communications media spread every novelty immediately, and demonstrate the—sometimes extreme—differences of opinion and attitude prevailing in the fields of social life, sexuality and the family, politics, the economy, religion. In theory and practice, ideas and behaviour, we live in a chaotic situation in which it is very difficult to follow the right track, to hear the call addressed to us by the Lord through the Spirit and the church, the people of God, today. In all this commotion, how are Christian communities to discern the authentic voice of the Spirit directing us surely along the right road (see John 5:5–15)?

(c) The Human Sphere Invaded

In the biblical vision, God is paradoxically both distant and close. God is the utterly Other, the Absolute, the First and the Last, an unfathomable Mystery so unutterable that not even the flights of the mystics can describe the reality of God; it simply cannot be seized in human words. On the other hand, God is closer to us than our innermost selves and God's love knows us better than we know ourselves. The religious imagery of the Old Testament has given us the lovely symbolism of God walking in the garden in the evening breeze; the Psalmist hears God's voice in a storm, making the oaks shudder and shaking the wilderness (Gen. 3:8; Ps. 29).

When in the fullness of time the goodness and love of God, our saviour, appeared in our midst (Titus 3:4), and God's grace became manifest in Jesus of Nazareth, the voice of God took on a more human form than it had in the prophets, speaking human language in ordinary everyday words. In Johannine theology, Jesus was the Word with God, who became flesh and dwelt amongst us, full of grace and truth (John 1:1–14). Jesus is identified with the truth people seek on their journey through this world; he is truth personified, as he is the sure way and the life that will never fade (John 14:6). To those who follow him and listen to his voice, he gives the Spirit of truth who will teach all truth and tell us of things to come, giving human beings the guidance they need in life (John 16:13).

In Christ Jesus, the voice of God not only became human, but invaded the whole sphere of the human. Besides its transcendental urge, human existence has two real dimensions ever present: the cosmic and the social. Human beings belong to the universe of nature and to society, and, in their origin and evolution, depend on them. The people of Israel were very conscious that humankind belonged to the earth, being made out of clay; they knew that through the use of reason, will and energy, men and women were responsible for cultivating nature and organizing human society. Their own eventful history bears witness to this consciousness in a thousand deeds, successes and failures. In the letters of the apostles, above all, this consciousness-of-task receives its fullest expression. The whole universe, of which humankind is the centre, finds its end and its beginning, its Alpha and Omega, in Jesus. In him, the human being *par excellence*, all things in heaven and earth were made; he is the beginning, through which everything was created, and the first raised from the dead; he is Lord of all history past, present and to come (see Col. 1:15–20). In the experience of the community of his disciples that is the church, he was and is present with the power of his word and his bread of life in their midst, the one whom they, journeying and working, hope to meet so as to be presented "without fault, holy and blameless" to the Father (Col. 1:22).

(d) The Dramatic Risk

Understanding the human sphere in the light of reason and faith does not, however, guarantee a triumphal progress, a foretaste of perfect living, a sort of return of paradise lost. The human condition today is scarred by hunger on one side and waste on the other, by epidemics that should no longer be with us, by pain in all its forms, and by the death that comes to all, rich and poor, old and young. The double condemnation which Genesis places in Yahweh's mouth, to suffering in childbearing for the woman and in producing food for the man, seems simple in comparison with the multifarious human tragedies which leave us feeling how limited human life is, how transitory, beset with weakness, threatened with failure and altogether finite. St Paul may glory in his weakness and affliction, but he cannot deny them (2 Cor. 12:5–9).

The epicentre of the human drama, though, lies in the fact that the course of our life so often crosses with the mystery of iniquity and the inheritance of Babel. The project for humanity that Jesus began to carry out would be relatively easy to complete if all we ever did was praise God together in a combination of the song of the children in the fiery furnace and St Francis' canticle to Brother Sun. But this is not what human life is like. St Matthew shows Jesus facing up to three demonic temptations: to pleasure, to power and to the old Adamic temptation to self-sufficiency, leaving God out of account. The human struggle is not just against pain, suffering, failure and death, but against the forces of evil that lurk in our hearts and in today's world produce ever new forms of slavery, injustice, exploitation, lies and violence, setting brother against brother, class against class, nation against nation. The real state of the world around us all makes sense of the warning: "Therefore put on the whole armour of God, that in the evil day you may resist and stand your ground" (Eph. 6:13).

(e) Building on Rock

The church community and Christians in their personal lives, listening faithfully to the word of God imparted through Jesus Christ, build their houses on the rock of the Lord. Already in the early community in Ephesus, there was danger of believers being "like children tossed about by any wave or wind of doctrine, and deceived by the cunning of men who drag them along into error" (Eph. 4:14). This danger has not grown less today; it has rather increased, due to the complexity of the problems that arise, and the speed with which new ideas are spread.

Here we have the quiet reassurance of Jesus' words: "Anyone who hears these words of mine and acts accordingly is like a wise man who built his house on rock. The rain poured, the rivers flooded, and the wind blew against that house, but it did not collapse because it was built on rock" (Matt. 7:24–5). In the church community and in personal life, building that house still provides work for all, just as the floods and the winds continue to batter it. But through all the storms, the voice of the Lord echoes in the church and in the hearts of the faithful: "Why are you so afraid, you of little faith?" (Matt. 8:26).

That to err is human is ancient wisdom. In building the house, involving Christians in making decisions and adopting certain courses of action, there can be deceits and the need to turn back and start again. But when there is human will to remain faithful, which includes a will to correct oneself and change direction if necessary, then there is a basis for confidence in the promise contained in Jesus' words: "My sheep hear my voice . . . and I give them eternal life. They shall never perish and no one will ever steal them from me. What the Father has given me is stronger than everything and no one can snatch it from the Father's hand" (John 11:27–9).

2. CONVERSION

In the confused babble of the voices and appeals of the world today, Christian life is like fine-tuning the radio so as to receive the station one is really interested in. In order to hear the word of the Lord clearly, Christians must turn themselves in the direction it comes from, as Jesus began his public ministry by proclaiming: "The Kingdom of God is at hand. Change your ways and believe the good news" (Mark 1:15). God's invitation is addressed to everyone, calling us all to communion with the Son, Jesus Christ our Lord (see 1 Cor. 1:9). To those shut inside their own selfishness, this invitation in love is a call to a complete about turn, to respond through love by putting faith to work in action in building, with others, the Kingdom of God: "What really matters is to have faith working through love" (Gal. 5:6).

(a) Conversion as Awareness

In countries where the majority of the population call themselves Catholic and the Catholic Church is continually visible in public acts, conversion is a process that can easily be left out of account. Baptized as infants, most Catholics go on to make their first communion and then gradually lose their life-giving contact with the church community. When children they, like St Paul, spoke and thought as children. But once they have become adults, unlike St Paul, instead of putting away childish things, they stop developing, cling to certain infantile concepts, effectively throw out the seed of faith that has not borne fruit, or immerse themselves in a sort of vague syncretism in which anything goes. Despite the pervasive voice of the church, the religious climate of Latin America resembles a river with many tributaries which spreads straight into an estuary with numerous channels, without ever forming the one clear course of commitment to the gospel.

In these conditions, conversion takes the form of growing awareness by adults beginning to reflect on their calling and mission in the world in which they live and work. In this way, they grow in faith, in fidelity and confidence, and develop the courage to accept a Christian commitment in daily life, as mature and responsible individuals. This process does not usually come like the shock that made Saul fall off his horse on the road to Damascus; it is more like the slow growth of a tree, with roots spreading deeper into the ground and branches that regularly bear their crop of the true fruits of the Spirit (see Gal. 5:22–6).

But conversion is not just an individual story of dialogue between God and the Christian involved; it is also service to the church community of which she or he is a member. It can be brought about by an event through which a person is touched by grace: a setback, a bereavement, a friendship leading to deepening thought about one's reason for being in the world, one's relationship with Jesus Christ, God and the church. It always involves other people through their example, actions or appeal. Communicating with God is not exclusive: it usually includes the mediation of other Christians, of the local church community. St John was right to address his letters to the various local churches, praising them and rebuking them as groups. The behaviour of Christians depends largely on whether their environment is fervent or lukewarm, zealous or slovenly, whether it surrounds them with a community rich in mutual love or not.

(b) Conversion as Personal Story

The appeal which the Spirit of the Lord Jesus makes to all through the church demands a personal response, one that is ever in need of improvement. The gift of life is not given to Christians once and for all; it is a growth in which each of us is powerfully strengthened by the Spirit. It is a process of penetrating ever deeper, together with all Christians, into the width, the length, the height and the depth of the mystery of God, revealed to us through the love of Christ in this world (see Eph. 3:15–19). In Christ, through his blood, Christians have redemption, remission of their sins ever lavished on them through the greatness of his grace, and obtain the true freedom and joy of living as adopted sons and daughters of God (see Eph. 1:5–8).

The more Christians discover the greatness of God's grace and mercy in their lives, the stronger—and more comforting too—will be their consciousness of their dignity and their strength in facing up to their mission to carry out God's purpose of justice and peace for all in the world God made for all. They will not be without a share in the sufferings of Christ, or persecutions from false brethren, or temptations to weakness and discouragement, since the disciple is not greater than the master. With humble courage to serve the Lord, each through his or her own Magnificat, Christians will learn that with one another they form "a chosen race, a community of priest-kings, a consecrated nation, a people God has made his own to proclaim his wonders. For he called [them] from their darkness to his own wonderful light" (1 Pet. 2:9). Christians can be proud and not bow their heads before any human idol or power, because if God is with us, who can stand against us? And will the One who spared not his own son, but gave him over for all our sakes, not give us all else besides (see Rom. 8:31–9; Matt. 6:33)?

(c) Conversion in the Church

The process of Christian conversion extends beyond the individual sphere, being umbilically linked to the fruitfulness of community church life. Christians open their ears and heart to the word of Christ and grow in understanding of their mission in the world in which they live through common worship around the lectern and eucharistic table, and by the mutual services they render one another. In the celebrations of the local community, Christians feed one another with the word and the bread of life, giving freely to others what they have freely received and continue to receive (Matt. 10:8). Thankful, they render ever new, through their sharing, what St Paul wished for the community in Colossae: "With thankful hearts sing to God psalms, hymns and spontaneous praise" (Col. 3:16). As a prelude to the eschatological joy they hope to experience, Christians celebrate their feasts in the consoling knowledge that where two or three are gathered together in his name, Jesus himself will be in their midst (Matt. 18:20).

"No man is an island, entire of itself": no one journeys alone through the desert of life. In living Christian communities, a process of mutual edification takes place, in which the faithful open their hearts to one another, instruct one another and, if necessary, admonish one another with the freedom of children of God, putting their different talents to work building the body of Christ in the church (see Eph. 4:11–16). If the building work proceeds as it should, no one should have a monopoly of the word, nor should others merely listen, because the true building-up of the people of God, the church, is based on mutual solidarity among those who know themselves to be called in the same faith, the same hope, and above all the same love. In this open climate of solidarity, even criticism becomes fruitful, opening eyes and cleansing ears to the present reality, so that the whole community will be able to discern what is the will of God, what is good, what pleases God, what is perfect, and, therefore, what they have to bring about (Rom. 12:2).

(d) Conversion in a Divided World

St John's theology is summed up in the statement: "The Word was made flesh" (1:14). Faith in the risen Lord supposes acceptance of the human life of Jesus of Nazareth who took on the human condition common to all humanity, in all things except sin; he was like other men and was recognized as an ordinary man by the Nazarenes who knew his family (see Phil.

2:6–8; John 8:46; Mark 6:3; Luke 4:22). He was not some sort of satellite flying around in space, but bound by the conditions of his time and place, as are the Christians who seek to follow him. They have to fulfill their human potential within the confines of the geographical, historical and social space in which they live and work. No one is impervious to surroundings; we all depend on them in forming our thoughts and feelings, and we are conditioned by them as we make choices and decisions along our personal journey.

If our time and space are that of a divided world and unjust society, the process of Christian conversion cannot take place according to some vague universal ideas, but has to be conditioned by the actual situation in which the bulk of the people around us live, move and have their being, as best they can. Christians will make different analyses of the reality of which they form part, according to the knowledge and imagination possessed by each: a jumble of impressions and experiences drawn from the small, everyday round, or a more "scientific," systematic analysis trying to encompass the whole of human reality and look deep into the causes of the present situation. Perceptual viewpoints will be different, depths of analysis vary, ways of expressing can range from hard words like exploitation, injustice, hunger, marginalization, oppression and torture, to more lyrical forms of expression describing the face of people, suffering, unemployment. But becoming aware of the actual situation of the church in the present-day social, political and economic climate is something inherent in the very process of adult Christian conversion. Without this, conversion is just incipient, not knowing how to transplant the tree of knowledge of good and evil into actual human lives in this human—all too human—world.

Knowledge of God, of Jesus, of the human condition in the world, is always knowledge on a human scale, limited, incomplete, a map of the universe with great areas left blank. Human knowledge is a light in the dark world of ignorance. There is an old saying that two heads are better than one; arrogance alone sets itself up in an ivory tower. So Christians, in order to understand the place they occupy in this world shared with others, need to exchange impressions, ideas and knowledge with others. The church community is the first place in which to meet and exchange thoughts and ideas, to develop a more complete and precise understanding of the universe we belong to, and to acquire elements of an answer to the ever-repeated question: "What shall we do, brothers?" (Acts 2:37).

3. MISSIONARY COMMITMENT

Like everyone else, Christians are born knowing nothing. They soon discover that their dawning desires, whims and wishes are surrounded by a mass of censors, rules, prohibitions and ordinances. Parents, neighbours, school, society and the church not only offer possibilities for growth, for enlarging one's personal space, maturing and starting to fulfill one's potential; they also block one's way through this world of men and women with a thousand and one warnings, laws and sanctions. In the human condition, the business of living together is not just a product of free and creative spontaneity—important though this is; it also follows a detailed map already drawn up showing us what to do and where to go on our journey through life. And in the Christian morality derived from many a manual, this map is full of no entries, roads blocked and security zones in which it is absolutely forbidden to set foot.

(a) Commitment to the Lord Jesus

In this complicated, sometimes confusing and oppressive situation, the high road and final guide for the behaviour of Christians are their missionary commitment to the Lord Jesus, his message and cause. The commitment, taken on at baptism and renewed every year in the Easter liturgy, cannot stop half way, as Peter's did (Matt. 16:13–28): he confessed his faith in Christ, but faced with Jesus' announcement of his cross and death, he followed the thoughts of man, not of God. Or as the apostles did: they left everything to follow Jesus, but then competed amongst themselves as to who would be greatest in the Kingdom of heaven (Mark 9:33–5 and parallels). For a time they lacked the power of the Holy Spirit that would turn them into committed witnesses to Jesus and make them open the gates on the world that belongs to all.

In Christian experience, commitment has its own inner paradox. On one hand, it is fraught with risk, because the gate that leads to destruction is wide and the road there broad, while the gate that leads to true life is narrow and the road rough (Matt. 7:13–14). Jesus' life knew a triumphal entry, but also a great deal of incomprehension, resistance and the plotting of adversaries, leading to prison and death on a cross. Since disciples are not greater than their master, they too have to complete in their own flesh the sufferings of Christ, in the cause of building up his body, which is the church (Col. 1:24). On the other hand stands Jesus' continual invitation: "Come to me, all of you who work hard and who carry heavy burdens . . . for my yoke is good and my burden is light" (Matt. 11:28–30). He himself will be with his disciples, through the power of his Spirit, till the end of time (Matt. 28:20). Even if disciples fail and betray their commitment, Christ demonstrated the mercy of the Father who is still ever awaiting the return of the prodigal son and still pardons him afresh, completely forgetting what is past, to celebrate in the feast of pure angelic joy (Luke 15).

(b) The Elements of Commitment

At a time when individualism and the spirit of "each one for himself" are increasing with material prosperity and growing social status, commitment too runs the risk of being defined in terms of a self-seeking and sterile spirituality. Then Christian life comes to look like a business of accumulating graces, merits and heavenly favours, as though God were a banker in whose bank Christians held deposit accounts. Such narrow egoism forms a flagrant contrast with Jesus' commitment to his Father: he gave his life in service to his friends and in freeing them from all evils. His death on the cross was the ultimate consequence of his living in this way, which made him prey to the hatred and cowardice of the religious leaders of his time. His commitment and that of all Christians opens beyond the narrow limits of self-interest to embrace these elements:

(i) The mystery of God. Commitment carries Christians, as individuals and in communities, within the mystery of God. For us today, used to the word "mystery" in terms of detective novels, thriller movies and tales of the supernatural, it is perhaps

difficult to appreciate the significance of the word as used in New Testament Greek. The simple people still retain some feeling for the original mystery of God: when afflicted with suffering or death, they say: "We don't understand, but God knows why." There is an element of resignation, coupled with the self-abandonment of faith which trusts in the One who is a good Father to the people.

Christians, set free in the name of Jesus, always and everywhere share in the Christian and effective dynamism of God who is the whole created universe from its beginning to its end. God is the utterly other, but also with us. With God all things are possible, without God nothing is, as popular wisdom has it. A little with God is a lot; a lot without God is nothing. The commitment of the people of God is the ever more intense celebration of God's new covenant with the people, sealed by the blood of the Lamb; it is the firm and faithful will to collaborate in the building of the Kingdom of justice and love which God planned without us, but wishes to go on building with us, as a historical work of our hands and God's.

After God, the productive efficacy of commitment depends on the maturity of Christians, determined by the extent of their responsibility and their power of decision-making. Development to this maturity is hampered by two obstacles: their ignorance of or weakness in faith, and the infantilism or deformation of their moral conscience. This problem made its appearance early in the first Christian communities: both St Paul and the Letter to the Hebrews refer to Christians who "need milk, not solid food," who are still moral infants, not having been tested in the ways of justice and not having trained themselves to distinguish between good and evil (Heb. 5:11–14; cf 1 Cor. 3:1–4). Using the same imagery, though in a different sense, Peter shows that maturity is not a stable adult "state," since all need to grow to reach salvation, tasting ever deeper of the goodness of the Lord (1 Pet. 2:1–3). It is not a system of external rules that should come first, but the depth and intensity of the discovery, made through the experience of faith, that God is love and truth.

(ii) Following Jesus. Through the free giving of their commitment, Christians enter God's "field of force" via the mediation of the Lord Jesus. In the line of faith that comes from Judaism, he

is the true high priest who builds the bridge linking God to God's people through his incarnation and eucharistic celebration. Jesus became like all other human beings, one of us, in order to be the merciful and faithful high priest who would expiate the sins of the people and help them in their struggle for life (Heb. 2:17ff). Taking on humanity in his flesh and taking up all creatures in the bread and wine, he gives historical embodiment to his ministry of mediator of the new covenant, in which all, great and small alike, come better to know the Lord their God (Heb. 8:6–13).

What Jesus of Nazareth did and said forms a wide fan of attitudes and positions within which commitment to God can be incorporated and become human history in this world. But this is not to say that Jesus' exemplary power and attraction form a simple paradigm to follow. Through baptism, Christians are themselves made sharers in the mystery of God, whose complete epiphany in the world is conditional on those who find their own dignity and basis for action in Christ. Jesus is not outside us; despite being a historical figure from another age, another culture and a different type of society, he is within us through his Spirit, working within every individual and in all Christian communities, as a voice and a light in the sanctuary of moral consciences (see GS 16).

(iii) Building the church. Commitment to Jesus the Lord is not simply an interpersonal, I-thou, closed-circuit relationship, but leads us into his house, the church, and makes us take on responsibility for the communal task of building that house. Drawing close to Christ, the living stone, and incorporated in him, Christians have to build the house of God with living stones so as to proclaim the wonders of God who called them out of darkness into God's own wonderful light (1 Pet. 2:4–10). Being the apostle and high priest of the faith we profess, Jesus lives and works in his own house, of which he is also the builder. We, the disciples, make up his household, provided we stand firm in the hope and courage proper to us (Heb. 3:1–15). With each one of us performing his or her own proper function, we build up the body of Christ, the church community, with sincere love (Eph. 4:11–16).

Building this church space in community requires disciples to take two of Jesus' sayings as a moral programme: "If you choose to save your own life, you will lose it; and if you lose your life for my sake and for the sake of the gospel, you will save it," and: "If anyone wants to be first, he must be the very last and make himself the servant of all" (Mark 8:34–8; 9:35 and parallels). The price of the game of winning and losing, of being less to be more, is constant struggle to overcome concentrating on oneself. Self-seeking, self-preservation, self-defence are inborn instincts and carry great force. Neither the law of "an eye for an eye" nor the principle of "do as you would be done by" could tame their explosive power. Jesus' demand, however, backed by the example of his own life and death, is that those who would be his brother, sister and mother must focus their vital energy on love for others (Mark 3:31–5; John 13:34ff; 15:9–13; Matt. 5:38–47). This love knows no limitations of persons or rank; it embraces all, even our enemies and debtors.

A multiplicity of rules and guidelines has grown up in the church over the centuries, uneven in weight and quality. In the specific, sometimes painful situations Jesus' disciples, members of the church, find themselves in, two principles always illuminate the path to right decisions and right actions. The first is the primacy of love or charity which makes others our neighbours through the service we perform for them, following the key Jesus gave us in the parable of the Good Samaritan (Luke 10:25–27). The practice of neighbourly love is the prime way for Jesus' disciples, following the example he set; it is the only form of servitude Christians must accept (1 Cor. 12:31—13:13; Gal. 5:13). The other is the primacy of humankind over the Law (Mark 2:23—3:5 and parallels). While no society can live without a backbone of law to enable it to function, harshness of law can lead to hardness of heart. Moral rules have the transitory nature of the image of this world, while the nerve centre of human beings is their absolute liberation even to death. Rules can serve only one overriding purpose: that all human beings should be saved and come to know the truth that is Christ (1 Tim. 2:1—6:4).

(iv) Open communication with "the world." In the world, the church is sacrament and sign of credibility, drawing those outside it to share in the mystery of God and become disciples of Jesus, the Lord. To carve out its true identity in the world

of today and to deepen its message of justice, love and peace for a human race suffering from hunger, exploitation, injustice and violence, the people of God need to take stock, analyze where they are going and plan their future, if they are to be true to their Lord.

This inward movement, though, has to be balanced with outward movement. Its missionary character is the very face of the church; it would be untrue to itself were it to turn in on itself, forming a closed, self-sufficient group in countries with a Catholic majority with influence in the political and cultural spheres. In accordance with the purpose of its Lord and Head it is the servant also of those who are not of the fold of the one true shepherd and who have to be rescued from their slavery and from the clouds among which they wander (John 10:11–18; Ezek. 34:1–16). Without this openness to the whole of humankind, bearing the seeds of Christ, Christian commitment risks drawing on itself the accusations made against the shepherds of Israel: "You have not strengthened the weak, cared for the sick or bandaged the injured. You have not gone after the sheep that strayed or searched for the one that was lost. Instead you ruled them harshly and were their oppressors" (Ezek. 34:4).

Christians are not other-worldly or unworldly beings: they remain human in every way, as much immersed in the culture, politics and environment of their countries as anyone else. There has been a tendency to oppose church and world, personifying both as antagonists, but nothing human should be alien to Jesus' disciples. On the contrary, the "otherness" of others is grounded in the common humanity of all; Christians recognize that what all persons and all peoples share in common is more important than what separates them, estranges them and sets them in opposition.

The final command in Matthew 28:18–20, to go and make disciples of all nations, the mission Jesus left to the ecclesial community, has to transcend what went before, in extension and intensity. The Christian commitment is to be perfect, as our heavenly Father is perfect (Matt. 5:8), but this perfecting is brought about to the extent that Christians make all peoples into disciples of Christ and lead them, by observing Jesus' directives, to that fullness of humanity that extends beyond the end of the world itself. In this missionary endeavour, the dialogue is not between religions, systems or cultures, but between persons in an exchange of contributions valid on both sides and mutually enriching.

It was the Holy Spirit who led the first apostles, shut up in the house out of fear, to open the doors and go out to proclaim the wonders of God in language understood by all (Acts 2). By comparison, recent centuries have been rather negative, with Christians developing a certain degree of schizophrenia between their religious practices and their lives outside their churches. A light that shines only on itself is useless, and yeast apart from the dough is sterile. Vatican II returned to the tactics of the apostles on that first Pentecost; this led and still leads to reactions of fear, since human weakness is a powerful force for seeking the assurance of security. Christian commitment is made by human beings according to the measure of their individual capacity, but its constituency is the whole human universe. The link between the two is Christ's promise: "I am with you always till the end of this world" (Matt. 28:20).

(v) The correct balance. The sequence God-Jesus-church-humanity has its logic within the parameters of theological tradition. In practice, however, the four elements are continually combined in a series of different interfaces in the lives of individuals. Isolating one prejudices the others and concentration on one impoverishes the overall commitment. The experience of history shows that worshipping God can form a tight compartment, filled with the pious letting the rest of the world go where it will, for fear of contamination. The church can shut itself into an elitist, self-regarding group, not only forgetting its missionary calling, but no longer discerning the truth, justice, love, good will, dedication and generosity in service to others that exist outside its ranks. The only text that gives specific form to the last judgment of humanity presents a series of human actions that in no way require baptism or belonging to any particular denomination. On the other hand, wasting one's energies exclusively on service to this passing world, even doing what is noble, just and honest, is like living in a room with the windows closed: we also need the eschatological breath of air

promised by the Lord Jesus.

The four elements constantly complement one another in the form of the commitment that all Christians have to express and carry out in their way of life and actions. The classic tension between the contemplative and the active life, between belonging to a particular religious congregation or being a lay person in the world, can help to guide each of us toward formulating a personal style of commitment. In the end, the balance we strike between each of the elements is our personal responsibility, which we have to adjust to our calling and to our capacity to deal with the situations in which we find ourselves—situations that change constantly and sometimes suddenly. The rhythm of life lived in action will always have particular stresses proper to the person doing the living and acting.

(c) Commitment to Doing

Catholic moral theology has traditionally made clear formal distinctions of kind within the multiplicity of norms transmitted from one generation to the next in one way or another. The manuals define the concepts of law of God, ecclesiastical law, natural law and civil law. These elements are usually intermingled in existing categorizing formulations of norms. A better understanding of the historical genesis of each norm will usually shed light on what principles of discernment and which authorities contributed to its formulation.

Without examining this historical evolution, we are liable to lose sight of the living broth of experience accumulated in human history, a broth which contains the folk wisdom we find in the Wisdom books of the Bible and in proverbs and sayings still current among simple folk today. For a generation that learns the rules first and then tries to obey them, this practical grounding is all the more important, as is the need to develop new directives and moral guidance in a world full of rapid changes and new discoveries. The rule-making body is like the individuals whose faith and reason filter the rules: they develop, change, mature, adapt, but remain the same people.

(i) Doing, the basic element. In an attempt to clarify the complex processes represented by people and their specific,

historically situated actions, traditional moral theory evolved two treatises: one on human actions and another on norms. This way of thinking involved the risk of giving a false impression of human reality, as though it were made up of two distinct entities, whereas daily experience places people of flesh and blood at the centre of moral experience; they bring their own understanding of norms and their freedom to decide and act. Norms are not carried out, do not become true, simply because they are formulated from a certain angle; a mixture of reason and will cannot of itself produce the moral values of humanization, justice, sincerity or love in the world. It is actual people, conditioned and situated as they in fact are, who do truth and thereby show that their "works have been done in God" (John 3:21).

Following Jesus' example, Christian commitment cannot simply be a fine way of looking at things, of thinking good thoughts, of having right desires; it takes real shape through doing what Jesus did. Before giving his disciples the new commandment to love, he loved them "with perfect love" (John 13:1). Therefore, the questions Christians have to keep on asking themselves are: What must we do to enter into the Kingdom? What must we do to build the community of the church? What must we do to make the world more human? In the words of the New Testament, it is not crying "Lord, Lord," nor faith without works, nor declaring our love for God, that will set Christians free through the grace of Christ. Christians themselves have to actualize, embody what is in their hearts and on their lips, through the services they render to others and through the effective collaboration they bring to achieving a truly human society, one in which the truth of the Kingdom of God can be made manifest.

Christians are helped and strengthened to take on their responsibilities and collaborate in God's plan by growth in faith, deeper understanding of the mystery of God, and a better appreciation of human society and the world in which they live. In this task, persons are inseparable from their actions. With Jesus too, the actions he performed, the works he carried out, were the witness to his true identity. His words are valid for all disciples: they will be recognized by their fruit, whether good or rotten (Matt. 7:16–20). If it is to give light, a lamp needs oil (Luke 13:24–8). In relation to God, to themselves and to others, Christians may live in joy and consolation, or in affliction searching in the dark and crucified, but their dynamism of doing goes on: the tree may lose its leaves in winter, but the spring brings new growth and eventually fresh fruits.

(ii) Doing together. What the multiplication of the loaves showed and eucharistic celebration confirms each time anew is that Christian doing is carried out in solidarity and collaboration, building and confirming the community character of the project Jesus set in motion. Around Jesus the "doer," disciples distributed the loaves and then gathered the remains into baskets. All Christian "doing" forms an ascent to the eucharist, from which flow new graces and powers to enable Christians to do better; but the doing itself has an inescapable content of cooperation, in which living in common becomes sharing in common, struggling in common, building humanity in common. God's earlier purpose of forming one people becomes, through the new covenant in Christ's blood, the purpose of uniting all peoples to form one body in Christ, ever more inclusive, more united and more productive in all its members.

This aspect of collaboration in solidarity and reciprocity in service in no way detracts from the personal responsibility of each one of us, according to our talents and position in society as a whole. The popular saying that "trouble shared is trouble halved" also means that joy shared is joy doubled. Faced with the great challenges of setting the whole of humanity and all creation free, not even the passage of Jesus of Nazareth through this world sufficed to give a complete response once and for all. The sufferings of God's creatures, like the pangs of childbirth (Rom. 8:22), continue crying out for relief, till the Lord comes. His coming, however, will depend in history on the communal openness and the practical and effective collaboration of disciples who, doing, working, serving, wait for their Lord.

(d) The fire of hope. The grace of hope which Christians receive in their hearts and live out in community is something like a fire rising from wood. At its base are the ashes of burnt-out bitterness: the evils, frustrations, failures and sins found in every life and in society; these have been cast out by the purifying

fire of hope for something better, more just and more human. Like the pillar of fire which went before the Israelites on their journey of liberation through the desert, Jesus the Lord is the new, paschal fire which lights our way and encourages us on our journey. Hope does not mean waiting passively for the sign from heaven; it means taking on the commitment to journey in the direction of the one hoped for, collaborating with others so as to make our lives together in this world an ever better expression of the true face of God's love, justice and peace, and thereby being prepared for the final meeting with our Lord.

Chapter VIII

God's Virtue and Human Virtues

Nowadays, outside manuals of moral theology or treatises on asceticism, the words "virtue" or "virtues" have somewhat lost their sense as ideals of humanity on both personal and social levels. Classical and medieval tradition gave the virtues an iconography in the shape of glamorous young ladies who somehow fail to fit modern concepts of beauty. As Max Scheler puts it, today they look more like "quarrelsome, toothless old hags" (though this might be something of an exaggeration in Catholic circles). In any case, handing on the dead letter of the past shows not just a lack of courage or adaptability, but a lack of creative faith in church communities which have to express God's "virtue," strength and power in new situations and under new conditions corresponding to the world in which they breathe and work.

It is not easy to discover what we do mean now when we speak of "virtue" or "a virtuous person." It is not just a question of putting a modern veneer on an old theory of goodness or innocence; the key question is what it means in practice. How does one become virtuous and give the fruits of the Spirit in a society that seems to function according to other ideas: how to get more money, rise in the social scale, penetrate the market, worship power, climb over those lower down the scale, obtain more possessions, have more power over others? If the moral climate of today is not the absolute antithesis of the Christian ideal, it at least looks contradictory and ambiguous. Not that this ambiguity is a modern product: the double standard traditionally applied to masters and slaves, to men and women (with another double standard applied to "good" and "fallen" women), not to mention the scarcely camouflaged discriminations against blacks and other ethnic groups, have been with us for a long time and have never provided a favourable climate for a balanced practice of the virtues expected of Jesus' disciples.

1. PRACTISING THE VIRTUES: AN APPRENTICESHIP

Virtues belong to our inner selves, are expressed in what we do, grow and put down roots through what we do. No one is born with a ready-made collection of virtues; we always have to wonder how any infant is going to "turn out." Catholic tradition (as embodied in St Thomas' systematic treatment of the subject in his *Summa Theologiae*) has a place for the concept of "infused" (supernatural) virtues. But the simple communication of God's virtue does not in itself guarantee that the seeds sown will fall on good ground, to produce fruit a hundred, sixty or thirty times over (Matt. 13:23). In the course of personal development, one can learn to be virtuous and to remain firm in virtue; but the contrary can equally happen: acquired virtues can gradually atrophy, lose their inspiring and directing power and be "exchanged" for defects and distortions, more or less constant shadows of what was once virtue.

Christian faith views the apprenticeship to a virtuous life and its historical evolution as a process of two poles drawing together and interacting. On one side is the generosity of God, communicating the strength—*virtus*—of God to men and women of good will, so that human virtues are true fruits of the Spirit, clothing human weakness in the strength that comes from on high (see Gal. 5:16–25; Luke 24:49). On the other is the discipline exercised by disciples, the effort they make to lead the life of disciples faithful to the Spirit of their Lord. The word "discipline" itself combined the concept of disciple—apprentice—and that of effort made and zeal shown in following in the footsteps of the Master.

For Christians-disciples, meeting Jesus begins with their birth, is intensified in baptism and nourished by the bread of the word of God and the eucharistic bread. A true and faithful friendship develops through a constantly renewed series of meetings; in these the two partners move ever closer together and enter into one another. On Jesus' part, this movement is the progressive revelation of the Spirit of God who advances in the hearts of the faithful and the communities of faith and assures them they are children of God (Rom. 8:16). On their part, Christians move and draw closer to Jesus through their lives lived like a pilgrimage that has still not reached the shrine at its end. Living in the world and passing through it, they seek to penetrate the mystery of the God of love, to know the width, the length, the height and the depth of this God, even if for the present they see but dimly as in a faulty mirror (Eph. 3:18; 1 Cor. 13:12). Through collaborating with grace, they have to set themselves and all creation free from the slavery of corruption, carving in themselves the hidden image and likeness of God, the hope of perfection.

(a) Human Society and Virtues

Human society is like a vast, complicated piece of machinery: if a piece is missing, a spindle clogged or a wheel broken, the whole machine falters, and eventually comes to a halt. Comparing the church to a body, St Paul observes that if one member of it suffers, all of them suffer, and that if one receives honour, all rejoice (1 Cor. 12:26). The same connections apply in world society. What anyone does for good or ill, justly or unjustly, has repercussions on the whole of society and makes ripples, like a stone thrown into a calm lake: the ripples spread till they reach the shores. In human society people are valued for what they do; they may not be known beyond a small circle of family and friends, but their goodness or badness affects the larger circle made up of all members of society.

While the machine is running well, no one pays attention to the parts, but once the gears begin to grate, all the parts are oiled and inspected, because there must be a defective piece somewhere. The worse society works, the greater its injustices and violence, the greater too the temptation to go along with it, to join the common dance of corruption; but the greater too is the responsibility falling on each one of us to help repair the social machine and, through leading an honest, just and moderate life, help human beings to live together in a manner that benefits all, especially the poor and the weak. And in a class-structured society, the responsibility for spreading virtues is greater for those who occupy the highest rungs and whose decision-making potential is greater. If the corruption of the best is the worst, their virtue also has a greater penetrative range.

The catalogues of virtues provided by the New Testament are applicable not just on an individual basis, but need to be practised in community. Christians who sincerely try to live their faith inspire hope in others; they are honest, just, straightforward, open-hearted in their dealings with others; they have paradigmatic strength in the community and attract others by their genuineness as human beings. As St Paul sees it, they build others, as they are built by others, and together they build the church on the cornerstone who is Christ (Eph. 2:19–22). People do not learn virtues by themselves; they acquire them from the early examples they find in their family, their community and their local environment. Neither do they practise virtues for the sake of their own miserly enrichment, but for the sake of their neighbours, to bring them joy and help them grow (Rom. 15:2). The body of Christ comes into being through mutual effort, through the coordinated work of all its members. So the church spreads God's power and light on humanity and helps it in seeking goodness and happiness.

Both inside and outside the church, living with others involves the risk of temptation and seduction by the evil that impels people downward, since evil has its own contaminating attraction. The power of evil works in all Christians, saints and sinners alike, and it is from inside that the evils which stain and intoxicate us come (see Mark 7). But there is something stronger than fear of contact with others: solidarity with others, based on the power of Jesus Christ, making all grow and excel in good deeds (Titus 3:8). The world is full of scandals brought about by human malice and weakness, but those who love their brothers and sisters walk in the light and need not be afraid of stumbling (Matt. 18:1–9; 1 John 2:10).

(b) The Virtuous Prototype

Human beings have a front and a back. They face forward toward the future, reflecting on the way to follow, making decisions and moving on, and behind them lies a past, their origins, their historical roots, the sources from which they drew life and the experiences of their ancestors, like them sons and daughters of Adam and Eve. Carrying the past on our backs, we journey toward the future.

Through the faith living in them and through the eucharist they celebrate in their communities, Christians continue to make new the memory of the Lord Jesus. One of us, this Jesus, was born of a Jewish girl called Mary, of the race of Abraham, Isaac and Jacob. Among his people, he grew in wisdom, stature and grace before God and human beings (Luke 2:52). He drew crowds, many of them following him maybe for the free bread and hope of a cure for their sufferings, but others because of the strange power that came from him and infected those who were closest to him. His personality, his manner of acting and dealing with people, his message concerning the great novelty of the Kingdom of God, already begun: all these enthused his followers, who gave up their old lives to follow him, since he had the words of eternal life (John 6:67). Through his virtue-strength, Jesus not only filled human life to the edge of death, but crossed this mortal frontier and made others cross it, since his Kingdom is without end.

The first disciples had to endure the shock of his death on the cross and regain their firmness of faith through belief in his resurrection. Faced with evil and death, the temptation for those who follow Christ today, those virtuous and strong in their faithfulness to Jesus, is still to let their light go out and their salt lose its savour. This temptation is aggravated by a spirituality of sweetness and consolation, a blond-haired, blue-eyed spirituality that may correspond to some longings of an oppressed and suffering people, but that does not correspond to the virtuous prototype found in Jesus of Nazareth, who was a mixture of kindness and firmness, of humility and haughtiness, of merciful patience and demanding radicality. He never bowed down before any human authority, but knelt to wash his disciples' feet. He never prostrated himself before anyone, but fell on his face to confess his weakness in the Garden of Olives. His strength lay in sacrificing his life to death on the cross, dying for our sins, in order to lead us to God (1 Pet. 3:18).

As the history of Christian art and spirituality shows, the image of Jesus as prototype of virtue has varied with periods and their preferences. The life of Christians is reflected in the way they see Jesus, their example. Disciples will meet and recognize their Lord through attentive reading of the Bible and celebrating the eucharist in their communities, as the two disciples did on the road to Emmaus, and will determine their actions—in accordance with the conditions they find themselves in—in the conviction that Christ will be with those who love him till the end of time.

(c) God's Virtue

For Christians, the apprenticeship to a virtuous life is not a simple process working from the outside in. In the final analysis, it works from the inside out, from God's virtue working in Christians, and in all men and women of good will, to form their way of thinking, deciding, acting in the world and communicating with others. Christian pedagogy has developed methods and techniques for training people in the practice of virtue, but it is Christ who is the vine and produces the sap, and it is the Holy Spirit who comes to the aid of human weakness and transforms us into reflected images of the glory of God (2 Cor. 3:18; cf Rom. 8:26).

This creative power of God runs through the Bible like a golden thread. Human language has given it a variety of names: breath, power, strength, virtue, spirit of God. . . . In the New Testament, it opens out toward the mystery of the Holy Trinity dwelling in us, working in us and revealing itself in the weakness of human clay, so that this all-surpassing power of true virtue may be clearly seen as coming from God and not something we can create for ourselves (2 Cor. 4:7). God is the great sculptor who frees enslaved men and women from the marble of their prison, from sin and death, shaping them to enjoy the freedom of children of God, "slaves of one another through love" (Gal. 5:13). In God's hands, we are unfinished work till our death, which is why St Francis of Assisi could say at the end of his life: "We are finally about to begin, since we have done little till now."

There is no repetition in the virtue of the figures that God the artist creates. From classical Greek philosophy on, we in the West with our limited schemes of thought have been forced to create schemes of virtues, with definitions, divisions and subdivisions—admittedly useful in both theory and practice. God does not use ordinary models or produce works in series; the originality of God as artist is expressed in the singular uniqueness of every human being, and in the configuration of his or her virtues. We are all the work of one and the same Spirit, who gives to all as they so desire (1 Cor. 12:11). Saints, whether great or ordinary, everyday ones, are never uniform, since, through the power of the one who called us from darkness to his own wonderful light, we all proclaim the wonders of God in our own particular way and form a particular image of God from our position among humankind (cf 1 Pet. 2:9).

(d) Obstacles on the Way

Treatises on virtues sometimes give the impression of being a sort of supermarket full of canned goods. One only needs to buy some cans, open them and eat their contents, for personal health in terms of virtues to be guaranteed. Yet better theoretical understanding does not automatically produce growth in virtue: knowledge in itself does not necessarily build; it can merely "puff up" (1 Cor 8:1), or store energy that is released only when we begin to put what we know into practice. Christians should take note of Jesus' reply to the woman who blessed his mother: "Blessed, rather, are those who hear the word of God and keep it" (Luke 11:28). Theory has the smoothness of a plan on paper; practice discovers the bumps and potholes in the road of life, here and now.

The modern world in which Christians have to give virtue practical form is extremely complex and changing at an accelerating rate. It is no longer the little village in which time stands still and the pattern of behaviour and social relationships is more or less straightforward and fixed. The world we live in today is a complex, and largely invisible, network of relationships of production, exchange and demand. So complex has it become that the analytical methods of sociology, political studies and economics can no longer describe its inner workings and frequently contradict one another. In the same way, human beings have also become more complicated and find themselves faced with problems which do not allow them immediately to see the correct path for true virtue to take. Within the church, too, attitudes and positions contradict one another and do not always come together in a commonly agreed practice.

Another aspect is indicated by what a truck driver wrote on the fender of his truck: "I am ashamed of being honest." Where corruption has become a social epidemic spreading from the top down; where the impunity of the powerful before the law is proverbial and the prisons are full of poor people; where sex has become an article for sale, an object of commercial promotion; where violence has become institutionalized in numerous forms of oppression and the marginalization of large sectors of the population; where the friends of those in power receive all the favours and advancement and the harshness of the law is reserved for their enemies; where dishonesty has become virtually a condition for survival: in such conditions, how are we to swim against the tide and become virtuous?

Worse still is the devaluation of the virtues themselves that is now the popular view. Humility has been distorted into an attitude of cringing submission to authority; obedience means obeying superiors' orders, however violent or unjust. Despite being blind, justice knows very well who is who and seems to apply a double standard, as the poor know to their cost. The recent past exalted chastity (curiously enough) into the queen of virtues—applied to women. Prudence became the armour of those who were not prepared to take risks and became a sort of cowardice preventing the virtue of fortitude from facing courageously up to life today. Even charity, the first of all virtues in the Christian book, was sometimes reduced to almsgiving or giving a crust of bread to some "poor devil," with the result that the slogan of popular movements has become: "We want justice, not charity."

2. THE GREAT THREESOME

To counterbalance the devaluation of the concept of the virtuous person, whose prototype was Jesus of Nazareth, and to resist the temptation to take part in the general dance of corruption, disciples need to deepen the favours they receive from God, giver of all graces, in the form of faith, hope and charity. Moral theology is concerned not so much with focussing on grace freely given, even though the communication of God's virtue is a continual motive for thanksgiving and praise. It is more concerned with the path Christians take, with their development on the basis of the gifts they receive from God, consolidating the practice of these three—faith, hope and charity—in their daily lives. The paradox of life is that we freely produce what has been freely given.

This dynamic process requires constant vigilance, especially in countries that call themselves Catholic, whose reality is more often than not akin to what St John found in some of the communities of his time and described in Revelation 2–3. The general tone is one of coolness, indifference—Catholic in name only. Parish-based renewal movements and the base communities have managed to rekindle Christian faith and make the charity of certain groups more productive. But the shortage of ordained ministers, the moral and religious dislocation produced by migration, the inroads made by secularization into traditional religious mentalities, the impoverishment and marginalization of so many millions, all prove serious obstacles to deepening faith, empowering hope and effectively exercising charity. Lack of research means that individual impressions, clouded with either optimism or pessimism, prevail over real knowledge where the actual state of the faith of the people is concerned.

If the conjuncture of faith, hope and charity is to be dynamized, this has to be done by the people of God in community and by individual Christians. There has recently been a fortunate level of cohesion between pastoral renewal programmes initiated by many bishops and priests inspired by Vatican II and grassroots initiatives coming up from base communities. Here too the enemy has sown darnel among the wheat and created confusion (Matt. 13:25), and Gamaliel's wise counsel (Acts 5:35ff) has not been heard. But a series of pastoral plans, backed by the Medellín and Puebla documents, has borne and is continuing to bear fruit in an intensification of community life, with the generous help of many lay people.

At the same time, the need is growing for all Christians to take on the personal responsibility of disciples of the Lord Jesus and to become active and lively members of his mystical body, the church. Traditional majority Catholicism had a strong dose of social conditioning and inculcated group cohesiveness. Today, with greater pluralism and privatization, the practice of Christian faith, hope and charity depends far more on the commitment and effort each baptized person makes to live up to their demands. As social control over religious practices—and over life in general—diminishes, so the resulting weight of personal conviction, supported by the local community, increases.

(a) Strengthening Faith

The spread of Bible reading and improved organization of catechesis and the liturgy are helping to strengthen the faith of many, but this is not to say that their faith discerns and embraces the whole panorama of God, Jesus, the Holy Spirit, the church and the world, such as is found in catechisms. No human being can command the whole of this panorama: the experience of faith allows for different views, some of which will necessarily be broader than other, more restricted ones. Each period and type of culture emphasizes some aspects at the expense of others; the existential conditions of different individuals and groups influence the way they form their faith and manage their behaviour.

According to the New Testament, the first Christian communities were already troubled by false prophets and the vagaries of human wickedness (see Eph. 4:14; Col. 2:4–8; 1 Tim. 1:3–7; 2 Pet. 2, etc.). In today's complex society, distorting influences on faith are far more subtle and impersonal, so more difficult to recognize and correct. In Latin America, conquered by the sword and the cross, societies grew up with clearly divided and opposed classes, which left their mark on the way Catholicism evolved on the continent. This Catholicism was responsible for upholding the power and possessions of the ruling classes, and for sublimating the resigned submission of the lower classes through religious motives. The same anti-evangelical system functioned in the sphere of sexual morality, with one rule for men and another for women, who were divided into "well brought up" women and girls and marginalized prostitutes. The recent conversion of the church in Latin America makes it possible to see such deformations of the faith for what they are, even if they still persist because of the slowness with which weak human beings change their ways. What is more difficult to discover is how an evangelical faith can be brought into being in today's conditions.

The superstitions that still hang round so many Christians in a dark ring are parasites on faith dating from way back, attempts to solve problems and take care of the future deriving from personal weakness or an undeveloped faith. They pose a pastoral problem which is perhaps not best solved by frontal attack: in Latin America the most effective approach would seem to be support of the base communities in their efforts to deepen the true faith of their members; the more intense the experience—especially shared experience—of trust in Jesus Christ, the less need there is for looking for superstitious props for the uncertainties of life.

(b) Hope in Action

"Hope is the last thing to die" is a significant saying, and one ingrained in the consciousness of the people. Amidst all the forms of resignation found in the oppressed social classes, there are as many examples of courage—mostly undocumented—in facing up to the problems of life. Parents may see no chance of change for the better for themselves, but hope for better things for their children. There is always something to hope for, and hope forces people to find solutions and ways forward. They may be tempted to discouragement and despair, but the will to survive is usually stronger and, whatever the cost, overcomes the inclination to lie down and die.

In its religio-moral dimension, hope is often inclined to the passivity of people waiting for a train, sitting with their baggage in a station. Those who wait in this way may not do the same sort of harm as those members of the church in Thessalonica criticized by Paul (2 Thess. 3:6–12) for wasting their time in idleness, since poor people usually work, and work very hard, spending their energy and health on often brutal tasks. Their problem is rather one of the deficiency of Christian eschatological thinking. The poor live close to death and with their dead, despite the pressures of modern life which try to hide these away. They tend to feel that the end of the world is nigh—a feeling they share with many elements in Western culture as each century draws to a close—but fail to appreciate that the Kingdom of God also comes through being brought about by cooperating in the good men and women do.

Doing good is the way we build the road, filling valleys and laying hills low, to the summit of the mountain of time when the Lord will come to judge the living and the dead and the fullness of the Kingdom will be revealed. Hope is not simply waiting for the Lord to come, but is strengthened and realized in the good things people do. Through the love they practise, the hope they inspire, the peace they bring, the sincerity of their dealings with others, the justice they do to all, the courage with which they comfort comrades in the struggle, not to mention the simple gesture of giving a glass of water to someone who is thirsty, they go on building up the Kingdom which has already come into our midst with Jesus, as a sort of overture to God's great opera whose last act is yet to be played.

(c) Charity and History

The Scriptures make clear that God is love, and therefore the basic directive for all human action is solidarity that makes us neighbours one of another. All love that makes others grow as human beings is a reflection of God's love for men and women and originates in this. Because of this link, as Jesus showed on the cross, even weak and sinful men and women can come to forgive their enemies and executioners. The same God works everything in all: the perfection of human love and friendship, especially for those who have most need of them, is the preeminent way of showing the presence of the Kingdom of God among men and women (see 1 Cor. 12–13).

In past centuries, Christian love has produced and maintained works of charity and mercy in all parts of society. Under Christendom, such incarnations of love in hospitals, hospices and orphanages had virtually no equals. This situation changed with the rise of modern states which, more and more, took over services devoted to the well being of the population, with all the deficiencies and bureaucratic complications that such institutions are liable to, especially in underdeveloped countries. By making deeper analyses of reality, the collective conscience gained a better appreciation of the true causes of the poverty, destitution and precarious state of health of the masses of the Third World, thereby creating a greater willingness to attack the root causes of such evils.

Popular movements found that many problems affecting the well-being of the people could not be tackled on a small scale; this would simply be pouring drops of water on to a blazing fire. The broader view acquired in struggling for a place in the sun showed that the only choice was to take part in national politics, make a clearing in the traditional area of power held by the ruling classes and hammer away at the question of human rights from a social standpoint. Nowadays, the love of interpersonal relationships extends beyond the small circle of one's daily round, reaching out to the whole field of politics, with its companions, plans, programmes and campaigns.

Historically, charity has not only been characterized by generous giving and dedication without counting the cost, but also by a paternalism which does favours to the less fortunate and leaves them in the state of dependency they were in before. The people have learned to sing that love makes free; this liberation involves respect for others, especially the weakest and neediest. Insofar as possible, they need to be helped to stand on their own feet, take their place in the life of the community and become autonomous in supporting themselves. If economic concerns are put first, these concentrate on maximizing the number of arms and heads available as production units within the capitalist system. Love, on the other hand, gives people the sense of being "persons" who can communicate with others on a basis of equality and play a responsible role in forming a new civilization based on humanizing love for all.

In a context of widespread social injustice, the only effective way of embedding this impulse in society is through political action. This can mean choosing to support a particular political party—where such choice exists—since love cannot remain neutral. The love shown by the Samaritan means making a commitment in favour of those classes euphemistically called less-favoured, to help them achieve full humanity with all its rights, to make them active participants in society, not only as producers but also as sharers in the fruits of their work. If the law of Christ obliges us to help one another carry our burdens (Gal.

6:12), logic points to the need for those who are most heavily burdened on the journey through life to be helped first.

3. FOUR SISTERS TOGETHER

In Aristotelian-Thomist iconography and presentation, the four "cardinal" virtues of prudence, justice, temperance and fortitude can give the impression of being independent and autonomous of one another. In fact, as their name (from Latin *cardo*, meaning hinge) implies, they all hang together to form the framework of human action: together, they are the backbone of virtuous behavior, the trunk of the tree through which flows the sap to give human actions their energy, balance and just measure. From classical Greek philosophy onwards, there has been a long tradition of commentary on these four qualities demonstrated by all virtuous human activity. Times change, and bring new requirements, so rather than repeat earlier analyses here, it seems more useful simply to comment on aspects made especially relevant by the state of modern society. Virtues, like the people who perform them, are not independent of time and space, but take shape and are practised in specific historical situations.

(a) A Critical Attitude: The New Face of Prudence

Criticizing, though as old and widespread as the human race, is generally looked at askance by the people: it suggests negativity—condemning, rejecting, refuting, denying and the like—in the sense of being mere personal attack or disturbing the established order. In the authoritarian tradition that has dominated Latin America, in politics and the church, the concept of constructive criticism has had a hard time emerging. The emphasis has been rather on the word of authority being received with submission and obedience. Now, with emergent ideas of democracy, the idea of "loyal opposition" current in Western countries is beginning to make headway, but it still tends to mean that criticism is constructive as long as it reflects the dominant mentality. And how does one formulate "constructive" criticism of police repression, torture, exploitation of workers and the destitution suffered by the masses?

Criticism is an innate quality in human beings. The story of

Adam and Eve attests to its symbolic presence in the shape of the tree of knowledge of good and evil. Its original Greek root means to separate, to winnow out the wheat from the chaff; to examine to see what is valid and non-valid; to distinguish what is true, worthy, just, honest and virtuous from what is false, unworthy and malicious in the complexity of the human condition, which is always a mixture of light and shade; to discern the good from the bad and to act in accordance with this discernment; to judge what has been done and what has to be done; to form an opinion, take a stance in a given situation. From this it follows that this basic human activity takes on greater importance in a situation of crisis, for the individual or for society as a whole. There is deep existential significance in the fact that "criticism" and "crisis" both derive from the same Greek root, *krinein*.

We make criticisms in a number of different ways. There is the cold reason which observes facts, analyzes reality, makes enquiries, judges according to pre-set criteria, laws or rules, uses objective arguments, or at least arguments presented as objective. There is the common sense with which the people often manage the sequence of seeing, judging and acting in their daily lives. There are the heart, sensitivity, emotions—sometimes so strong that the only explanation of a critical stance is: "That's how I feel." Scenes of violence, starvation, injustice provoke us to critical indignation, since the more "critical" a situation is, the more criticism it arouses. Christians possess a special critical faculty through their ecclesial faith which implies the judgment of the church.

The touchstone of a critical attitude is capacity for self-criticism, or the ability to include the subject in critical thinking. Greek philosophy, and modern empirical sciences still more, make objectivity the centre, to the point where the subjectivity, the thinking, observing, judging human subject, is marginalized. In negative terms: "Take first the plank out of your own eye; then you will see clear enough to take the speck out of your brother's eye" (Matt. 7:5); in positive terms (applied to a particular situation): "Let each one, then, examine himself before eating of the bread and drinking from the cup" (1 Cor. 11:28).

In a society with pronounced class divisions or hierarchical power structure, this rule is more vital still, since social position determines the optic from which one views the complex of human affairs and so determines the critical process, and acceptance or rejection of the criticism of others, which one brings to bear on society. One's perception and judgment are affected by mental make-up, existential experience, personal history, group or class history. So criticism supposes that those who make it look around them and instinctively analyze themselves in the observed universe, using their own eyes to raise their own consciousness.

Including oneself in the critical process has another consequence: effectiveness. There is nothing easier than to deliver critical verdicts from one tribunal or fence without concern for the consequences. The responsibility of the people of God for the progressive implementation of the Kingdom of God does not allow us the comfort of being mere speaking heads, producers of discourses. The phrase "there are no innocents in history" may be shocking, but it can at least warn Christian consciences not to repeat Pilate's gesture. Criticism involves those who make it in events, either helping humankind on its way through active collaboration, or breaking away from one course to establish another which is more evangelical and human. Criticism includes loyalty in cooperation as well as courage to row against the tide, since the present state of both church and society shows a confused mixture of good and bad, life and death.

(b) Justice and Rights

When we talk of justice today, we think first of rights: the Universal Declaration of Human Rights, economic, social, political and cultural rights, workers' rights, civil rights, rights won and those still to be generally accepted as rights. The basic quality of justice, which should operate in all human actions and systems, is today most specifically configured and defined in the concept of rights, even though these by no means exhaust the concept of justice in theory, and still less in practice: we are still very far from achieving the ideal of a just society or a harmonious church in which the rights of citizens and faithful will be perfectly expressed and fully developed. Reality still lags far behind the expression of rights on paper, and the latter still needs further development.

The central question that needs tackling is the relationship between rights and duties. What usually happens in practice is that when one person claims rights, he or she is reminded of the corresponding duties. But the relationship between right and duty goes far beyond this simple exchange, with three main elements:

(i) Those who have rights have the duty to take good care of them. If these rights are just theoretical, they must work to turn them into reality. The transition from what Roman jurists called the *ius ad rem* to the *ius in re* has to be made first through responsible action by the individual or social group concerned. It is no use standing by with one's arms folded waiting for others to fight for one's rights.

(ii) The golden rule (Matt. 7:12) suggests that human rights are not private property but imply reciprocity. What people demand as their rights, they must recognize and respect as also the rights of others. The sense of justice seeks the equality of all, with no distinction of person or classes, no discrimination on grounds of sex, colour or race, because human dignity is something that belongs to everyone.

(iii) Christian love requires solidarity, especially with those whose legitimate rights are denied them, and this means struggling alongside them so that they can win space in which to live and freedom to share in building a just society. Carrying out this project often exacts a high price. The prime example of this sort of solidarity is that of Jesus of Nazareth, who sacrificed his life to free all his brothers and sisters—of then, now and times to come—from all evils and even death.

(c) Courage to Live

St Paul's "act like men" (1 Cor. 16:13) is designed to be an invitation to fortitude, but the Greek original, the Latin Vulgate and modern translations, with their concentration on the masculine, strike an unfortunate note in many societies today, those still dominated by *machismo* and those influenced by feminism. Bourgeois idealization of the past projects an image of meekness, delicacy, tenderness and readiness to serve on to women, but this ill fits today's women, who have to be strong enough to bring up their children, do most of the work of the home and, usually, work outside the home as well. Fortitude is hardly an exclusively masculine characteristic when women have the double courage of facing up to the present in their own lives and to the future in those of their children: the strong woman of Proverbs (31:10) is a more fitting image for them. Fortitude goes with human actions, provides people with energy to act, and this applies at least as much to women as to men.

United with other qualities in human actions, fortitude tempers and channels the aggressivity people feel in the face of obstacles in life, the violence and injustice they suffer in their own lives or see being inflicted on others. It is the antithesis to the attitude of simply shrugging one's shoulders, of deciding that there is nothing to be done, that things just are that way and have to be left that way. In our passage through life, it lets us forget the past, bury traumas, rise above what has happened without regret or resentment and leave the past to bury its dead; it leads us forward toward our goal, step by step, fulfilling our calling from God in Jesus Christ and building God's Kingdom, making the world a better and more honest place till its fullness comes and we reach our final goal (see Phil. 3:12–15).

In the understanding of the people of Israel, strength to live and prevail in life was rooted in the powerful strength of God, whose weakness is stronger than any human strength (1 Cor. 1:25). The Psalmist expresses this faith, so often experienced in historical events: "I love you, O Lord, my strength. The Lord is my rock, my rampart, my deliverer and my God, the rock in whom I take refuge. He is my shield, the horn of my salvation, my stronghold" (Ps. 18:2–3). And gratitude for this continual communication of God's strength leads to acceptance of the law graven on our hearts: "And you shall love Yahweh, your God, with all your heart, with all your soul and with all your strength" (Deut. 6:5; Matt. 22:37 and parallels).

The people of the God of the new covenant continue to live and struggle in this conviction, finding the strength of their salvation and freedom in the gospel (see Rom. 1:16). They know that the prudent person builds his or her house on the rock that is Christ, the strength of God incarnate (see Matt. 7:24). In our pilgrimage through this world, the powers of the darkness to which even Jesus fell victim also operate (Luke 22:53): so great is their strength that St Peter compares it to a roaring lion, seeking whom he may devour, and St John to a wild beast who receives his strength, power and throne from the dragon (1 Pet. 5:8; Rev. 13). But through the grace of the Lord Jesus, Christians stand firm, knowing that tribulation produces constancy, constancy proves fidelity, and proven fidelity produces the hope that will not fade, because the love of God has been poured out into their hearts by the Holy Spirit who has been given to them (see Rom. 5:1–5).

(d) The Taste of Life

The fourth inner quality of constructive human achievement is temperance. The term carries a historical charge of suppression of desires and pleasures, brake on spontaneity, list of prohibitions, sins and taboos. Perhaps the best image to give it back its true value is the care taken by a cook to adjust the seasoning so as to give the food its maximum taste. Temperance means the correct measure, the right balance, avoiding the excesses that harm people and overload the already complex construction of society and church.

The present world to which we all belong, in one way or another, is a great unbalanced framework of shocking contrasts. Freedom is the central value of individuals and the basis of their morality, but not only do we see violations of human rights in totalitarian regimes of all colours, but also abuses of freedom in the shape of exploitation of the weak, manipulation of public opinion, treatment of others as objects and the other forms of egoism rife in supposed democracies. Consumerism leads to saturation with massive extravagance and waste for some, while others scavenge in garbage cans for food and find shelter in cardboard boxes under city bridges. In the sexual field too, extremes of taboo and licence rub shoulders; sex has become a leisure pursuit, with no assumption of responsibility for a lasting and deepening relationship between persons.

The vital energy of persons and peoples driving them on to self-fulfillment, to create societies and cultures, embraces a vast spectrum of human activities and includes a whole range of motives from the love of Christ (2 Cor. 5:14) to the basic need for food and shelter. It shows the grandeur and the misery of the human condition, the heights we aspire to and the depths we reach, the virtues and vices accumulated by human experience in our history of peace and war, love and hate. The desires, impulses and propensities people feel and the forces that play on them guide their course to good or evil, to liberation or destruction. Without these, human beings do not live and achieve nothing; with them, they need a full harness to control the steeds on which they ride through life and to help them to move forward without falling or pulling up.

The old adage that virtue lies in the middle way implies temperance as the pointer to all moral action. In practice, this pointer does not work in the same way for all; it varies in accordance with individuals and situations. Temperance is like body temperature, which can vary slightly from normal without affecting one's health. God does not work with clones, but with living children who, maturing step by step, need to keep a constant balance as they carry out the projects to which the Spirit inspires them. They will not lack upsets, either from inside or from outside, but, shaking off the chains of sin and arming themselves with patience and sobriety, they can face up to the challenges set before them, with their gaze fixed on Jesus, author and goal of their faith (see Heb. 12:1).

CONCLUSION: HUMILITY AND PATIENCE

In the carnival of life, Adamic pride wears a thousand masks and is constantly devising new ones. So its opposite, humility, goes through a long process of apprenticeship, vital to Christian life, that ends only in death. Covetousness of all possible goods and values, self-admiring narcissism, vanity and envy are not dissolved by the humiliating setbacks imposed by living in a harshly competitive and critical society. Their flames may die down from time to time, but they continue smouldering among the ashes.

Humility is hard to define, but means a realistic and honest recognition of oneself: where one is, where one is going and how one relates to opportunities that arise. Through the strength of their faith, which seeks a sincere and deep-seated response to the question of who they are, Christians grow smaller in relation to the mystery of God invading their hearts and deeds. We are worth what we are before God: no more and no less. Humility is the garb in which, as creatures and sinners, Christians bow down before the powerful hand of God, in whom they can place all their worries (1 Pet. 5:5–7).

The faith experience of the Old and New Testaments provides many texts which give a unanimous witness. God's strategy is to cast down the mighty from their thrones and exalt the humble (Prov. 3:34; Ps. 33:10; Luke 1:52; etc.). The only attitude proper to disciples is to follow their Master, who doubly and inimitably humbled himself. Though he was divine in nature, he emptied himself to take on the condition of a slave; and being in human form, he humbled himself by being obedient even to death on a cross (Phil. 2:5–11).

Christian humility is not the same thing as being downtrodden. The poor people of Latin America think of themselves as "lowly," but this is more an attitude that has been imposed on them by the ruling classes, more a form of precaution, a means of survival, than a real feeling of themselves as people. In the light of faith, Christians stand up to those who challenge them. Peter himself, who found himself through the miraculous catch of fish at his first meeting with Jesus (Luke 5:8), was also convinced that we are a chosen race, a royal priesthood, a holy nation, a people made God's own in order to proclaim God's wonders (1 Pet. 2:9). Through becoming conscious of their dignity, poor people today can learn to show the same courageous pride before present-day Pharisees and Pilates that Jesus and the apostles showed before their adversaries; they can learn not to show more obedience to those who oppress and maltreat them than to God, the common Father of all (see Acts 4:19).

Finally, virtuous men and women are not made overnight, at the touch of a magic wand. The people know that things take time, and they learn this more from their own experience than from reading the history of their own remote past in the Bible. Weeds grow fast; hardwood takes time to mature. The task of becoming a virtuous person is like scaling a steep mountain. At first sight, the peak looks near and easily reached; but the more ridges one crosses, the further off it becomes, always asking further effort and sacrifice. The climb is finished only when death brings the definitive meeting with Jesus Christ.

In order to grow and become strong, the human body needs exercise as well as nourishment. To grow in virtue, we need the nourishment of the eucharistic celebration with our companions, and the exercise of the Holy Spirit promised by Jesus the Word, constantly stimulating us on our journey. But there is no timed training programme that will fit us for virtue: if love is what ties everything together and makes it perfect (Col. 3:14), the golden rule is to do good to all in all circumstances and to play the part of Simon of Cyrene in helping others to carry their crosses. Through exchange of mutual services, not only are people formed in virtue, but the church too is built up, and the Kingdom of God revealed in a more peaceful, just and equal society.

Chapter IX

The Struggle against Modern Idolatries

The Israelites, freed from their slavery in Egypt, sang and danced around the golden calf, which they had made with their own hands (Exod. 32). This sad memory from the past provides a clue to the way we live now. When worship of the true God weakens and the practice of love grows cold, the human need to adore and submit creates other gods and other practices, which mean no more than new forms of humiliating slavery. This shows the duplicity of the human heart, crying after freedom yet at the same time hankering after slavery, as though Egypt were nothing but fleshpots. So the uses and abuses of modern society carry on the age-old struggle between spirit and flesh: between freedom, justice and mutual love, and sin and the power of death (Rom. 8:1–17; Gal. 5:13–26). Though often vague and camouflaged, the boundary between the two goes through the human heart and through the whole of modern society.

1. GENERAL OBSERVATIONS

(a) The Difficulty of Identifying Idols

Though idolatry is an ancient scourge of humanity and the false gods constantly change their clothes and their manners, the temptation to adore them remains the same. The quest for security and protection, the urge to flee from oneself or to dominate others, all lead to the creation of modern idols, from the sex symbols of the movie world to a thousand types of superstition and the false ideologies that favour the few and mean slavery and death for the many (see Puebla, 405, 493, 500). With contagious power and seductive subliminal propaganda, modern idolatries spread their tentacles through the whole of society, not sparing the space marked out by the church, which, as an entity made up of the sons and daughters of Adam and Eve and incarnate in this world, also bears the historical marks of what St Paul called a sting of the flesh and an angel of Satan (2 Cor. 12:7).

Modern idols are far more complex and a lot less obvious than the golden calf forged by the Israelites in the desert. According to the Psalmist, the old gods could discern nothing, having eyes that cannot see and ears that cannot hear (Ps. 115:12–15). Modern ones may not have eyes, but they are nonetheless quite capable of perceiving human reality; they may not have ears, but they can follow public opinion; they may not have mouths, but they know how to manipulate the masses. They are all cloaked in the respectability of plausibility and integrated into social life to an extent that makes it difficult to unmask and situate them, and still more difficult to defend oneself against this type of contamination and reduce its seductive power. It is one thing to distinguish the darnel from the wheat and produce documents condemning certain systems of power, production and consumption; it is another to melt down the golden calf and reduce the malign influence of idolatry in social intercourse, politics, the economy and culture.

The old Greek and Roman religions had a series of idols, each with its own image and appropriate symbols. Modern society lacks this clarity and hides its idolatry under a jumble of continually shifting images. Analysis has to try to sort out what is fluid and mixed in reality, to put into some order what overlaps in fact. We have chosen to examine the idolatries of power, money, technology, pleasure and superiority, set in the overall context of the struggle for a truly Christian faith-praxis.

(b) The Hard Struggle

There is a deep and irreconcilable opposition between Jesus' praxis and the idolatries of our time, with the former serving as an instrument for measuring the false gods among us. The gospel, put into practice in the church community, provides the means of discerning today's idolatries, so that they can be melted down and ground to powder (Exod. 32:20). Moses did not have to make much effort to locate his idol; Christians today have a harder task, for idolatry now is like air pollution: it poisons without being noticed.

The struggle is hard not only because the seducers are hidden, masked and infiltrated into hearts and minds, including those of Christians, but also because it takes time and trouble to create valid alternatives to systems condemned in theory as idolatrous, dehumanizing and death-dealing. The human mind can detach itself from a specific context and take refuge in abstractions, but we can work on and reform reality only from within present history, and from our condition in time and the limitations and possibilities of our own situations. A defective machine can be stopped for the fault to be put right or a piece replaced, but history does not stop, being made of living people of flesh and bone; history goes on, while its actors keep changing course.

To destroy idols, it is not enough for prophets to go about brandishing axes, even if they do so in the name of the gospel. Christian communities need to take stock of the way they themselves have been contaminated, be converted and show in their own practice an attractive example of how to humanize society. Without this genuine common effort, the most accurate condemnations will be mere words and more words, instead of being leaven, light and salt to stimulate, light the way and kindle the hope of those who look to Christians for answers (see Matt. 5:13–16; 13:33; 1 Pet. 3:15).

2. THE IDOLATRY OF POWER

The expression "power corrupts" is perhaps suspect, as it must have originated among victims of the abuses of power with which history is strewn. The numerous forms of authoritarianism found in all human groupings, from the family to the state and international organizations, are usually justified in Christian circles by reference to God the Creator, or the Lordship of God; those who make such justifications just as facilely forget that those who carry authority are also sons and daughters of Adam and Eve and know what happened with Cain and Abel. In the West, power is symbolized by a sword, which is ambiguous, since it can suggest struggle for justice and the common good as well as recalling violence and slaughter.

(a) Abuses of Power

From the time of their colonization, the peoples of Latin America have been deeply scarred by authoritarianism of all sorts: the petty tyrant in his own home, the colonel with power over life and death, the dictatorial regime. Nazism gave authoritarianism its formula: what the leader says is the truth; what the leader does is justice. It matters little if petty or great dictators still invoke divine providence and power, or simply rely on the ideology of national security. The results are always the same: oppression, persecution, violence, torture, forced exile, extermination, death squads, disappearances—the whole familiar gamut of the consequences of arbitrary totalitarianism with no right of appeal. The root cause too is always the same, despite its different historical camouflages: humankind's Adamic pride absolutizing its own power.

This makes totalitarian use of power a form of idolatry (Puebla, 500). In politics above all, the idol becomes a Moloch on whose altar individuals, families, human rights, liberties and the common good of entire nations are sacrificed without scruple, since the executioners are easy in their consciences, simply carrying out orders from above. Besides violence and violations of human rights, absolute power usually brings wide-scale corruption in its wake, victimizing the humble and benefitting only the potentates and their fair-weather friends. Often, in order to stay in power, authoritarian regimes seek the protection and support of great political and economic powers, at the expense of the legitimate development of their people and culture (Puebla, 501).

Looking at the broader world picture, evidence continues to pile up in the political, economic and cultural spheres, to show the dependent, satellite role that most nations play in relation to the East-West power struggle. After the Second World War, there was a rapid process of juridical decolonization; but economic, political and ideological colonialism continues, more disguised but just as effective. Theory and rhetoric give sovereignty and autonomy in accordance with international statutes; in practice the two superpowers make the rest of the world an extension of their political and military spheres of influence.

The North-South dialogue, seen increasingly as a vital necessity by people of goodwill everywhere, fails to grow in volume, while political dependency, and the divergence between developed, wealthy nations and underdeveloped, poor ones remain the same or grow even worse. At present, the iron fist of power may wear a velvet glove, but its egocentric pressure still provides a virtually insurmountable obstacle to the development of real humanizing and just reforms in the dependent countries of the periphery, shut out of the decision-making process where the great decisions affecting the well-being and security of the human race are made.

(b) The Situation of the Church

Church history is not exempt from absolutism either. The world with its power structures in which the church moves has its seductive influence. Since the slow decline of the Roman Empire, church authorities have seen themselves obliged to step into areas formerly organized by the civil power. The Middle Ages reached a particular combination or composition of cross and crown which, together, ruled over the same clientele, called the people. This situation has traditionally continued in Catholic countries, in which the two powers, ecclesiastical and civil, have generally worked together, exchanging favours and support between their respective leaderships. Rubbing shoulders in this way as they have, small wonder that there has been a certain symbiosis and assimilation of manners of exercising power—and finally of abusing it.

Since the Second Vatican Council and the Medellín conference there has—as Puebla confirms—been a great change in the way authority is exercised in the Catholic Church in Latin America, with a new accent on service and sacrament (Puebla, 260). In various countries the church has at first distanced itself from authoritarian regimes and then moved into outright opposition to them, repeatedly denouncing the arbitrary assaults on human rights made by military dictatorships. Many base Christian communities have evolved new forms of sharing and participation—two key words in the Puebla document—on the basis of consultation, distribution of tasks, new forms of ministry and co-responsibility in solidarity. Pastoral councils have made their appearance in the organizations of dioceses and parishes too, as signs of openness and hope that inherited structures are capable of being transformed.

Nevertheless, there is sense in the popular saying that smoking a pipe leaves one's mouth twisted. A long tradition of clerical monopoly of the word and authority will not disappear simply by wishing it away. The evangelical criticism of the Pharisees is still applicable to the church: "They prepare heavy burdens that are very difficult to carry and lay them on the shoulders of the people. But they do not even lift a finger to move them" (Matt. 23:4).

(c) The Practice of Jesus

Faced with his disciples' desire for power, promotion and favours, Jesus addressed harsh words to them: "You know that the rulers of the nations lord it over them and the powerful oppress them. It shall not be so among you; whoever wants to be more important in your group shall make himself your servant. And whoever wants to be first must make himself the slave of all. Be like the Son of Man who has come, not to be served, but to serve and to give his life to redeem many" (Matt. 20:25–8). The paradoxical play the synoptics make on least and greatest is particularly applicable to those who are in positions of authority: those who seek to be the greatest must make themselves the least (see, e.g., Luke 22:26).

Here the New Testament term most applicable to civil and ecclesiastical authorities is *exousia*, variously translated as "power" or "authority" (e.g., Matt. 28:18–20; John 1:12; 19:11; Rom. 13:1; 1 Cor. 6:12; etc.). Its meaning is not to be seen in terms of human beings having absolute autonomy to command and impose in a vertical structure of higher above lower, since this belongs to God alone, but in terms of possibility, competence, authorization, the creative freedom to act and marshall resources so as to serve and attend to the needs of others. For those who exercise human power, being in authority means having authority to the extent that one's decisions and rules express the truth that is Christ and the justice that is God, our justice, in biblical terms. Without this close and limiting correspondence, all exercise of power and all requirements to obey are false and unjust, since they take away the freedom that, through Christ, belongs to God's children. This applies just as much to the civil authorities, whose power still comes from God, inasmuch as they are servants (*diakonos*) of God (Rom. 13:1, 4, 5).

(d) The Contrary: Fear

The abuses of the powerful spread the poison of fear and anxiety to the rest. Dictatorships large and small, in nations and families, force people to adopt the tactic of covering their heads with their hands in the hope of warding off the successive blows of violence and humiliation. What does one do when faced with a tank in the street, a torture chamber, the constant threat of losing one's job, one's home, one's life itself? Of course, some are heroes. But authoritarian regimes generally spread a cloud of fear among the people, in which they cannot breathe; they foment worry and uncertainty and close in the horizons of freedom and the courage to act. And in its wake, this cloud leaves mutual mistrust and the perversity of the slave mentality, the slaves licking the feet of their ruler.

In recent centuries, a fearful Christendom in retreat has produced an atmosphere of anxiety and fear among the faithful in the West. Instead of celebrating the prelude to Easter and cultivating paschal joy, moral theology has multiplied sins, temptations and prohibitions and created a reign of terror through hell and its demons. Many have felt as though they lived in a house with no doors or windows, reeking of sulphur, threatened by enemies from all sides. Popular devotional books pictured hell beckoning with all its paraphernalia of flames, tortures, screams and despair. Since Vatican II the gates have been opened and fresh air let into Christian life, but the distortions produced by fear have still left their traumas on the Catholic faithful.

Popular wisdom may regard fear as salutary, but Jesus' actions conveyed the contrary of fear, of anguished concern with sin and evil. He opened up a horizon of freedom, joy, hope and courage to live. Continuing the prophetic tradition of the Old Testament, his watchword was "Fear not." Sleeping peacefully through the storm, he chided his disciples for their lack of trust. His strength is like the sun which finally breaks through and scatters the dense cloud cover darkening the horizon of life.

It is not hard to imagine the joy of the people he set free from their sufferings and sins: the satisfaction of the crowd, when the disciples gathered up the remains into twelve baskets (Mark 6:43); the immense relief of the woman taken in adultery or the sinful woman in the Pharisee's house, who could hold their heads up in society once more, freed from their sins and anxieties; the feelings of the crucified thief who heard his neighbour on the cross say: "Today you will be with me in paradise" (Luke 23:43). Jesus' presence makes hearts burn (Luke 24:32); it removes fear, sets free. The dignity with which Jesus faced his judges, the soldier who struck him, Pilate, inspires courage and trust in his promise that when the hour comes, the Spirit will speak in his disciples (Matt. 10:17–20).

3. THE IDOLATRY OF MONEY

The dominant economic system in Latin America, which leaves such deep marks on the population and society of this continent, is far more than a mere system or theory called liberal capitalism. A theory is an agglomeration of ideas, words and phrases which, in printed form, serves to swell libraries. Here what counts is the pervasive, systematic exploitation of raw materials, capital and labour. This is what actually produces the true face, composed of suffering, ambivalence and sharp contrast, of the multitudes who throng the cities and rural areas, supposedly as free citizens with equal rights.

Factories are symbols of the system, and the banks, with their marble and smoked glass, its temples. But ethics is concerned with actual people and the situations they find themselves in: they relate to factories, workshops, banks, shops and supermarkets, but they also, and primarily, represent the grandeur and misery of the human condition. There is a popular saying that money has no smell; the overall human and socio-economic framework into which this observation fits is not just a matter of notes, figures and percentages of profit or inflation, but the product of individuals and groups of human beings, and the victims the system produces are equally human.

(a) A Society of Contrasts

Up till now, capitalist economic dynamism has reproduced the statue of Janus, the old Roman god with two faces, whose temple was opened only in times of war. One face is the minority of privileged rich, amassing land, banks, factories and service empires, and with them the power to decide the destiny of the great mass of workers, whose only possessions are the strength of their arms and the brains in their heads. The masters take full advantage of all the benefits of economic development: they live in mansions, surround themselves with servants and bodyguards, go to exclusive clubs, can spend at will and even control the administration of justice. It has long been said that small-scale robbers are thieves, large-scale ones are barons: the former go to prison; the latter off to their yachts. At the pinnacle of society, individuals may come and go, but the structure that keeps the group in place does not change, so that power is virtually anonymous.

The other face is made up of the mass of poor labourers and clerical workers and their families. For most of these, their wages are insufficient to keep their families, and their situation becomes steadily worse through enforced policies of wage restraint. Security of employment, housing, transport, sustenance, social welfare, basic and further education are minimal. The shanty-towns and so-called "pockets of poverty" (a fine euphemism) are standing reproaches to the ostentatious riches of the minority. The backwardness of the rural areas forces many families to the cities in search of a living, and the infrastructure of the cities cannot cope with the population growth resulting from this migration. Sociological studies of migration give many tables and figures, but are unable to convey a sense of the human misery it produces for so many of the poor.

(b) A Society in Conflict

Janus' two faces belong to a single person; so the extremes of classes belong to a single human society. The wealth, power, prestige and privileges of a small minority are not independent of the poverty, marginalization and crying needs of the majority of the population. The growing wealth of some is not simply a parallel development to the growing poverty of the masses since the accumulation of wealth in the hands of a few is often at the expense of the exploited many, who lack the power to claim their share in the political and economic process (see Puebla, 30; 1135n; 1209). The conscientization and political organization of the workers are slow processes, constantly broken off by armed or bloodless coups by the ruling classes.

Many people will not label this situation of permanent conflict of interests "class struggle" because of its Marxist connotations. It is not worth quibbling over labels; the facts are plain to see. Perhaps the most telling index is the expectation of life: for most of the population this is reduced by hunger, high levels of infant mortality, disease, air and water pollution, agricultural chemicals, assassination for the sake of acquiring land, industrial accidents. . . . The fact that the overall life expectancy is increasing cannot hide the great difference there is in this respect between rich and poor.

(c) Increasing Frustration

Marginalized in politics, in the economic system of production, reduced to living from hand to mouth, the poor feel increasingly frustrated, dehumanized, lacking recognition as human beings outside the immediate circle of family and friends. To make things worse, they are constantly bombarded with commercial propaganda from billboards, radio and television, presenting them with a mirage of well-being and luxury their finances can never stretch to, however "soft" the loans on offer. The oldest are perhaps used to a life of sobriety and austerity, with few possessions, but the young are more easily swayed by fashion, so their frustration mounts up as they see the ever-widening gap between their wants and their realistic life expectations, inevitably seeking an outlet in anti-social behaviour and crime. There is always a certain tension between expectation and realization in life, but if the tension becomes too great, the human cord between them snaps.

Frustration leads to weakness, an inability to resist any offer of betterment. The collective frustration of the working classes, battling, like Don Quixote, against the windmills of economic and political power, lays their flank open to any theory offering them hope, progress and advancement. Workers, peasants, "cold-snackers" and casual labourers may not know anything about Marxist analysis or dialectical materialism, which are food for intellectuals to quarrel over. The victims of the productive system are in a different situation: they feel suffering, resistance, exploitation and frustration in their flesh and family life. Subjected to real situations of sin and injustice, defenceless, they are open to any siren song and often at the mercy of impostors, from dictators and demagogues to popular preachers (see Eph. 4:14).

(d) The Leaven of Jesus

The two accounts of the Sermon on the Mount both include the beatitude of poverty. At first sight, Matthew seems to spiritualize it, as though it were enough to be poor in heart and the amount of material possessions were unimportant (Matt. 5:3). Luke, through the antithesis he puts in, is more direct. While he makes it clear that the fortunate ones are the poor who are hungry, who suffer and weep, he is harsh to those who are full, who laugh now, whom people speak well of (Luke 6:20–26). But Matthew in fact leaves no doubt that Jesus made poverty a requirement for entering the Kingdom. Jesus' advice to his disciples, not to pile up riches on earth, since they will corrupt and be stolen, becomes the invitation/challenge to the rich young man: if you want to be perfect, go sell all you have and give to the poor (Matt. 19:21; see 5:48; 6:19–21). And the continuation of Jesus' discourse is as clear as the midday sun: "Yes, believe me, it is easier for a camel to go through the eye of a needle than for a rich man to enter the kingdom of heaven" (Matt. 19:23 and parallels).

Like the Old Testament prophets before him, Jesus clearly saw the risks and abuses of riches in the society before him: misappropriation, fraud, corruption, avarice, pride, exploitation of the poor. The more goods we possess, the greater the risk of closing our hearts and eyes and, dressed in the latest fashion and feasting every day, failing to notice the presence of so many Lazaruses lying stretched out in our doorway (see Luke 16:19–21: the Old Testament framework of the rest of the parable does not obscure what it says about God's judgment on the rich and the poor). The apparent security provided by possessing money, armaments and land makes the rich forget the mortal finiteness of their life and their economic calculations (see Luke 12:16–21). This is why Jesus was so pleased by the conversion of Zacchaeus, who confessed his frauds and wanted to share his goods with the poor (Luke 19:1–10). Liberation from one's goods is the open door to the Kingdom. Without renouncing them, no one can be a disciple of Jesus (Luke 14:33).

Historically, a cloud has fallen over Jesus' clear view. His challenging words on poverty were effectively monopolized, in the West, by religious with their vow of poverty. For lay people, the requirement laid on all Jesus' disciples, if it has not quite lost all its meaning, has become a distant symbolism, at best something extraneous to real life, an extra task. Instead of following the *kenosis* of the Lord (Phil. 2:7), the manuals of moral theology sought to provide them with every sort of justification for private property and the sort of financial transactions the capitalist system has developed over the past centuries, with never a mention of the radical gospel texts. It is only in this century that the quest for a lay spirituality has begun to recover the Lord's words on the poverty expected of his disciples. Although the origins of this quest lie in the middle classes, its results have been apparent in the lives of the poor, who already led lives of simplicity and sacrifice, guided by the light of their faith.

(e) The Kingdom of Justice

Seek first the Kingdom and its justice and all the rest—things like food, drink, housing—will be added on, as a result of the productive collaboration between Jesus' disciples and the creative power of God (Matt. 6:25–34). Under the influence of Roman legal thinking, the concept of justice is often linked, in moral treatises, to the question of rights and duties, of paying each according to his or her deserts. But the richness of the Greek biblical term *dikaiosyne* far transcends this restricted interpretation, since God's action in the world, which is what the word refers to, is far broader, more varied and, above all, gratuitous, than human beings, working from their own experience of justice, can imagine.

The epiphany of God's justice, appearing throughout the Bible but above all in the person of Jesus Christ, is the creative and coherent actions of the Father of all, characterized by gratuitousness, endless generosity, fidelity, patience, forgiving more than seventy times seven, so that St John could conclude that God is love—*charitas* (1 John 4:8). Communicating with the people through the covenant, God gradually carries out the plan of building new heavens and a new earth, where justice will reign (1 Pet. 3:13). In this unfolding plan to set the whole of creation free, there is a place for men and women, who accept the driving force of grace, acting and working in the direction proposed by God. This collaboration with God's plan includes the cross which leads to iniquity and death (see 1 Pet. 2:21–5); but it also includes confidence in the eventual triumph of our God's justice.

In such a vision it is clear that "no one can serve two masters . . . God and money" (Matt. 6:24). Money makes people selfish and idolatrous, through seizing goods that were originally common to all and destined for all. God's justice, brought about through human collaboration, opens hearts, hears the cry of the needy and shares everything, applying the words of the parable: "All that I have is yours" (Luke 15:31). Since the church in Latin America made its preferential option for the poor against their poverty, its praxis can no longer remain on the level of general principles; through accurate analysis of the economic and political causes of the mass poverty that afflicts us, it has to achieve effective political action on behalf of those most in need.

The main obstacle to this has been a certain apocalyptic dualism between earth and heaven; as it took shape in Western Christianity, this led to disdain of and withdrawal from the world, which was seen as merely an enemy and an obstacle. Vatican II produced a more balanced view, but the mentality that separates earthly values from heavenly things still persists. Instead of seizing on objectivized abstractions which seem to give autonomous existence to human goods and values, reifying them, Christian morality should place human persons, as individuals and as making up society, in their rightful historical place, in the centre. They are the element that provides continuity, be their tents earthly or eternal, and they have to bear the fruits of justice through Jesus Christ, for the sake of their brothers and sisters (see Phil. 1:9–11).

The consequence of the dichotomy between heaven and earth is that the gospel is still preached in a mutilated form, without its economic, social, cultural and political implications. Such a mutilation implies a certain degree of collusion with the established order and its idols of money and power, and dialectically conditions opposite—equally distorted—positions (see Puebla, 558).

4. THE IDOLATRY OF TECHNOLOGY

If we take the mass of the population of Latin America as a starting-point, it is clear that a deep change in mentality is taking place, directly affecting their religious view of existence. We do not merely exist on and derive material support from this earth; we are part of it, made from its dust, part of mortal nature and destined to return to the dust. Belonging to the earth in this way, however, is not merely a question of passive growth and decrease, birth and death, being tossed about like leaves in the wind. From Old Testament times, people of faith have not seen themselves as blind playthings of natural forces or the processes of history; they have understood their given role of facing up to nature, controlling the earth and using it in accordance with the needs of increasing population numbers.

In order to survive and create an environment in which all can survive, we have to work the land, make use of nature, cultivate the soil with our hands and our strength and make the world a worthy human habitat. Israel's faith saw God's blessing on this mission: "Fill the earth and subdue it, rule over the fish of the sea and the birds of the sky, over every living thing that moves on the ground" (Gen. 1:28). Through human pride, however, work has become burdensome, even death-dealing for many (Gen. 3:17–19). The blessing and curse of work have increased to such a point that the world is now covered with a vast network of factories, machines, communications and transport systems, involving the earth and its raw materials as well as human beings.

Its overall name is technology, now so widespread that even education is said to have its technologies.

(a) The Traditional Image

The dominant idea of the universe was one of established order, fixed forever. Human life unfolded on a vast stage, with the firmament for a roof and the horizon for pillars. On this stage, human beings too had their own prescribed and limited roles: to work, produce a family and live in harmony with others. Differences of class, between rich and poor, authorities and subjects were accepted as simply always having to be so. From a religious aspect, the world was in the hands of God, patron saints and guardian angels; the devil, destiny, blind fate and the evil eye had their place too. In this play of supra-human forces, human beings had little space in which to manoeuvre and so their dominant feeling was one of dependence. Sun and rain, harvest and plague, health and sickness, well-being or disaster were all set in the religious sphere, so that the means to bring about good results and defend oneself against evil ones were also religious in nature: prayers, vows, penances, processions, blessings, exorcisms.

This world view brought a division of responsibilites with it. Human beings' knowledge of their world and their role in it was fixed from infancy. The same applied to their behaviour: this was controlled by the "it's always been that way" tradition, sanctioned by God. Outside these spheres, everything belonged to God: the favours and caprices of nature, order, good luck, calamity. This static, immutable interpretation of the universe, still current among the masses of the people, produces respect, admiration for and submission to the rhythm of time and nature, on one hand; on the other, it produces serious resistance to the introduction of change, whether in the methods and techniques of production, or in the traditional codes of family and social behaviour. Faith in a creator God made it difficult to allow for dynamic evolution or human creative inventiveness, since everything in life was fixed and firm from beginning to end.

It is probably unjust to label this underdevelopment of popular faith as idolatry; it is rather a distorted image of the true God, with the effect of reducing the human role in the universe. The ordinary people are not the milieu in which to look for atheism, but deformation of faith is also a problem.

(b) The Opposite Extreme

Since the end of the Middle Ages, a different cultural current has been forming, with profound effects on the position human beings occupy in the overall scheme of things. Instead of seeing ourselves on the same level as animals, as creatures dependent on our creator, a new Promethean will has emerged, facing up to cosmic, biological and social nature so as to change it at our pleasure. Scientific and technical progress increase the power, control and ability to manipulate, not only of human beings as a whole, but of certain groups who take control of new knowledge and discoveries and their practical applications, and sometimes monopolize them. The capitalist system, with its accumulation of economic, scientific and technical capital in the hands of a few, has been the main historical factor in the material development of the modern world, creating a worldwide network of services and communications and producing an endless supply of consumer goods and commodities.

This is the broth in which the new virus of idolatry of technology has been cultivated, a virus which has now spread its tentacles throughout the world, invading the traditional territory reserved to the creator with its inventions and initiatives. Throughout at least the Western world, including the ruling and middle classes in traditionally Catholic countries, God has been marginalized, reduced to a "God of the gaps," disappearing as a point of reference in most human plans and activities.

The historical advance of technology has had other adverse effects on the world. It has led to an increase in the contrast and conflict between rich and poor, between developed and underdeveloped countries, within nations, between peoples, not to mention the socially conditioned destitution of the "Fourth World." The new idol has been no less cruel to nature: its depradations in quest of raw materials for industry, the senseless destruction of the rain forests, forced urbanization without proper planning, infrastructure or means of transport, are all serving to reduce the quality of life. Erosion, desertification, water and air pollution, the poisoning of the oceans, are as great a threat to human life as nuclear weapons. In their present embodiments, today's technological undertakings claim many lives and threaten the eco-systems of whole regions of the planet.

There are two facets to the installation of technology as a modern idol. One is the presentation of technology as autonomous, a self-generating process, whose only law is that what can (technically) be, may (morally) be. All that *homo faber* knows how to do and sets out to make, create or manipulate is justified, and may therefore be done. The other is that technological projects, generally linked to desire for maximum profit, usually take only the interests of those who plan and execute them into account, with no respect for the rest of the population or for nature as the common and essential human habitat for all.

(c) The Balance of Christian Faith

In the faith experience of Israel and the church, the relationship between human technology and nature differs both from that produced by the distorted image of God in traditional religiosity, and from the idolatry of technology which sets humankind on the pedestal of sole creator. In the universe Christians occupy through their faith, intelligence and creativity, there is no simple juxtaposition of God and humankind, each working independently in a separate sphere, nor does God retreat as the constructive and organizational strength as humankind advances. Though they form part of nature, the sons and daughters of Adam and Eve stand in a special relationship to nature, giving names to all the animals, plants, rivers, trees, valleys and mountains, because these belong to the whole of humanity and are the common basis of its survival—or were before the Western colonizing onslaught. The world of nature is the workplace in which human beings create culture and well-being for all, organizing their dwelling space in justice, peace and mutual respect.

For Christians, the creative power of God, in which they live, move and have their being (Acts 17:28), stretches through the whole evolution of the cosmos and the whole of human history heading for its final consummation. In the covenant of love proposed, God remains the creative agent in the universe. The ritual rest mentioned by Genesis does not indicate a withdrawal, since the Spirit of God is still present and, step by step and age by age, inspiring the transformation of nature and the progress of humankind, bringing them all to fullness. Through the incarnation principle of the crucified, dead and risen Jesus, God continues to create the world through the agency of the Son, the first-born of all creation. As image of the invisible God, Jesus enters history to make humanity evolve from within itself to complete liberation, carrying the whole of creation forward in this continuous movement as it anxiously awaits the manifestation of the children of God. To the Son, all power in the universe has been given, so that nothing remains outside his dominion and everything is kept in being by the power of his word (see Rom. 8; John 1:1–3; Heb. 1–2; Col. 1:15–20; Eph. 1:10–14; Matt. 28:18).

(d) The Responsibility of **Homo Faber**

In Christian belief, human beings occupy a special place in God's creative process, and therefore have a special responsibility. God is the utterly Other; on the other hand, through the Spirit sent to us, God dwells in us, adopted children of God, and is deeper inside us than we are ourselves. In the light of this inspiring and creative indwelling of the mystery of God in us, in the Pauline sense (Rom. 16:25; Col. 1:26; etc.), we become co-creators, co-workers and co-explorers of God in the evolution of the universe and in the development of history. Through our intimate mediation, the creator continues to unfold this work of love, initiated in the Son, till God comes to judge the fruits of human discovery and productivity in this world. The great risk God takes is the ambivalence of human nature, capable of freeing and enslaving, using and abusing. But God's patience reaches where it will and human beings learn even from their errors and selfishness.

In the task of building a viable human habitat for all, in the best possible way, the human mission is to be inventive, innovative and creative in a universe that is still open and in the process of formation. The responsible human role is to free the forces of nature and human potentialities for the good of the whole world. This is how human beings fit into the great project of love and justice which God, the creator, began without them but wishes to make evolve and complete with them. Autonomous in their intelligence and freedom, human beings must seek, in their works, discoveries and technical accomplishments, to show the creative generosity of God who seeks the salvation of all, who wishes all to be freed from the forms of slavery that have historically ensnared and maltreated them.

The Augustinian paradox always comes back: "man the maker" has to work as though God did not exist, and give thanks as though God did everything. In technical work, Jesus' words "Without me you can do nothing" tell the Christian conscience that in him who comforts us (John 15:5; Phil. 4:13), we are capable of everything. The greatest wonders of technical and scientific progress will always have their dark side, exacting a price in sacrifice and harmful results. Through God's grace, the proud egoism of the children of Adam will learn the golden rule and follow the spirit of Jesus who came not to be served, but to serve others, his brothers and sisters (Mark 10:45). True justice in human conditions on earth means a fair distribution of rewards and duties, benefits and losses.

5. THE IDOL OF PLEASURE

Pleasure is something eminently human and inherent in life itself: joy, satisfaction, contentment, laughter, happiness, celebration, enthusiasm and ecstasy are proper to human beings and their histories. Human pleasure runs a vast gamut of variations and types, from little to great, passing to lasting, superficial to deep. In all cases, its liberative power is such that those other companions of human life, sadness, suffering, hurt, hardship, are incapable of suppressing it, since it always finds a way to break out, in individuals and communities.

Catholicism has long shown a stoical-ascetic tendency to eliminate pleasure and train its adherents to perfect self-control, indifferent to the joys as well as the sorrows of life. Even now, much devotional writing views this human—sometimes all too human—area of experience with suspicion, as danger, temptation and sin. The people can sing of the joys to come in heaven, but have to move through this life as though in a vale of tears, sufferings and penances. Pleasure is easily linked to hedonism and so surrounded with taboos and inhibitions in an attempt to suppress it.

(a) The Features of the Idol

Human beings are born with basic needs: they grow, mature and survive thanks to their balanced satisfaction of these needs. But a simple comparison between the sober, uncluttered life of the poor and the opulent abundance of consumer goods and comforts "needed" by the rich shows the great scale of variation of need in the modern world. Western consumer goods and leisure industries, backed by persuasive and insistent promotion, have developed and distorted basic human needs to a point where immediate consumption, "having more," has become, for many people, more important than "being more," as persons. The imbalance has led to an over-valuation of the pleasures within the reach of those who have money, coupled with the hunger, homelessness, lack of dignity and inability to make ends meet of the majority of the world's population. The destitution of the modern world spreads like a huge sea of unsatisfied desires around a little island of conspicuous and uncontrolled consumption.

What is presently happening and being promoted in the sexual field can, of course, be explained partly as an explosive reaction against centuries of repression and inhibition. In Latin America, the sexual exploitation of women in slavery and traditional prostitution also form part of the background. But the production and consumption of "canned" sex in the forms of shows, pornographic magazines and the general exaltation of female nudity, has other social factors at work too: the easy profits to be made from this sort of exploitation, and human superficiality, which shrinks from more lasting and deep relationships. The provocative power of sex displayed on this level hinders rather than helps the normal maturation process in men and women.

Throughout history, human sexuality has always shown its lights and shadows, beauties and abuses. But modern society, competitive, demanding and alienating, has complicated the normal pattern of human relationships. The numerous tensions it provokes make transient sexual encounters, free from responsibility, a little resevoir of freedom and licence, one of the few left. The immediacy of sexual pleasure, even imagined, diverts attention from real social problems and dissipates the aggressive energies of those who feel unjustly treated, oppressed and marginalized in the established order (or rather disorder) of things, and look for their own place in the sun. The old Roman tactic of providing bread and circuses has many faces in the modern world, but its mechanism remains the same.

(b) The Search for a New Equilibrium

In the light of faith, all true joy is, in its gratuitousness, a showing through of God's joy in loving us and giving us good things till we are received into God's dwelling. Hoped for, worked for, or simply appearing as though fallen from heaven, pleasure forms part of the formative journey of Christians who seek the state of perfection, the full measure of Christ, in this world (Eph. 4:13). It is in this process of full humanization that pleasure and satisfaction find their measure and balance. Through being faithful to their mission of building the Kingdom of love, justice and solidarity, Christians not only find joys on the way, presences of God's mystery in history and foretastes of the glory that will be revealed (Rom. 8:18), but also communicate these to others. Pleasure is not egocentric, but effusive.

St Paul's words, nevertheless, also remind us that exclusive concentration on pleasure makes no sense in the context of Christian life, since the sufferings of the present time form an inevitable part of actual living conditions in human society. A student is not above his teacher, nor a servant above his master (Matt. 10:24). By way of contrast, the modern world with its myriad sources of pleasure, throws the hunger, destitution and unhappiness of millions of futureless families into starker relief.

Their faith in God gives the simple people a fine sensitivity to the transitory nature of both pleasure and suffering. The fleeting nature of human life and this world itself relativizes the procession of pleasures, joys and happinesses that flit through this life, in comparison with the ultimate future that

Christians, working the while, wait to see revealed. This eschatological expectation of the Kingdom pushes the people of God onward to help in its full realization, which is not yet known. In this constructive movement which makes the new society of solidarity and sharing germinate, many possibilities of easy and transient pleasures are sacrificed, because there are more important things to do. If one's heart is set on the pearl of great price, one sacrifices everything to buy it, and the hardships embraced today become the stepping stones to future joy. Only those who see nothing before them live for the moment.

6. THE IDOLATRY OF SUPERIORITY

Despite its majority Catholicism, Latin American society is a mass of contrasts and discrimination. Around a relatively small number of families who monopolize its wealth and power, revolve the great mass of urban and rural workers, who are thrown crumbs, who are systematically silenced, who have little or no say in political and economic decision-making processes. On top of this, women suffer obvious discrimination: they may be taking a larger part in the production sphere, and can find service employment, but at lower wages than men and with far fewer career opportunities, besides still being regarded as good only for "bed and kitchen" by a society still dominated by *machismo*. The black population, originally depersonalized as imported slaves, have freedom under the law now, but are still marginalized, hemmed in by social prejudices and with no chance of being treated on an equal footing. The Indians, the only autochthonous inhabitants of the continent, are not even considered as citizens with full rights; their lands are stolen from them, and with them their means of survival, so they are threatened with extinction, as peoples and as cultures.

Behind all this lurks the false sense of superiority of the whites. There is officially no racism in Brazil: this is something practised by Hitler, the North Americans, and the South Africans. But no amount of social propaganda about upward mobility can camouflage the reality, though it may colour soap operas: in fact it only serves to strengthen the many forms of superiority shown, consciously or unconsciously, in daily life.

How to overcome social discrimination is an old problem that the people of God have still not solved. St Paul rebuked the Corinthians for the inequality shown at their "eucharists" between the rich who had plenty and the poor who had nothing to eat (1 Cor. 11:20–22). Instead of the strong helping the weak or at least tolerating them, they were marginalized in the community from the earliest times (see Rom. 14; 1 Cor. 8:7–13; Gal. 6:1). St James too observed the distinction made between persons, and inveighed against the attention given to the rich and withheld from the poor as incompatible with faith in the glorified Lord (James 2:1–9). And still today we discriminate against women in the church. . . .

"There is no longer any difference between Jew and Greek, or between slave and freedman, or between man and woman, but all of you are one in Christ Jesus" (Gal. 3:28) and so children of the same Father. This text may reflect expectation of an imminent *parousia*, but its declaration of equality is still valid. Furthermore, Jesus' practice focussed on precisely the weakest, the poorest, those who were suffering, sinners, outcasts who longed to meet someone who would treat them as "persons" and show them human love. Fidelity to Jesus cannot mean simply carrying on the patterns of social discrimination in which we were caught up at the time we became conscious of belonging to Jesus Christ and being part of his body. Being leaven does not mean getting lost in the mass, but fighting to bring all closer to the same level, cutting down social distances and helping others to hold their heads high.

7. CONCLUSION: THE GOOD FIGHT

In ordinary everyday life, today's idols do not stand up clearly to be recognized; on the contrary, they are nebulous and difficult to see, like air and water pollution, which are perceived only in the damage they do to organisms. Since they live in the world with others and like others, Christian communities are open to contamination by idolatry and nostalgia for slavery. The defence strategy against such contamination can be to shut themselves up in a castle and save their integrity at any price, as though the people of God could be the one pure, spotless light shining out in this world of darkness and sin. Guided by the Spirit of truth, however (John 14:17), Christians do better to take on the challenges thrown at them by the world in which all are called to become followers of the Lord, looking carefully at the specks of dust in other people's eyes, but still more carefully at the planks in their own eyes, the idolatries in their own way of life.

The better the people of God understand the times in which they are living, the more valid they can make St Paul's words: "Let us discard, therefore, everything that belongs to darkness, and let us take up the arms of light. As we live in the full light of day, let us behave with decency; no banquets with drunkenness, no prostitution or vices, no fighting or jealousy. Put on, rather, the Lord Jesus Christ . . ." (Rom. 13:12–14). Sobriety of life and vigilance against the tentacles of idolatry that reach out for Christians in the modern world (see 1 Pet. 5:6–11) are not enough, however. Christians, church communities, have received from the Lord the mission to go through the world preaching the good news and announcing the Reign of God through their words and, above all, through the way of life that promotes justice, love and solidarity in peace. It is through the growth in fervour of community faith and the effectiveness of good works meeting modern human needs that the power of idolatry will be swept away and banished. Without this productive vitality, reaching deep into the world and remaking human society, the fine phrases of popes, bishops, councils and conferences are but tissues of words.

Chapter X

Moral Theology and a New Society

Despite local variations and profound contrasts, moral problems are increasingly similar the world over. Television, radio, telephone, telex, fax and aviation are—at least apparently—turning the world into a global village, though in fact they also paradoxically serve to heighten differences. Economic interests, the spread of technology and the extension of world trade give an illusion of a *pax economica*. While political de-colonization spread rapidly after the Second World War, a new economic colonialism now binds the world into a web of domination and interdependence. International organizations, while serving as meeting points for the exchange of ideas, are dominated by the East–West and North–South conflicts.

Perhaps without realizing it, people, social groups and nations are increasingly drawn into an extending web of economic, technological, political and cultural conditions which affect their traditional moralities and provoke similar waves of crisis in all parts of the world. Reading the episcopal documents emanating from the Synods gives the impression that as far as moral questions are concerned, we all face the same problems; survival, well-being, happiness: these present the same challenges and force us all to look for a new meaning to life and a new form of society.

The great problems facing humanity are presented in

increasingly radical terms: the most obvious are perhaps the contrasts between desire for peace and the threat of nuclear holocaust; between consumer abundance and chronic hunger; between concentration of political and economic power in a few hands and the poverty and alienation of the masses; between the wealthy nations and those of the Third and Fourth Worlds, underdeveloped, sunk in debt and alienated from their native cultures. But there is one basic question underlying the outstanding problems of our time (GS 10), and this is the religious one: not just because of atheism and post-religious humanism, but because of the diversity of religions, the divisions within Christianity and the "parties," in the Pauline sense, within the church itself, detracting from its evangelical power.

Three dominant systems claim to have the answers to the "outstanding problems of our time."[1] All are, or seek to be, worldwide; all have great influence and an extensive "clientele"; all promise that their "truths" will bring happiness, freedom and joy. The three are capitalism, Marxism and the teaching of the church. They are locked in with one another in a state of mutual antagonism, each presenting itself as a moral alternative to the other two for the salvation of humanity. It took the church a long time to come to criticize liberal capitalism as strongly as it did at Puebla, where it was described as a system marked by sin, generator of injustice and atheism in practice (see 92, 437, 546); the anti-religious atheism of Marxism made it an immediate target, and it was only later that the church came to accept that atheism also arose as a reaction against a way of teaching and living the Christian faith that hid the true face of God (GS 19, 21).

Looking at the three systems from the moral aspect, one has to take the double meaning of "morality" into account. It can be studied as a rule-giving theory, a matter of intention, something prior to the action that produces historical effects; or it can be seen as the morality of history, the lessons drawn from the real effects and consequences produced by a system of norms imposed on individuals and groups, large and small. So North American and European protagonists of capitalism as the only economic system capable of producing widespread prosperity will seem to be describing something quite different from the situation of inhuman poverty which the system has brought to Latin America. The idealism of Marxist theoreticians is a long way from describing the totalitarianism states professing it have produced in practice. The church too has the same problem: it preaches Christ as the image of the sacrament of union with God and all humanity; it speaks of showing forth the Kingdom of God through witness, service and community. But the historical facts, as seen in the daily lives of Christians or in the analyses made by religious historians and sociologists, explain why every eucharistic celebration has to begin with a rite of penance and reconciliation. What is pure and ideal in theory presents a sad, confused mixture of virtue and failing in practice.

Medieval art was fond of the triptych, consisting of a centre panel and two side panels, which could be folded across the centre panel. The images painted on these either contrasted with or complemented that on the centre. Perhaps we can see capitalism and Marxism as two side panels of the overall picture of a new society, with Christian moral aims as the centre. If we were proposing a full-scale dialogue with the other two here, this would be somewhat insulting, but our purpose is rather to describe a model of Christian action, using influential characteristics of the other two systems as a means of defining it. Our purpose is not to attempt a historical or philosophical analysis of the three, but simply to see what creative strength they have for producing a better humanity in a more human world.

1. THE CAPITALIST SIDE PANEL

Because of its name, capitalism is usually simply identified with capital: money and other forms of accumulate wealth, an economic system of production, business, the market, profit, consumption. But its historic rise links it indissolubly with liberalism, its ideology (LE 40), and the rise of secularism in the West. Basically, too, it means a way of looking at individuals, their lives and the way they act in the world. This basis shows how it can affect matters beyond the world of work and production processes: fields such as sexuality, leisure, culture, politics and communications media, leaving its particular mark on all of them.

(a) The "Ethos" of Capitalism

The spirit of capitalism, on the level of ideals, is made up of a series of qualities and attitudes which together constitute its "ethos." These begin with the self-sufficiency of the owners/entrepreneurs: no longer content with their old place in relation to the earth and nature, they set themselves up against them to control them, draw the maximum benefit from them and so satisfy their ever-increasing needs. This leads to a new attitude to productive work, in which the aims become growth and profitability, with workers as part of the productive process, needed as long as machines cannot do the job more cheaply. What is produced—food, armaments, etc.—is immaterial as long as it can find a market and produce a profit.

This social organization of work requires a freedom of action uncircumscribed by the state, by competition or by the market. Freedom to act is seen as the mainspring of progress and growth; it transcends economic activity to become the banner of how to live in society. But this system also involves giving free consent to being governed through democratic processes in which the citizens take part by right.

The organization and efficiency of the capitalist work ethic are rooted in an asceticism: thrift is an indispensable component of its economy. Indeed, in common parlance, "economizing" means spending little, saving for the morrow, as opposed to spending for the moment. Capital is built up by the exercise of thrift and sobriety, qualities usually envisaged when "Victorian values" are being extolled: indeed the sober, thrifty, God-fearing capitalists of the last century would not recognize the consumer-orientated societies of today as their true successors. Their predecessors, on a more modest scale, perhaps, were the medieval monks, whose combination of hard work and personal austerity led to the contradiction between evangelical poverty on the personal level and the accumulation of wealth on the community level. Many capitalists do not get rich without being ascetics first.

(b) Two Basic Principles

In capitalist theory, all human activity follows two typically individualistic principles: each individual seeks his or her own happiness, and the achievement of this happiness or well-being is the best means of safeguarding the common interest and contributing to universal harmony.[2] In economic activity and social life in general, the ultimate aim is personal profit, gain, advantage, success. In their autonomous freedom, individuals with their personal qualities and possessions are the epicentre of the productive process and of the promotion of well-being in society. So not only they themselves, but the material goods they accumulate, constitute the central value. The duty of the state is to protect their persons and private property, which are sacrosanct, and to support the private sector in business, leaving it full freedom to produce and market its products as it thinks fit.

The "ethos" of free market capitalism was formed within the dynamic context of recent Western history. Despite its successive crises, it continues to dominate the lives of millions, especially in the poor countries. In the wealthy countries, the selfishness of the capitalist classes is somewhat restrained by laws regulating the relationship between capital and labour, though these do not attempt to change the basic structure, which has produced inhuman and scandalous results. These results were stigmatized in the last century, but continue to show their effects in millions of impoverished and alienated victims of the system. The system's perversity, however, does not lie merely in its deadly results; it is at the source of the structure itself: its carefully theorized blindness in the face of the obvious fact of social inequality (RN).

It does not take a detailed examination to show that the goods of the earth, and with them individual and political freedoms, are unequally divided. Capital has been and still is (despite recent policies designed to "widen the base" in some countries) in the hands of relatively few, while the bulk of workers still have only the strength of their arms to sell. The capitalist "ethos" is typical of a false and falsely universal ideology, since it is an abstract and self-seeking extrapolation from the narrow base of those who possess capital and with it the power to downgrade others, the workers, to selling their labour and being forced into a position of social and political marginalization. By exalting the creative freedom of the individual, it justifies control of millions by the few, into whose pockets flow the profits deriving from the labour of the many. "Money can buy everything," we say. But Jesus said, "No one can serve two masters, God and money" (Matt. 6:24; see 1 Tim. 6:10).

2. THE MARXIST SIDE PANEL

Although Western capitalism developed into an atheism in practice (Puebla 546), it never seems to have tackled the question of God seriously. The cultural environment of the West was still so impregnated with religious values that neither the emancipation of modern states from the tutelage of the church nor the rise of the capitalist system brought a radical separation from Christianity—the rich and powerful even had their privileges within the churches. Neither did utopian socialism, which evolved in the same environment, reach the ultimate sort of secularization in which there is no space for religious ideas and practices. It took Marxism, with its this-worldly philosophy, shorn of the eschatological horizon of Christian tradition, to deny the existence of God, or at least the God of nineteenth-century Western society.

(a) The "Ethos" of Marxism

The radical anthropocentrism of Marxism does not deny the value of morality, even though traditional Western morality was founded on a religious view of human existence. On the contrary, Marxism used its humanistic concept of humankind, the world and history to produce its own "ethos" in which tradition and novelty fused, in opposition to the dominant capitalism of the time. This historical conditioning did not deprive the new "ethos" of strength: it has proved sufficiently consistent and convincing to produce real consecration to its cause in millions, arousing a spirit of sacrifice and ascetic self-discipline which is the more impressive for lacking any hope of recompense in another life.

Marxism proposed a new ethic in which rational realism would take the place of ideologies that falsified the "production" of human values. In this process the proletariat was to play a special role, since it had carried the whole weight of oppression and alienation: "In its quality as oppressed class, the workforce has long since accepted the moral values imposed on it and which keep it in its servitude: conformism, humility, passive acceptance, and so on."[3] Marxists saw traditional morality as molding workers' dignity and social position into a patient, resigned acceptance of existing conditions of work, motivated by the promise of an (illusory) reward after death—the "opium of the people."

The new ethos was to break this mental pattern and encourage the oppressed classes to create their own human values, with the virtues of freedom, comradeship, solidarity, resoluteness, honesty, fidelity to the Marxist cause, dedication to work, a critical and self-critical faculty. Not only the workers were victims of oppression and alienation: women too were relegated to a secondary, submissive and exploited role, with no recognition of their social place in history. For both sectors, the process of becoming aware was to take the place of humiliating resignation and lead them to recognize their true situation of domination and subjection, so as to accept their own responsibilities and free themselves from their inhuman slavery through the courage, clarity and discipline of their actions.

According to this vision, human beings are always in movement, towards the future, which depends on them, since they have to construct it. Their progress does not lead them to an imaginary other world, but to one that is just ahead of them, one that they will bring into being through their work, struggle and sacrifice. In this way they will increase their sense of power over material things and natural forces, as well as their rational capacity to organize human society collectively, overcoming the present subhuman conditions in which most of the population live. Human creative vitality, expressed through work, leads people constantly to extend their sphere of power and overcome the obstacles and challenges presented by the world. It is by breaking out of these constraints on freedom that people fulfil themselves in their relationship with society and nature.

(b) Praxis and Practice

In its aim of producing a just society, the key Marxist term is "praxis," used in the sense of the specific, effective, progressive action in history of the "freed" men and women who will emerge from the oppressed classes to overthrow existing limitations and alienations. Through work, technology and planned production, praxis works to dominate nature for the common benefit of humankind. Through political, militant, revolutionary action, it will—one day—make human society a reality that demonstrates the fullness of human potential. When that day will come is not specified; present generations may well not live to see it, but the value of their praxis derives from this unknown, unforeseeable fullness, and is evaluated in relation to it.

Human beings make their society and history as autonomous beings. This does not make them into demiurges, since they remain part of nature with its organic and physical limitations, and subject to chance and fate. So human and social life is more complex than the spheres embraced by ideas, initiatives, plans and decisions. But praxis continually enlarges the area of human creativity and reduces that of natural determinism, dependence on chance, and limitation through ignorance.

When one looks at the historical progress made by nations in which Marxism has won political power, however, at how it works in practice, the picture is not so clear. Marxism aims to give the product of society back to society, along with the benefits of culture, education and social welfare. It seems to have failed to achieve this aim, despite the draconian measures often adopted: totalitarianism, persecution of dissidents, state control of the communications media, abuse of human rights, domination by party bureaucracy. But capitalist states can often show these abuses too, and specific Christian criticism of Marxism has to look more at its limitation of the horizon of human existence to humankind as the absolute centre of the universe. Jesus replied to the tempter, in words deriving from the faith of his people: "Man does not live by bread alone, but by every word that comes from the mouth of God" (Matt. 4:4).

3. THE CHRISTIAN CENTRE PANEL

Even given such summary treatment, these two models can be seen to offer significant material for Christian moral reflection. Both move from economic and political theories to affect all dimensions of human existence; so too Christianity is far more than an ethics of economics or a social theory: it involves the totality of persons and society in this world and aims to show the true meaning of life in this world. The two secular models have prompted Christian moral thinking to enunciate certain principles which stand out from the overall panorama of moral and social teaching. Though still limited by their own generality, and by the fact that human survival will be decided not by discourses or theories, but by praxis, by the responsible, effective and organized actions of human beings in history, they are worth examining. They are the principles of incarnation, of praxis and of solidarity, and together they provide some pointers for the future.

(a) The Principle of Incarnation

The epiphany of God in the history of salvation comes in the form of a successive evolution of creation, covenant, incarnation, coming of the Holy Spirit and the hoped for second coming of the Lord; in the faith of Christians, this epiphany becomes the present, effective actuality of God in the forms of Lord, protector, incarnate God, Paraclete, giver of life, hope. In all eucharistic liturgies, summit of convergence and starting point of all Christian praxis, God reveals all these facets of the grace that sets humanity and the world free, symbolized by the bread and wine, fruits of the earth and work of human hands. Celebrating the memory of the Lord is always a sort of new opening of the source of energy that gives freedom to all creatures, still enslaved and alienated from their human dignity and earthly value.

The exercise of trusting faith lends a new element to human life, incarnate in this world, transitory and mortal. If God has not only created the universe and found it good, has not only become our ally despite our sins, but has become truly one of us, taking on the human condition including temptation, suffering and death, then human life on earth and humanity's historic journey are enriched to an extent beyond what is immediately visible and palpable. In all its critical complexity, the modern world is yet more striking evidence of the ambivalence of the human condition, in which nausea and despair are as much an existential option as hope and joy. Through faith in the incarnation, human society and individuals are no longer thrown back on themselves, shut in between birth and death, but are caught up in the great movement of life, which comes from God and will return to God.

The incarnation of the Son of Man in the time and space of this world forces Christians fully to accept their existence in the flesh and their belonging to the conditions of this earth, here and now, with all the risks and responsibilities this existence implies. Christians do not lead a schizophrenic life, with their feet on earth and their heads in heaven; they are simply themselves, today and tomorrow, living, working, taking part in human society as it exists in the present configuration of this earth, indissolubly bound up with the categories of time and space and conscious of their limitations in understanding, power and achievement. Tomorrow will be death and resurrection in Christ, but it is always the same incarnate person, though with a glorified body, who continues to live in fullness.

To "spiritualize" Christian revelation, marginalizing the earth and our bodies, taken from the earth, and devaluing them, is ultimately to deny the incarnation, the fleshly, worldly reality of human existence today, and to alienate human beings from themselves and their world. The substantive unity between persons and their physical and biological make-up, and their real incarnation in this world, are not only the bases of our mission to organize the world and make it humanly viable, a "habitat" fit for all; they are also the reason for doing away with the old opposition between verticalism and horizontalism. Verticalism spiritualized faith to the point where, in its narcissism, it saw others—those who were hungry, sick or enslaved—merely as means to heavenly self-advancement. This false identification between human beings and heaven saw horizontalism as exclusive preoccupation with the things of this world, lacking the transcendental hope of the Christian faith. Both upset the harmony of the open humanism brought by Christ through his incarnation in this world as one of us.

The mystery of the incarnation, the source of the worth belonging to human life on this earth, did not end with the death of Jesus, nor with his resurrection from the dead. Through the Spirit, he formed and is still forming the body of the church, whose flesh and blood members are the sacrament of the union of earthly humanity with God. To call this a "mystery" is perhaps to suggest something transparent, volatile, lacking in material substance. Jesus, however, could be seen and touched, like anyone else; he ate, drank, conversed, slept, felt pain and died, like all his brothers and sisters who make up the church. So the church as mystery, inspired by the breath of the Spirit and hoping in the Lord, is also an earthly human reality. Neither the Spirit nor the Lord take away human conditions, the living together of living, mortal Christians in this present world. When the end comes, when every rule, authority and power are destroyed, then Christ will place himself under the Father who subjected all things to him, so that God may be all in all (1 Cor. 15:20–28).

Incorporated as they are in the church, Christians cannot be errant spirits who drift into the world's orbit; they are more than ever tied to others and to the world in which all live and act. Nothing human, earthly, physical, is alien to them; it is all theirs, as part of their belonging to this here and now. Their faith enables them to penetrate deeper into the mystery of humankind and the world than pure rationalism or empirical sciences. In the Judaic and New Testament tradition, there is no room for *fugus mundi*, for cutting oneself off from, for fearing, despising, being judgmental about human realities and potentialities in this world. On the contrary, the first phrase to learn is "God saw that it was good." There are situations of suffering and horror in which this filial trust demands an extreme effort and forces Christians to say "Never again," to decide to change them radically and prevent their repetition. But the energy of indignation comes from the same faith in the goodness of God and our mission to express this, ever more effectively, in the way we live in ourselves and together with others.

Human experience knows the ambivalences of knowledge

and ignorance, strength and weakness, power and limitations, autonomy and dependence; it knows the sad law of doing the evil that one does not want to do and not doing the good one does want to do (see Rom. 7). Moral good finds its enemy in human wickedness and weakness; the opposite of human virtue is human sinfulness. It is through the light of faith that we begin to understand the mystery of evil and its tentacles, but all sins, whatever their names—injustice, exploitation, libertinage, infidelity, lies, corruption, violence—have a human face. Christian fortitude, however, tells us that not even sin can extinguish the mercy or exhaust the patience of God.

Belonging to the church extends human life incarnate in this world inwards and forwards: inwards, because the depths of a person are also the meeting-place with the God-with-us; we can be solitary, but never alone, and where two or three are gathered together in the name of Christ, he is in their midst (Matt. 18:20); forwards, because the dynamic of their life enables Christians to overcome decadence, slavery and iniquity and to conquer death itself, following the example of Jesus who was crucified, died and rose again. These two movements define the mission of the people of God: to be the leaven and light of human society as it exists in the world today, through the exercise of the gospel, so that historical human reality may ever better express the image of the the true God-man and the whole universe become an environment formed for the well-being of all humankind.

(b) The Principle of Praxis

Originating in the classical Greek which has kept its general meaning till now, the word "praxis" is doubly exposed: on the one hand, there is the specialized meaning given it by Marxism, which leads Christians instinctively to reject it; on the other, its link with "practice" suggests routine, custom, usage, uncritical repetition and so on. But as it enjoys such wide currency in international intellectual circles today, it would seem even more hazardous to abandon it and search for an equivalent.

Its Christian sense stems from its association with the verb "to practise," in its traditional meaning of doing, carrying out, undertaking, working—all of which imply more than the current idea of a "practising Christian" as one who regularly attends

Sunday worship. . . . Applied to Christian morality, it means the courage and perseverance of Jesus' disciples, inspired by him and guided by his Spirit; their capacity to make the historical reality of this world something better: more human, more just, more honest, more balanced, more viable for a greater part of the human race than it is at present.

As the Gospels testify, Jesus "practised" the Jewish religion; he lived as a Jew critical of various aspects of life: he gave bread to the hungry, healed the sick, saved an adulteress from stoning, defended the weak and the poor, set people free from the demons that possessed them. To John the Baptist, fretting in prison, Jesus sent word of the signs that the Kingdom had already come about: "The blind see, the lame walk, the lepers are made clean, the deaf hear, the dead are brought back to life, and the good news is reaching the poor" (Matt. 11:5). The rule for the disciples is to do things, even something as simple as giving a cup of water to someone who is thirsty. Evildoers will be excluded from the Kingdom, even if they say "Lord, Lord" and work miracles. The blessed are those who do good to the humblest (Matt. 7:21–3; 25:31–46; Luke 13:25–8).

The central plank of Jesus' praxis was total service to others. With his authority and power, he always gave an effective response to all human needs: for bread, for health, for support, for peace, for forgiveness. He expressed his compassion for the crowds who surrounded him, tired and scattered like sheep without a shepherd, and defended them against the abuses of power of their leaders (Matt. 9:36; 12:1–12; 15:1–14; 23; etc.). In the Word made flesh, it is the whole of humanity—all persons, all peoples—that is taken up, with no separation between body and soul, earth and heaven. The mission of the Son of Man was not to be served, but to serve and to give his life as a ransom for many (Mark 10:45; Luke 22:27). Faithful to this mission, he did not free himself from his captors and the death sentence imposed on him but acted to set other captives free and liberate the oppressed of this earth (Matt. 26:23; Luke 4:18).

The history of the church, made up of those who follow Jesus, however, shows that insistence on the praxis of the disciples is not sufficient in itself, since it can still be tinged with an unfleshed spiritualizing which sets aside and despises the present human, bodily condition and thinks human problems can be resolved with words. Christian praxis can also be manipulated in an individualistic direction, producing the self-centredness of disciples helping others, the poor and needy, through works of charity, but in a paternalistic spirit in which the ultimate aim of the help given is the personal salvation of the giver, and the recipients are left in the same dependent state as before. The blind Jesus helped began to see with their own eyes, the lame to walk on their own two feet, the dumb to say what they wanted to say. Pardoned sinners were at most warned not to repeat the evil they had done. The liberation practised by Jesus was to give freedom to others, to enable them to take responsibility for their own lives, pulling them out of the prison of their faults, their sins, and the marginalization in which they had been condemned to live.

Debates about the spiritual dimension of aid have at least had the effect of making church authorities recognize that evangelization and therefore Christian praxis have to include economic, social and political activity, and cannot be reduced to the individual and family sphere. The two interlocking arms of Christian liberation are the organized effort for people to change themselves into agents of their full personal and community development, and the systematic effort they make to change socio-political mechanisms of domination, injustice and marginalization into an equal, just and free society (Puebla 480).

In view of the fact that the most extensive areas of Christian activity in this world fall outside the churches, in the areas of family life, productive work, political affairs and the like, praxis cannot be mirrored in the specific tasks befalling the priestly ministry in the church today. Praxis is based on the autonomy of earthly things (GS 36) and the responsibility proper to lay people, in the theological-juridical sense of the word. Whatever the function of ecclesiastical authorities in these areas may be, the historical process of see-judge-act is always actually carried out by those who get their hands dirty, as they say.

There are two obstacles to Christian praxis involving this earth, this present-day society, and doing so in the best and most efficacious way possible. The first is that, at least in

Roman Catholic circles, the production of moral knowledge has been reserved to the clergy. When the positive and social sciences began to develop, the reaction from the clergy was often distrust and polemic, which have not entirely vanished despite the openings made by Vatican II. In practice, clerical authorities still find it difficult to trust in the competence and responsibility of "the laity" in the autonomous fields of politics, economics, culture and family life.

The second difficulty follows from the first: it is that those who have been silent for so long are now afraid to speak out. The leadership of the church has heard the cry of the poor and has officially taken on the defence of the poor, the oppressed, the marginalized, the victims of all sorts of discrimination. The action programme is that these should be given time and space to live their lives with human dignity and, through participation and in communion, take their proper place in the economic, social and political orders that are to be made. The problem is not so much that this change of attitude on the part of the clergy leads to their being suspected of opportunism; it is that the Catholic people have lost the place to speak inside the Catholic Church, and have perhaps lost interest in doing so. But the growth of base Christian communities is providing signs that they are recovering their speech and their interest. The future will show whether the life experience of poor people and the intellectual contribution of lay people will really contribute to the mobilization of Christian praxis in this world, and to the development of theological moral theory.

The idea of Christian praxis extending to all areas of human coexistence so as to transform them into an incarnate expression of the Reign of the God-man is not simply a result of the church bringing itself to adapt to the conditions of the modern world so as to have space in which to act. Of course modern society is far more complex than it was in Jesus' time, and understanding it requires the tools of modern scientific analysis, not just the impressionism of experience. Its complex structure cannot be divided into static compartments of individuals here and institutions there, of religion here and politics there, because all its existential dimensions are interwoven and work on each other in terms of hegemony and dependence, dominion and submission, in the whole economic, social, political, cultural and religious complex that makes up society. Scientific analysis will uncover a whole mass of conflicts, latent or open; this not only produces a better understanding of historical reality, but forces one to take sides, instead of hiding under a false neutrality.

(c) The Principle of Solidarity

Crises and conflicts tend to sharpen the principle of *sauve qui peut*. As dangers and threats to physical and moral survival increase, the instinct of self-preservation tends to make individuals and social groups close in on themselves in search of a way out, without considering the state other people are in. If one adds the ethos of liberal individualism to this, then the risk of narcissistic self-regard, concern with one's own life, well-being, security, identity, is greatly increased. Behind much searching for one's own identity lies the thought that we are not, thank God, like others (see Luke 18:11), as though life were a continual competition to see who was most entitled to go first.

The state of the world today means that morality has to be considered in terms that apply worldwide. As a common space for action, the world today is both big and small. Small, in that communications media reduce physical distances in time and space; big, in that there are impossibly large gaps between powerful and powerless, between ruling and oppressed classes, between the interests of the centre and those of the periphery: a mass of apparently growing conflicts with their attendant dangerous and explosive tensions.

The concentration of religious as well as economic and political power in the hands of a few has reached the point where the lives, well-being and security of millions of people, of families, of whole nations, depend on decisions taken above their heads. The public at large sees a leader or spokesperson on television; the real power-brokers are elsewhere and often unreachable. As a reaction against this verticality, increasing numbers of initiatives are being taken among the people who make up the wide base of society's pyramid: unions, national and local associations, pressure groups, minority rights groups and the like. The strength that holds them together is solidarity. Before the term became widely known from the "free" Polish trade union, it was used in moral law in cases involving restitution for wrongs done. Vogue words can easily lose their original power and fascination, but the courage of the Polish union and the inspiration it has been for similar movements around the world make the concept of solidarity a worthy subject for reflection in faith.

Jesus' own praxis offers two pointers through the play he makes on the words "neighbour" and "brother." The question was: What must a person do to inherit eternal life? Jesus replied with the central tenet of the morality of the Old Testament: love God and your neighbour. He did not place this "love" in a vague, lyrical context, hovering like a scented cloud over the universe and the whole of humankind, without distinction. Love is something for each person to practise concretely in the situation/challenge that presents itself, using one's capacities to respond effectively to the actual needs of others. The parable of the good Samaritan is an illustration of Jesus' practical sense: two people see the victim of assault lying wounded and bleeding and pass by without doing anything; a third, a foreigner, takes care of him with the means at his disposal.

Jesus' own question points to the change in emphasis Jesus makes from a vague, generalized love to a specific and practical love. He asks: Who was the neighbour of the man who had been attacked? Instead of following the idealist course, which would see everyone as neighbour to everyone else, Jesus states that it is by doing good to someone that one becomes a neighbour (Luke 10:25–37). Being neighbours is not something natural or automatic; it comes from rendering service to others, being a present help to them in their actual hour of need. As his praxis constantly showed, Jesus saw love as something more than a pious wish that all should be brothers and sisters to one another; it meant expending physical and psychic energy to do good, to serve, to help, to collaborate with, to work at bettering the lives of other inhabitants of the globe. It is practical services, meeting "cases," the situations and demands of the others of this world, that build "togetherness," that make people into brothers and sisters, and turn those who perform these services into the blessed ones of the Father, those who will finally take possession of the Kingdom (Matt. 25:31–46).

The second pointer Jesus offers as regards solidarity has to do with the way he changes the meaning of the words "brothers" and "mother." He dramatized this change when his relatives came to take him away and talk to him privately, thinking he was out of his mind (Mark 3:20–35 and parallels). Jesus' reaction was not to obey the call, but to continue his conversation with the crowd around him, with the question: "Who are my mother and my brothers?" He himself then gave the answer, looking at those around him: "Here are my mother and my brothers," going on to explain: "Whoever does the will of God is brother and sister and mother to me." In relationships among persons, there is something more important than ties of blood, interests or friendship; this is the meeting, then the journey together, of those who seek to carry out the aim of the God of the new covenant. It is this quest that creates bonds, binds together and makes those who share in it the sisters and brothers of Christ.

Of course, it is not difficult to find a series of moral indicators addressed to all in the Gospels, beginning with the golden rule and the programmatic proclamation in Mark: change your ways and believe the good news (Mark 1:15; cf Matt. 7:12). For Jesus, solidarity is not primarily an abstract notion or an ideal; it is definite action, historical movement, mobilization of persons and peoples. Explaining his message of the Kingdom and doing good to all, he opened himself to his audience, trying to reach all and attend to their needs.

This movement did not produce just mental divisions: people and groups of people began to draw away from Jesus and form an obstructive opposition to him among themselves, to organize a resistance to him that was ultimately to lead to his condemnation and death. As Simeon had prophesied, Jesus himself stated that he came to bring not peace, but a sword that separated (Luke 2:34; Matt. 10:34 and parallels). Faced with this separation among those who listened to him, he spoke decisively: he who is not with me is against me.

In many situations, to maintain an "impartial" equidistance is to take the stance of the priest and the Levite in the parable of the good Samaritan; people fail to see how they are carried along by the prevailing current and hesitate to counter it for fear of getting their hands dirty. Christian responsibility in the world of today also means responding, through the position one takes and the work one does, to the mute call of the great masses of those who are weak, poor and suffering, shut in the wings of the stage of history, though on paper possessing the same human rights as everyone else.

Because they take part in the affairs of the world and society today, Christians have eyes with which to discern reality as it is, the critical intelligence to analyze it and the strength to help in changing it, while remaining aware that their morality is a two-edged sword. As a tool for action, it discerns good and evil in others, in historical situations, in society today, produces courageous denunciation of injustices and discriminations, and works to eliminate them; but its other edge is turned on one's own judgment, separating what is authentic and sincere from what is false and merely "comes out of the mouth" in our own lives. Demagogy and Pharisaism are historical possibilities, but they do not usually deceive people for long. Solidarity means exposing oneself to the criticisms and accusations of Greeks and Trojans, adversaries and companions. Self-criticism can easily turn into self-defence. By accepting criticism from the poor and weak, and amending their ways in accordance with this, Christians consolidate their identification with these, the beloved of the Father.

As a moral principle, solidarity operates in all human spheres, narrow and broad. If the basic question is how to relate to "the other," then both singular and plural are involved: being one's "brother's" and one's "brothers'" keeper both play a part in moral development. Approaching moral problems on a worldwide scale, affecting the whole of human society, however, does produce a broader view of the concerns, rights and hopes of collectivities victimized and dominated by discrimination, injustice and various forms of slavery. Then one can see the little world of family and immediate circle as part of the big world in which the great decisions on the exercise of human rights, economic sharing and political and religious participation have to be made.

Through its dynamism, solidarity overcomes the old antagonism between egoism and altruism by constantly seeking the "us": meeting, coming together, communicating, through the effective participation of all. So it moves beyond the temptation to organize an isolated "steering group," though this may be required as a temporary pressure group. Equally, it does not look just for a change of power, a shift in control, which can involve a series of twists and turns that leaves those at the bottom of the social heap in the same position as before. Its ultimate aim is to find ways of living together in which growing freedom, mutual respect and social tolerance create a quality of community life in which both individuals and groups can feel more at home and more fulfilled, insofar as human conditions in this world allow.

(d) Looking to the Future

Modern theological writing lays a renewed stress on hope. The extension of human power in the modern world, the demands made by the accelerating rhythm of life, and even the threats to the survival of humanity, are integral features of this development. Hope is the grace with which God calls human beings forward, and the eschatological horizon on which the mystery of God, now scarcely visible through a clouded glass, will be made clear in its fullness. But hope also has a human face and works as a tenacious strength, being, as the popular saying goes, the last thing to die. It has a special role to play in the face of present-day challenges.

Christian hope is a process of apprenticeship which rethinks and reformulates all that the past has handed down, and reshapes all that Christian praxis has produced till now. We cannot say that moral theory has reached its highest point, as the situation of humanity/inhumanity in the countries where Christianity has spread and taken root shows. Just as all human beings are unfinished and mortal, so are their works. Hope pushes us forward, since the human situation as we know it now fails to satisfy and does not yet merit the final prize, either on the personal or on the social level. St Paul is right when he counsels us not to be happy with the world as it is, but to "be transformed through the renewal of your mind," so as to "discern the will of God, what is good, what pleases, what is perfect" (Rom. 12:2).

Renewing moral understanding does not mean opening the gates to anarchy and nihilism. Outside the Christian environment, the moral inheritance that comes from the past is a basic factor for human stability, going from the golden rule and the ten commandments to modern international formulations of human rights on the individual, cultural, economic, social and political levels. Seen from the standpoint of faith, human fulfillment and the humanizing development of society are based on the rock that is Christ, on what he did and what he continues to inspire through the Spirit of God (1 Cor. 3:11–16). The symbolism of God blowing the breath of life into man's nostrils is continually actualized by the Holy Spirit, who works in the here and now of history, which human beings form through their actions (see Gen. 2:7).

Faced with new moral problems that arise and old ones that appear in new guises, hope moves steadfastly in two directions: to a deeper understanding of these challenges, to the extent that today's scientific analysis can provide this; and to community living of faith in Jesus Christ within the present historical context, with all its contradictions and conflicts, in which the incarnate church community lives and endeavours to discover what God, its Father, expects of it. The long history of humanity which the present generation carries within itself does not either determine or guarantee the future: it is the future we hope for that stimulates the creative imagination to move onward from what has been done up till now.

Hope can take time; it knows that Rome was not built in a day. In the conditions of this world, human beings, unfinished and ambivalent as they are, will not finish their work through some miraculous stroke. There is no magic pass through the rapidly changing history of our time, by which complex human society will suddenly change structure and direction. Those who take up their responsibilities in their personal lives and society today will have to face a lot of resistance without grace, a lot of cross without mysticism, and will often have to work without seeing direct results. On this "endless" journey, hope prevents the spirit of struggle from going rusty, corroded by the frustrations, failures and setbacks that are part of the human condition. On the positive side, hope is a pledge of fidelity, firmness and perseverance, enabling us not to give up but to stand firm in good heart: "Have hope and be cheerful" (Rom. 12:12).

Firmly planted in history, hope knows our limitations, the possibilites offered by the present time and the human resources available, without losing sight of the fact that its full realization lies beyond the horizon. Moral actions are always provisional, like climbing a mountain whose summit can often not be seen. We can have dreams of the future, but our next step always starts from where we are and how we are, which may be weakened, wounded, damaged by the traces of the past. Freedom lies ahead, glimpsed through a veil, the deep, if vague, aspiration of human existence, whose present is the hard, ongoing struggle to win a little more true freedom for oneself and to help, in solidarity, in the liberation of one's neighbours. Hope will not deceive us, "because the love of God has already been poured into our hearts by the Holy Spirit given to us" (Rom. 5:5).

Glossary

CONSCIENCE/CONSCIENTIZATION—Conscience is one of the most important concepts in moral theology. Together with Scripture, tradition, the magisterium, human nature and the natural law, and the signs of the times, it forms the framework within which Christians try to discern God's actual plans. There are various types of conscience and it can operate on different levels of profundity. Often called "the voice of God," conscience is at once immediate and difficult to grasp fully as a concept.

Conscientization (see note 2 to chapter VI) as developed over the past twenty years, particularly in Brazil, seeks to shed fresh light on conscience and its modes of action. Conscientization processes drew attention to new aspects of conscience and also to the implications of so-called "consciousness-raising." Properly assimilated, theories and practices of "conscientization can be useful instruments in cultivating a mature conscience. Though worked out in a sociological context, these theories and practices can also shed light on the theological aspects of conscience.

ETHICS/MORALS—Many people today would rather speak of ethics than morals, or would make a distinction between the two. Ethics sounds more appealing: morals smacks of "moralism," an impositional, condemnatory attitude. But the root of both terms is *ethos,* meaning house, dwelling, identity, coherence, authenticity. Both ethics and morals as disciplines seek to serve the humanizing of human beings. Ethics is sometimes restricted to the specific obligations of a profession.

IMMORALITY/AMORALITY—Immorality denotes infringement of moral norms from any aspect of human nature. Historical circumstances have led it to be associated above all with sexuality, but it is important to recognize that there can be immorality in other areas too: politics, business, etc. Amorality denotes a lack of moral sensitivity, a negative attitude to moral norms.

MORAL SCHEMAS/SYSTEMS—the development of moral "systems" was a feature of the seventeenth and eighteenth centuries.

They were like different schools or currents within moral theology. Today we prefer to call then "schemas" to indicate their provisory nature, to show an awareness that different theological currents are all engaged in a quest. This is to recognize that all theology is but an attempt to understand and follow God's will better.

NATURAL LAW—Today we are wary of generalizing about "human nature" and this applies equally to the idea of natural law. But this wariness stems from a misunderstanding. The expression "human nature" designates what identifies all human beings, of all times and all places; it is our "human-ness." But this nature does not exist in the abstract: it is always actualized in socio-cultural space. Natural law, in turn, designates what any person of good will accepts as a requirement of being human. "Do good and avoid evil" is a classic statement of a principle that no one would deny. Both human nature and natural law can be understood properly only in the light of a God revealed in many ways, but fully through Jesus the Son.

NOMINALISM—The term is linked to endless discussions in the eleventh and twelfth and more particularly fourteenth and fifteenth centuries over the validity or otherwise of so-called universals. "Humanity," for example, would be an empty word for nominalists, for whom only the individual, the actual person, would exist. In the field of morals, nominalists would hold that the commandments were like "universals"—lacking inner coherence. The commandments we know as God's law would be valid only in the sense of having been imposed by God, but by the same token would be arbitrary and could have been quite different. Moral theology, on the other hand, holds that the commandments are inner requirements of human nature as created by God. Even if they had not been formulated, they would have to be followed, since they are the way to human fulfillment.

ORTHODOXY/ORTHOPRAXIS—The best way to understand their meaning is to start from the root: *orthos* means what is right, correct; *doxia* refers to *doxa*, truth; *praxia* to praxis, actions. So orthodoxy is the right understanding of revealed truths, while orthopraxis is right action, acting in accordance with revealed truths. One concept is sometimes played off against the other, as though they were mutually exclusive. But in fact they go together, since right understanding does not exclude right acting, nor vice-versa; rather, they complement one another.

Notes

Chapter I: The Challenges to Moral Theology Today

1. M. Vidal, *Moral de atitudes* (Santuário, 1975), pp. 482–9. Trans. of *Moral de actitudes*, vol. 1, *Moral fundamental*, 4th ed. (Madrid, 1977).
2. See A. Moser, "Teologia moral e ciências humanas: antigos e novos desafios," *REB* 45 (1985), pp. 227–44.
3. See Ph. Delhaye, "La morale des Pères," *Seminarium* 3 (1971), pp. 623–37.
4. See GS 22.
5. See Vidal, *Moral*, pp. 13–44.
6. Ibid., pp. 15–34.
7. See B. Leers, *Jeito brasileiro e norma absoluta* (Petrópolis, 1982); H. Lepargneur, *Fontes da moral na Igreja* (Petrópolis, 1978).
8. There is now an abundant literature on base Christian communities. See, *inter alia*, in English, L. Boff, *Ecclesiogenesis: The Base Communities Re-invent the Church* (Maryknoll, N.Y., 1984); C. Boff, "The Nature of Basic Christian Communities," *Concilium* 144 (1981), pp. 53–8; the whole issue of *Concilium* 176 (1984) on the "Popular Church"; J. Comblin, *The Holy Spirit and Liberation* (Maryknoll, N.Y., and Tunbridge Wells, 1989), pp. 1–42—TRANS.
9. See G. Angelini and A. Valsecchi, *Disegno storico della teologia morale* (Bologna, 1972), pp. 61–209.
10. Delhaye, "La morale." 623–37.
11. See D. Figueiredo, *Curso de teologia patrística, I* (Petrópolis, 1983), pp. 119–20.
12. On the following historical aspects, see B. Häring, *Das Gesetz Christi. Moraltheologie*, vol. 1, 8th ed. (Munich–Freiburg, 1967), pp. 33–75. Eng. trans.: *The Law of Christ* (Westminster, Md.: Newman Press, 1961).
13. See M.-D. Chenu, *La théologie au douzième siècle*, 2nd ed. (Paris, 1966).

14. See Vidal, *Moral*, pp. 41–3.
15. H. Jone, *Katholische Moraltheologie auf das Leben angewandt. Unter kurzer Andetung ihrer Grundlagen und unter Berüchsichtigung des CIC . . .*, 17th ed. (Paderborn, 1961).
16. Vidal, *Moral*, pp. 72–5.
17. B. Leers, *Novos rumos da moral* (Belo Horizonte, 1970).
18. Ph. Delhaye, "The Contribution of Vatican II to Moral Theology," *Concilium* 75 (1972), pp. 58–67.
19. Such as C. Spicq, *Théologie morale du Nouveau Testament* (Paris, 1975); Delhaye, "La morale."

Chapter II: Renewed Morality: One Way Forward

1. See B. Häring, *The Law of Christ* (Westminster, Md.: Newman Press, 1961), esp. vol 3; M. Vidal, *Moral de actitudes*, vol. 1 (Madrid, 1977); R. Rincón Orduña, ed., *Práxis cristã. Moral fundamental*, 2 vols. (São Paulo, 1983–4).
2. See Vidal, *Moral*, pp. 47–75.
3. See J. Walgrave, "Is Morality Static or Dynamic?", *Concilium* 5/1 (1965), pp. 13–22 (UK); I. Lobo, "Towards a Morality Based on the Meaning of History," *Concilium* 5/3 (1967), pp. 13–23 (UK).
4. J. Alfaro, *Teologia del progreso humano* (Assisi, 1969), pp. 54ff; K. Rahner, "Zur Geschichtlichkeit der Theologie," *Schriften zur Theologie VIII* (Einsiedeln, 1967), pp. 88–100.
5. See J. Gründel, *Wandelbares und Unwandelbares in der Moraltheologie* (Düsseldorf, 1967).
6. Ph. Delhaye, "The Contribution of Vatican II to Moral Theology," *Concilium* 75 (1972), pp. 58–67.
7. F. Tillmann, *Die Idee der Nachfolge Christi* (Düsseldorf, 1934).
8. See J. Endres, "Genügt eine rein biblische Moraltheologie?", *Studia Moralia 2 (1964), pp. 43–72.*
9. See C. Spicq, *Théologie morale du Nouveau Testament* (Paris, 1975).
10. See J. Fuchs, *Moral und Moraltheologie nach dem Konzil* (Freiburg, 1967); R. Thysman, "L'éthique de l'imitation du Christ," *Eph. Th. Lov.* (1966), pp. 139–75; R. Schnackenburg, *Christliche Existenz nach dem Neuen Testament*, vol. 1 (Munich, 1967), pp. 87–103.
11. See M.-D. Chenu, *L'Evangile dans le temps* (Paris, 1964).
12. I. Ellacuría, "Historicidad de la salvación cristiana," *Revista Latino-americana de Teología* 1 (Jan.–Apr. 1984), pp. 5–43.
13. See J. Comblin, *Retrieving the Human: A Christian Anthropology* (Maryknoll, N.Y. and Tunbridge Wells, 1990).

14. See J.-B. Libânio, *Pecado e opção fundamental* (Petrópolis, 1975); A. Moser, *O pecado ainda existe?* (São Paulo, 1976).
15. Moser, *O pecado*, pp. 89–104.
16. A. Moser, "Mais desafios para a teologia do pecado," *REB* 40 (1980), pp. 682–91.
17. L. Boff, *A graça libertadora no mundo* (Petrópolis, 1976), pp. 191–208. Eng. trans.: *Liberating Grace* (Maryknoll, N.Y., 1979).
18. See R. Koch, "Vers une morale de l'alliance?", *Studia Moralia* 6 (1968), pp. 7–58; P. van Imschoot, "L'Esprit de Jahwé source de piété dans l'Ancien Testament," *Bible et Vie Chrétienne* 6 (1954), p. 19.
19. Schnackenburg, *Christliche Existenz*, pp. 109–30; B. Häring, *Christ in einer neuen Welt* (Freiburg, 1959).
20. Vidal, *Moral*, pp. 104–19.
21. See. M.-D. Chenu, *La théologie au douzième siècle* (Paris, 1966); *El evangelismo* (Bogotá, 1962), pp. 28ff; *La théologie comme science au treizième siècle*, 2nd ed. (Paris, 1943), pp. 37–71.
22. See J.-B. Metz, *Glaube in Geschichte und Gesellschaft* (Mainz, 1977); K. Rahner, letter of 16 Mar. 1984 to Card. Juan Landázuri Ricketts, Archbishop of Lima, in support of Gustavo Gutiérrez, original text, *Orientierung* 5/49 (1984), Spanish text in *Vida Nueva* 1425–6 (1984).
23. See Brazilian Bishops Conference, ed., "Saúde e fraternidade," *SEDOC* (Apr. 1981), 950.
24. As does L. Boff, *Do lugar do pobre* (Petrópolis, 1984), pp. 63–77.
25. John Paul II, Encyclical *Dives in Misericordia*.

Chapter III: Latin American Approaches

1. See Various, *Credo para amanhã*, 3rd ed. (Petrópolis, 1972), pp. 169–97.
2. L. Meulenberg, "A discussão aberta na Igreja Antiga," *REB* 45 (1985), pp. 16–31.
3. See G. Angelini and A. Valsecchi, *Disegno storico della teologia morale* (Bologna, 1972), pp. 61–209.
4. For a variety of approaches to crises see *Concilium* 200, *Truth and Its Victims* (1988)—TRANS.
5. C. Palacio, "A Igreja da America Latina, a teologia da libertação e a Instrução do Vaticano: um discernimento," *Perspectiva Teológica* 43 (1985), p. 308.
6. L. and C. Boff, *Como fazer teologia da libertação* (Petrópolis, 1986). Eng. trans,: *Introducing Liberation Theology* (Maryknoll,

N.Y., and Tunbridge Wells, 1987), pp. 11–21.

7. A. Moser, "Teologia moral e ciências humanas," *REB* 45 (1985), pp. 227–44.
8. M. Vidal, *Moral de actitudes*, vol. 3 (Madrid, 1977); I. Ellacuría, "Hacia una fundamentación filosófica del método teológico latinoamericano," *Liberación y cautiverio* (Mexico, 1976), p. 273.
9. Boff/Boff, *Introducing*, pp. 44–6.
10. Thus G. Staccone, *Teologia para o homen crítico* (Petrópolis, 1984), p. 76.
11. See J. L. Segundo, *Nuestra idea de Dios*, vol. 2 of *Teología abierta* vol. 2 (Buenos Aires, 1972), pp. 115ff. Eng. trans.: *Our Idea of God* (Maryknoll, N.Y.: Orbis, 1974).
12. See Puebla 1143; A. Moser, "The Representation of God in the Ethic of Liberation," *Concilium* 172 (1984), pp. 42–7.
13. Moser, "Representation of God".
14. A. Flores, "Antropologia da libertação latino-americana (Uma ética centrada no homen)," P. Meneses et al., *A hora da ética libertadora* (São Paulo, 1985), pp. 23–8.
15. See F. Moreno Rejón, *Teología moral desde los pobres* (Madrid, 1986). Eng. trans.: *Moral Theology from the Poor* (Quezon City, Philippines, 1988); idem, "Seeking the Kingdom and Its Justice: The Development of the Ethic of Liberation," *Concilium* 172 (1984), pp. 35–41; T. Misfud, "The Development of a Liberation Ethic in the Documents of the Church since Vatican II," *Concilium* 172 (1984), pp. 48–53.
16. Such as E. Dussel, *Caminos de liberación latinoamericanos*, 2 vols. (Buenos Aires, 1972–4); *Para una ética de la liberación latinoamericana*, 5 vols. (Buenos Aires, 1973–80).
17. Such as Moreno Rejón, *Moral Theology*.
18. In M. Vidal, "Is Morality Based on Autonomy Compatible with the Ethics of Liberation?" *Concilium* 172 (1984), pp. 80–86.
19. M.-D. Chenu, *El evangelismo* (Bogotá, 1962).
20. J. Braga, "Fazer teologia moral hoje," *Moral social* (São Paulo, 1984), pp. 10–11.
21. J.-B. Libânio, *As grandes rupturas socio-culturais e eclesiais* (Petrópolis, 1980), p. 73.
22. See A. Melo, "Classe média e opção preferencial pelos pobres," *REB* 43 (1983), pp. 340–50.
23. C. Clark, *Population Growth and Land Use* (London, 1967), p. 153.
24. Brazilian Bishops Conference, ed., "Saúde e fraternidade," *SEDOC* (Apr. 1981), col. 951.

25. Ibid., cols. 954ff.
26. Idem, "Terra de Deus, Terra de Irmãos," Brotherhood campaign, 1986.
27. John Paul II, "Love Christ and Men," homily in the Plaza de Independencia, Santo Domingo, 25 Jan. 1979, *SEDOC* (1979), col. 866.
28. Idem, "Right Social Order," address to the workers of Monterrey, 31 Jan. 1979, *SEDOC* (1979), cols. 924–5.
29. J. Alfaro, *Teologia da justiça* (São Paulo, 1978), p. 43.
30. Vidal, "Is Morality Based?", p. 85.
31. Ibid.

Chapter IV: The Covenant: Revelation of God's Purpose

1. See S. Triana, "Alianza y promesa en las tradiciones del Antiguo Testamento," *Servir* 107 (1984), pp. 328, 337.
2. Ibid., pp. 338–9; G. Cordero, "La noción de alianza en el Antiguo Testamato," *Salmant.* (1969), pp. 233–74.
3. See R. Koch, "Vers une morale de l'Alliance?", *Studia Moralia* 6 (1968), pp. 7–58; J. Salvador, "Alianças e Aliança no Antigo Testamento," *Rev. Cult. Bíblica* (1969–70), pp. 7–27.
4. L. Babbini, *L'Uomo e il decalogo* (Genoa, 1969), pp. 35ff.
5. P. Barget, *Le livre des morts* (Paris, 1967), pp. 158ff.
6. Koch, "Vers une morale?"
7. J. Trapiello, "Preocupación social en el Antiguo Testamento," *Angelicum* 55 (1978), pp. 161–92.
8. J. L'Hour, *La morale de l'Alliance* (Gabalda, 1966), pp. 105ff.
9. N. K. Gottwald, *The Tribes of Yahweh: A Sociology of the Religion of Liberated Israel* (Maryknoll, N.Y., and London, 1979).
10. Triana, "Alianza y promesa," p. 344.
11. R. Koch, *Il peccato nel Vecchio Testamento* (Rome, 1973), pp. 79–107.
12. R. Scott, *The Relevance of the Prophets* (New York: Macmillan, 1944).
13. L'Hour, *La morale*, pp. 115–20.

Chapter V: Jesus Christ: God's Purpose Fulfilled

1. J. L. Segundo, *The Historical Jesus of the Synoptics* (Maryknoll, N.Y., and London, 1985).
2. J. Comblin, *Jesus Cristo e sua missão* (São Paulo, 1983), p. 154.
3. L. Boff, *Jesus Cristo libertador*, 9th ed. (Petrópolis, 1983), p. 68. Eng. trans.: *Jesus Christ Liberator* (Maryknoll, N.Y., 1978).

4. See J. Sobrino, *Cristología a partir da América Latina* (Petrópolis, 1983), p. 138. Trans. of *Cristología desde América Latina* (San Salvador, 1976). Eng. trans. *Christology at the Crossroads* (Maryknoll, N.Y., 1978).
5. See S. Lyonnet, *La historia de la salvación en la carta a los Romanos* (Salamanca, 1967), p. 50. Trans. of *Les étapes de l'histoire du salut selon l'épître aux Romains* (Paris, 1969).
6. See Sobrino, *Christology*.
7. Such as H. Echegaray, *La práctica de Jesús* (Lima, 1980), ch. 1. Eng. trans.: *The Practice of Jesus* (Maryknoll, N.Y., and Melbourne, 1984).
8. Such as Boff in *Jesus Christ Liberator*; R. Pesch, "Jesus, a Free Man," *Concilium* 93 (1974), pp. 56–70.
9. Echegaray, *The Practice*, p. 92.
10. Comblin, *Jesus Cristo*, p. 156, see also 154, 155.
11. Ph. Delhaye, "The Contribution of Vatican II to Moral Theology," *Concilium* 75 (1972).
12. See P. Freire, "Educação popular: Ideário do Prof. Freire," *SEDOC* (1983), p. 480.
13. See F. B. de Avila and P. Bigó, *Fe cristã e compromisso social* (São Paulo, 1982), pp. 173–4.
14. See A. Fierro, *El evangelio beligerante* (Estella, 1975), pp. 361–8; J. B. Metz, " 'Politische Theologie' in der Diskussion," H. Peukert, ed., *Diskussion zur 'Politische Theologie'* (Munich–Mainz, 1969), pp. 267–301.
15. See P. Demo, *Conflito social. Perspectivas teóricas e metodológicas* (Petrópolis, 1973).
16. B. Häring, *The Law of Christ*, (Westminster, Md.: Newman Press, 1961), vol. 3.
17. See M. Rocha, "O seguimento de Jesus Cristo," *REB* 42 (1982), pp. 12–28.
18. Ibid., pp. 18ff; see also Echegaray, *The Practice*.

Chapter VI: "Conscientization" and Conscience: Between Humanity and Divinity

1. M. Bach, *Consciência e identidade* (Petrópolis, 1985), p. 11.
2. "The term 'conscientization' refers to learning to perceive social, political and economic contradictions, and to take action against the oppressive elements of reality"—translator's note to P. Freire, *Pedagogy of the Oppressed* (Harmondsworth, 1972), p. 15.—TRANS.

3. See H. C. de Lima Vaz, "A Igreja e o problema da conscientização," *Rev. de Cultura Vozes* 62 (1968), p. 493; J. Barreiro, *Educação popular e conscientização* (Petrópolis, 1980), pp. 472ff.
4. C. Boff, "Agente de pastoral e povo," *REB* 40 (1980), p. 217.
5. Ibid., pp. 219–30.
6. Ibid., p. 225.
7. Ibid., p. 230.
8. See A. Hortelano, *Problemas actuales de moral. Introducción a la teología moral.* Vol. 1: *La conciencia moral* (Madrid, 1979), pp. 426–55.
9. Bach, *Consciência*, p. 171.
10. See Ph. Delhaye, "Les bases bibliques du traité de la conscience," *Studia Montis Regis* (1971), pp. 229–52.
11. See ch. V, section 1.
12. M. Vidal, *Moral de atitudes*, vol. 1 (Santuário, 1975), pp. 268–71.
13. Delhaye, "Les bases."
14. St Augustine, *De Sermone Domini in Monte*, PL 34, col. 1283.
15. See O. Cullmann, *Christus und die Zeit*, 2nd ed. (Zollikon–Zurich, 1948), p. 203; G. Terrien, *Le discernement dans les écrits pauliniens* (Paris, 1973).
16. Hortelano, *Problemas actuales*, p. 257.
17. See Vidal, *Moral*, vol. 1, pp. 310ff.

Chapter X: Moral Theology and a New Society

1. A section in the original referring to the systems applied to Latin America has here been shortened with only the general points retained—TRANS.
2. An assessment of capitalism based on the excessive forms it has taken in Latin America has here been omitted—TRANS.
3. H. Lefebvre, *Der Marxismus* (Munich, 1975), pp. 48–9.

Select Bibliography

Alfaro, J. *Teologia del progreso humano*. Assisi: Cittadella, 1969.
———. *Teologia da justiça*. São Paulo: Paulinas, 1978.
Angelini, G., and A. Valsecchi. *Disegno storico della teologia morale*. Bologna: EDB, 1972.
Bach, M. *Consciência e identidade*. Petrópolis: Vozes, 1985.
Barreiro, J. *Educaçao popular e conscientizaçao*. Petrópolis: Vozes, 1980.
Bastaniel, S. *Autonomia morale del credente*. Brescia: Morcelliana, 1980.
Baum, G., and J. Coleman, eds. *The Church and Racism*. *Concilium* 151 (1982).
———. *Sexuality, Religion and Society*. *Concilium* 173 (1984).
Béaud, M. *Histoire du capitalisme*. Paris: Seuil, 1981.
Betz, O., ed. *Tugenden für heute. Zwischen Möglichkeit und Wirklichkeit*. Munich: Pfeiffer, 1973.
Bigó, P. *La doctrine sociale de l'Eglise*. Paris: PUF, 1965.
———, and F. B. de Avila. *Fé cristã e compromisso social*. São Paulo, Paulinas, 1982.
Boff, C. "Agente de pastoral e povo." *REB* 40 (1980).
———. *Comunidade eclesial, comunidade política*. Petrópolis: Vozes, 1978.
———. "The Nature of Basic Christian Communities." *Concilium* 144 (1981).
———. *Teologia e prática*. Petrópolis: Vozes, 1982. Eng. trans.: *Theology and Praxis*. Maryknoll, N.Y.: Orbis, 1984.
Boff, L. *Teología desde el cautiverio*. Bogotá: Indo-American Press Service, 1975.
———. *Do lugar do pobre*. Petrópolis: Vozes, 1984.
———. *A graça libertadora no mundo*. Petrópolis: Vozes, 1976. Eng. trans.: *Liberating Grace*. Maryknoll, N.Y.: Orbis, 1979.
———. *Jesus Cristo libertador*. 9th ed. Petrópolis: Vozes, 1983. Eng. trans. *Jesus Christ Liberator*. Maryknoll, N.Y.: Orbis, 1978.

———, and C. Boff. *Como fazer teologia da libertação*. Petrópolis: Vozes, 1984. Eng. trans.: *Introducing Liberation Theology*. Maryknoll, N.Y.: Orbis; Tunbridge Wells: Burns & Oates, 1987.

Calvez, J. Y. *La pensée de Karl Marx*. Paris: Seuil, 1956.

Caram, D. *Violência na sociedade contemporânea*. Petrópolis: Vozes, 1978.

Chatillon, J., et al. *Le pouvoir*. Paris: Beauchesne, 1978.

Chenu, M.-D. *La théologie comme science au treizième siècle*. Paris: Cerf, 1943.

———. *L'Evangile dans le temps*. Paris: Cerf, 1964.

———. *La théologie au douzième siècle*. 2nd ed. Paris: Cerf, 1966.

Comblin, J. *Teologia da missão*. Petrópolis: Vozes, 1980. Eng. trans.: *The Meaning of Mission*. Maryknoll, N.Y.: Orbis, 1977.

———. *O Espíritu Santo e a libertação*. Petrópolis: Vozes, 1987. Eng. trans.: *The Holy Spirit and Liberation*. Tunbridge Wells: Burns & Oates; Maryknoll, N.Y: Orbis, 1989.

Cordero, G. "La noción de alianza en el Antiguo Testamento." *Salmanticenis* (1969).

Cosmao, V. *Changer le monde, une tâche pour l'Eglise*. Paris: Cerf, 1979. Eng. trans.: *Changing the World*. Maryknoll, N.Y.: Orbis, 1984.

Curran, C., ed. *Readings in Moral Theology*. Vol. 1: *Moral Norms and Catholic Tradition*. New York: Paulist Press, 1979.

Delhaye, Ph. "La morale des Pères." *Seminarium* 3 (1971).

———. "Les bases bibliques du traité de la conscience." *Studia Montis Regis* (1971).

———. "The Contribution of Vatican II to Moral Theology." *Concilium* 75 (1972).

Delumeau, J. *Le péché et la peur*. Paris: Fayard, 1983.

Dussel, E. *Caminos de liberación latinoamericanos*. 2 vols. Buenos Aires: Paulinas, 1972–4.

———. *Para una ética de la liberación latinoamericana*. 5 vols. Buenos Aires: Paulinas, 1973–80.

Echegaray, H. *La práctica de Jesús*. Lima, 1980. Eng. trans.: *The Practice of Jesus*. Maryknoll, N.Y: Orbis; Melbourne: Dove, 1984.

Endres, J. *Menschliche Grundhaltungen, Ein Ordnungsbild der Tugenden*. Salzburg: Müller, 1958.

———. "Genügt eine rein biblische Moraltheologie?" *Studia Moralia* 2 (1964).

Evans, D. *Struggle and Fulfillment*. Cleveland: Collins, 1979.

Feiner, J., and M. Löhrer, eds. *Mysterium Salutis*. Vol. 5: *Zwischenzeit und Vollendung der Heilsgeschichte*. Zurich-Einsiedeln-Cologne:

Matthias Grünewald, 1976.
Figueiredo, D. *Curso de teologia patrística*. Petrópolis: Vozes, 1975.
Follmann, J. *Igreja, ideologia e classes sociais*. Petrópolis: Vozes, 1985.
Freire, P. *Pedagogy of the Oppressed*. Harmondsworth: Penguin Education, 1972.
Fuchs, J. *Moral und Moraltheologie nach dem Konzil*. Freiburg-Basle-Vienna: Herder, 1967.
Galbraith, J. K. *American Capitalism*. Boston: Houghton Mifflin, 1956.
George, R. T. de. *Soviet Ethics and Morality*. Ann Arbor: Univ. of Michigan, 1969.
Gestel, C. *La doctrina social de la Iglesia*. Barcelona: Herder, 1959.
Girardi, G. *Christianisme, libération humaine, lutte des classes*. Paris: Cerf, 1972.
———. *Marxismo e cristianismo*. São Paulo: Paulinas, 1968.
Goffi, T. *Etica cristiana in acculturazione marxista*. Assisi: Cittadella, 1975.
González Faus, J. *El engaño de un capitalismo aceptable*. Santander: Sal Terrae, 1963.
González Ruiz, J. *Marxismo y cristianismo frente al hombre nuevo*. Barcelona: Fontanella, 1972.
Gottwald, N. K. *The Tribes of Yahweh. A Sociology of the Religion of Liberated Israel*. London: SCM; Maryknoll, N.Y.: Orbis, 1979.
Granon, A. *Capitalisme et mode de vie*. Paris: Cerf, 1974.
Gutiérrez, G. *La fuerza histórica de los pobres*. Lima: CEP, 1981. Eng. trans.: *The Power of the Poor in History*. Maryknoll, N.Y.: Orbis, 1983.
———. *Beber en su propio pozo*. Lima: CEP, 1983. Eng. trans.: *We Drink from Our Own Wells*. Maryknoll, N.Y.: Orbis, 1984.
———. *Teología de la liberación*. Lima: CEP, 1971. Eng. trans, new ed., *A Theology of Liberation*. Maryknoll, N.Y: Orbis; London: SCM, 1988.
Häring, B. *Das Gesetz Christi*. 8th ed. Munich-Freiburg, 1967. Eng. trans.: *The Law of Christ*. Westminister, Md.: Newman Press, 1961).
———. *Frei in Christus*. Vol 1. Freiburg: Herder, 1979.
Heininger, E. "Ideologie der Rassismus." *Neue Zeitschrift für Missionswissenschaft* (1980).
Hildebrand, D. von. *Die Umgestaltung in Christus*. Einsiedeln-Zurich-Cologne: Matthias Grünewald, 1950.
Hinkelammert, F. *The Ideological Weapons of Death*. Maryknoll, N.Y: Orbis, 1985.

Hortelano, A. *Problemas actuales de Moral. Introducción a la teología moral*. Vol. 1: *La conciencia moral*. Madrid: Sígueme, 1979; Vol. 2: *Problemas actuales de Moral*. Salamanca: Sígueme, 1980.
Kerber, W., ed. *Sittliche Normen*. Düsseldorf: Patmos, 1982.
Koch, R. "Vers une morale de l'alliance?" *Studia Moralia* 6 (1968).
Kolakowski, L. *Die Hauptströmungen des Marximus. Entstehung, Entwicklung, Zerfall*. 3 vols. Munich-Zurich, 1977–9. German trans. of Polish original.
Leers, B. *Catolicismo popular e mundo rural*. Petrópolis: Vozes, 1977.
———. *Jeito brasileiro e norma absoluta*. Petrópolis: Vozes, 1982.
———. "A lei natural e sua problemática atual." *REB* 35 (1975).
———. "Moralistas e magisterio." *REB* 45 (1985).
———. *Novos rumos da moral*. Belo Horizonte: Lutador, 1970.
———. "O sacramento da reconciliaçao." *REB* 44 (1984).
———. "Violência e reconciliação." *REB* 42 (1982).
Lefebvre, H. *Der Marxismus*. Munich: Kösel, 1975.
———. *Sociologie de Marx*. Paris: PUF, 1966.
Lepargneur, H. *Fontes da moral na Igreja*. Petrópolis: Vozes, 1978.
L'Hour, J. *La morale de l'Alliance*. Paris: Gabalda, 1966.
Libânio, J. B. *Pecado e opçao fundamental*. Petrópolis: Vozes, 1975.
———. *As grandes rupturas socio-culturais e eclesiais*. Petrópolis: Vozes, 1980.
———. *Formaçao da consciência crítica*. 2nd ed. Petrópolis: Vozes, 1980.
Lima Figueiredo, E., et al. *Por que Marx*? Rio de Janeiro: Graal, 1983.
Lima Vaz, H. C. de. "A Igreja e o problema de conscientização." *Revista de Cultura Vozes* 62 (1968).
Lobo, I. "Towards a Morality Based on the Meaning of History." *Concilium* 5/3 (1967).
Lyonnet, S. *Les étapes de l'histoire du salut selon l'epître aux Romains*. Paris, 1969.
Maduro, O. *Religion and Social Conflicts*. Maryknoll, N.Y.: Orbis, 1982.
Matura, T. *Le radicalisme évangélique. Aux sources de la vie chrétienne*. Paris: Cerf, 1978.
Mieth, D., and J. Pohier, eds. *The Ethics of Liberation—The Liberation of Ethics. Concilium* 172 (1984).
Melo, A. "Classe média e opçao preferencial pelos pobres." *REB* 43 (1983).
Meneses, P., et al. *A hora da ética libertadora*. São Paulo: Paulinas, 1985.

Messner, J. *Die sociale Frage*. 6th ed. Innsbruck: Tyrolia, 1956.
Mesters, C. *A missão do povo que sofre*. Petrópolis: Vozes, 1981.
Metz, J. B. " 'Politische Theologie' in der Diskussion." In H. Peukert, ed. *Diskussion zur Politische Theologie*. Munich-Mainz, 1969.
———. *Glaube in Geschichte und Gesellschaft*. Mainz, 1977.
Moreno Rejón, F. *Teología moral desde los pobres*. Madrid, 1986. Eng. trans.: *Moral Theology from the Poor*. Quezon City, Philippines: Claretian, 1988.
Moser, A. "Aspectos morales da caminhada das CEBs no Brasil." *REB* 43 (1983).
———. "Conscientizaçao e mudança do ethos social Brasileiro." In *Mudanças na moral do nosso povo*. Petrópolis: Vozes, 1984.
———. "Mais desafios para a teologia do pecado." *REB* 40 (1980).
———. *O pecado ainda existe?* São Paulo: Paulinas, 1976. "Teologia moral e ciências humanas: antigos e novos desafios." *REB* 45 (1985).
Muñoz, R. *Solidaridad liberadora: misión de la Iglesia*. Santiago, 1977.
Negrâo, L. ed. *A religiosidade do povo*. São Paulo: Paulinas, 1984.
Nell-Breuning, O. von. *Kapitalismus—kritisch betrachtet*. Freiburg: Herder, 1984.
Pastor, P. A. *Existência e evangelho*. São Paulo: Loyola, 1973.
Pieper, J. *Kleines Lesebuch von den Tugenden des menschlichen Herzens*. 5th ed. Munich: Kösel, 1957.
Rahner, K. "Brief von 16.03.1984 an Kardinal Juan Landázuri Ricketts, Erzbischof von Lima, zur Unterstütstung von G. Gutiérrez." *Orientierung* 5/49 (1984).
Regidor, J. R. *Gesù e il risveglio delli oppressi*. Milan: Mondadori, 1981.
Ribeiro de Oliveira, P. *Religião e dominação de classe*. Petrópolis: Vozes, 1985.
Richard, P., et al. *La lucha de los dioses: los ídolos de la opresión y la búsqueda del Dios Liberador*. San José: DEI. Eng. trans.: *The Idols of Death and the God of Life*. Maryknoll, N.Y.: Orbis, 1983.
Rincón Orduña, R., ed. *Práxis cristã. Moral fundmental*. 2 vols. São Paulo: Paulinas, 1983–4.
Rossi and Valsecchi, eds. *Dizionario enciclopedico di teologia morale*. 2nd ed. Rome, 1976.
Santa Ana, J. de. *El desafío de los pobres a la Iglesia*. San José: DEI, 1977.
Schaff, A. *Marxismus und das menschliche Individuum*. Vienna-Frankfurt-Zurich, 1969.
Schackenburg, R. *The Moral Teaching of the New Testament*. London: Burns & Oates; New York: Herder & Herder, 1970.

Schrage, W. *Ethik des Neuen Testaments*. Göttingen: Vandenbreck & Ruprecht, 1982.

Segundo, J. L. *El hombre de hoy ante Jesús de Nazaret*. 3 vols. Madrid: Ediciones Cristiandad, 1982. Eng. trans.: *Jesus of Nazareth Yesterday and Today*. 5 vols. Maryknoll, N.Y.: Orbis; London: Sheed & Ward, 1985–9.

Snoek, J. *Ensaio de ética sexual*. São Paulo: Paulinas, 1981.

Sobrino, J. *Cristología desde Améica Latina*. San Salvador: UCA, 1976. Eng. trans.: *Christology at the Crossroads*. Maryknoll, N.Y.: Orbis, 1978.

Spicq, C. *Théologie morale du Nouveau Testament*. Paris: Gabalda, 1975.

Tepe, V. *Estamos salvos. O cristão diante das ideologias*. São Paulo: Paulinas, 1982.

Tillmann, F. *Die Idee der Nachfolge Christi. Handbuch der Katholischen Sittenlehre*. Vol. 3. Düsseldorf: Patmos, 1934.

Triana, S. "Alianza y promesa en las tradiciones del Antiguo Testamento." *Servir* 107 (1984).

Vagovic, S. *Etica comunista*. Rome: Gregorian University, 1959.

Vidal, M. *Moral de actitudes*. 3 vols. 4th ed. Madrid: Sígueme, 1977.

Walgrave, J. "Is Morality Static or Dynamic?" *Concilium* 5/1 (1965).

Weber, W., ed. *Macht, Dienst, Herrschaft in Kirche und Gesellschaft*. Freiburg: Herder, 1974.

Index
